Katharine Lee Bates, Lydia Boker Godfrey

English Drama

A Working Basis

Katharine Lee Bates, Lydia Boker Godfrey

English Drama
A Working Basis

ISBN/EAN: 9783743404793

Manufactured in Europe, USA, Canada, Australia, Japa

Cover: Foto ©Andreas Hilbeck / pixelio.de

Manufactured and distributed by brebook publishing software (www.brebook.com)

Katharine Lee Bates, Lydia Boker Godfrey

English Drama

English Drama.

A Working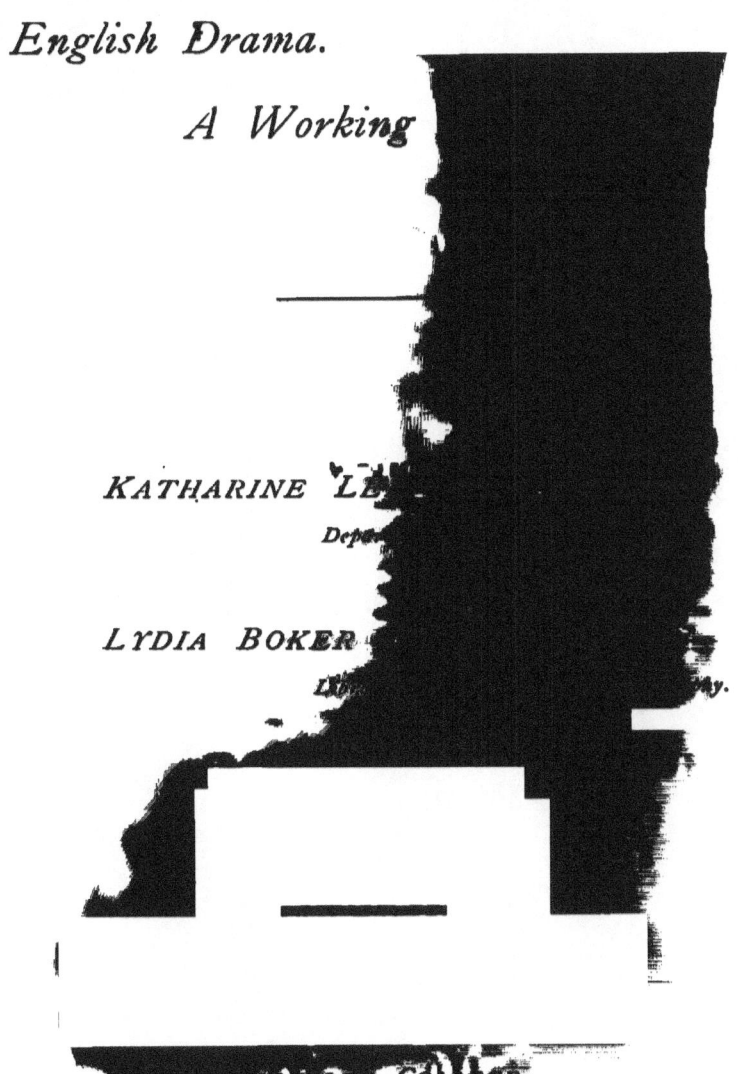

KATHARINE L...

LYDIA BOKER

...LLEY COLLEGE.
1896.

AUTHORS, PLAYS AND REFERENCES, FOR
>PRE-ELIZABETHAN DRAMA.
>ELIZABETHAN DRAMA
>JACOBEAN DRAMA.
>RESTORATION DRAMA.
>EIGHTEENTH CENTURY DRAMA.
>>The Reformed Drama.
>>The New Comedy.
>>Playwrights, Adapters and Triflers.
>NINETEENTH CENTURY DRAMA.
>>Georgian.
>>Victorian.

BOOKS OF GENERAL REFERENCE.
>1. Bibliographical.
>2. Dramatic History and Criticism.
>3. History of the English Theatre.
>4. Stage Polemics.

CONTENTS.

COLLECTIONS OF OLD PLAYS.
    (Chronologically arranged, with alphabetical index).

GENERAL INDEX TO COLLECTIONS.
    (By titles of plays alphabetically arranged).

AUTHORS, PLAYS AND REFERENCES, FOR
    PRE-ELIZABETHAN DRAMA.
    ELIZABETHAN DRAMA.
    JACOBEAN DRAMA.
    RESTORATION DRAMA.
    EIGHTEENTH CENTURY DRAMA.
        The Reformed Drama.
        The New Comedy.
        Playwrights, Adapters and Triflers.
    NINETEENTH CENTURY DRAMA.
        Georgian.
        Victorian.

BOOKS OF GENERAL REFERENCE.
    1. Bibliographical.
    2. Dramatic History and Criticism.
    3. History of the English Theatre.
    4. Stage Polemics.

NOTE. The English drama as here handled comprises only what may be termed secular drama. The bibliography of the old religious drama of England, exclusive of Moralities, is thoroughly treated by Prof. Francis H. Stoddard in his *References for Students of Miracle Plays and Mysteries*, Library Bulletin, No. 8, University of California. (See also my *English Religious Drama, Appendix*, Macmillan).

It is hoped that the work under the first two divisions is tolerably complete. The rest is necessarily done on the selective principle. Where, under the third division, a book is noted by author and title only,—as is the case with books several times cited—full data may be found in the fourth division, where the book occurs under its appropriate heading. Authorities on the general subject, as Ward and Collier, are not ordinarily given in individual cases, and, except for special reason, the obvious works of reference, as the Dictionary of National Biography and the Encyclopædia Britannica, are taken for granted.

K. L. B.

COLLECTIONS OF OLD PLAYS.

NOTE.—Compilations of "Beauties of the Stage," and the like, are not included here, nor the later collections of acting plays. Of these the most voluminous is Lacy's Acting Edition, continued by French. A partial list of the plays so issued, mostly modern, may be found in the card catalogue of the Boston Athenæum Library. Other collections not indexed here, because not accessible to the compilers, are

    Collection of New Plays. London, 1774.
    Cawthorn's Minor British Theatre. London, 1807.
    Galt's New British Theatre. 4 vols. 1814–'15.
    Sinnett's Family Drama. Hamburg, 1834.
    Dicks' Standard Plays. London, 1883.

ALPHABETICAL INDEX.

Ancient British drama. Scott. 1810.
Bell. British theatre. 1797, and supplement, n. d.
Best English plays. 1710 – '21.
British drama. 1853.
Bullen. Old English plays. 1882.
Bullen. Old English plays. New series. 1887.
Chetwood. Collection of old plays. 1750.
Child. Four old plays. 1848.
Collier. Five old plays. 1833.
Cumberland. British theatre. 1829.
Cumberland. Minor theatre. n. d.
Dilke. Old English plays. 1814 – '15. A supplement to Dodsley.
Dodsley. Old plays. 1744.
Dodsley. Reed's edition. 1780.
Dodsley. Collier's edition. 1825 – '27.
Dodsley. Hazlitt's edition. 1874 – '76.
Farces. 1792.
Fitzgibbon. Famous Elizabethan plays. 1889.
Gratiæ theatrales. 1662.
Hawkins. Origin of the English drama. 1773.
Inchbald. British theatre. 1808.
Inchbald. Farces. 1809.
Inchbald. Modern theatre. 1811.
Keltie. Works of the British dramatists. 1870.
London stage. 1824 – '27.
London theatre. Dibdin. 1815 – '25.
Maidment and Logan. Dramatists of the Restoration. 1872 – '79.
Modern British drama. Scott. 1811.
New English theatre. 1776 – '77.
Old English drama. 1825.
Old plays. 1816. *See* Dilke, Old English plays. 1814 – '15.
Oxberry. New English drama. 1818 – '25.
Scott. Ancient British drama. 1810.
Scott. Modern British drama. 1811.

Simpson. School of Shakspere. 1878.
Six old plays. Published by J. Nichols. 1779.
Tauchnitz. Doubtful plays of Shakespeare. 1869.
Thayer. Best Elizabethan plays. 1890.
White. Old English drama. 1850.

COLLECTIONS.
(Chronologically arranged).

Gratiæ theatrales: or, a choice ternary of English plays, composed upon especial occasions, by several ingenious persons. Lond. 1662.

A collection of the best English plays. 10 vols. 1710 — '21.

Dodsley, R. A select collection of old plays. 12 vols. Lond. 1744.

Chetwood, William Rufus. A select collection of old plays. Dublin. 1750.

Hawkins, T. Origin of the English drama, illustrated by specimens. 3 vols. Oxford. 1773.

The new English theatre. 12 vols. Lond. 1776 — '77. Containing the most valuable plays which have been acted on the London stage.

Six old plays on which Shakespeare founded his Measure for measure, Comedy of errors, Taming of the shrew, King John, King Henry V., King Henry VI., King Lear. 2 vols. in 1. Lond. 1779.

Dodsley's old plays. (Reed's Dodsley.) 12 vols. 1780. The second edition, corrected and collated with the old copies, with notes critical and explanatory, by Isaac Reed.

A collection of the most esteemed farces. Edinb. 1792. 6 vols.

Bell's British theatre. Consisting of the most esteemed English plays. 34 vols. Lond. 1797.

Supplement to Bell's British theatre. 6 vols., n. d. Consisting of the most esteemed farces and entertainments now performing on the British stage.

The British theatre; or, A collection of plays which are acted at the Theatres Royal, Drury Lane, Covent Garden, and Haymarket. Printed under the authority of the managers for the prompt book, with biographical and critical remarks by Mrs. Elizabeth Inchbald. 25 vols. Lond. Longmans. 1808.

A collection of farces and other afterpieces, which are acted at the Theatres Royal, Drury Lane, Covent Garden and Haymarket. Printed under the authority of the managers from the prompt book. Selected by Mrs. Elizabeth Inchbald. 7 vols. Lond. Longmans. 1809.

Scott, Sir W. The ancient British drama. 3 vols. Lond. W. Miller. 1810.

Scott, Sir W. Modern British drama. 5 vols. Lond. W. Miller. 1811.

Inchbald, Mrs. Elizabeth. 10 vols. The modern theatre; a collection of successful modern plays, as acted at the Theatres Royal, London. Printed from the prompt books under the authority of the managers. 1811.

Dilke, C. W. Old English plays; being a selection from the early dramatic writers. (A continuation of Dodsley's collection). 6 vols. Lond. Rodwell. 1814 — '15.

The London theatre. A collection of the most celebrated dramatic pieces correctly given, from copies used in the theatres. By Thomas Dibdin of the Theatre Royal, Drury Lane. 12 vols. 1815 — '25.

Oxberry, W. The new British drama; with prefatory remarks, biographical sketches, and notes, critical and explanatory. Being the only edition existing which is faithfully marked with the stage business and stage directions, as performed at the Theatres Royal. 22 vols. Lond. Simpkin. 1818 — '25.

The London stage. A collection of the most reputed tragedies, comedies, operas, melo-dramas, farces and interludes. Accurately printed from acting copies, as performed at the Theatres Royal, and carefully collated and revised. 4 vols. Lond. Sherwood. 1824 — '27.

The old English drama. A selection of plays from the old English dramatists. 2 vols. Lond. Baldwyn, 1824. Hurst, Robinson & Co. 1825.

Dodsley's Old plays. (Collier's Dodsley). A new edition, with additional notes and corrections, by the late Isaac Reed, Octavius Gilchrist, and J. P. Collier. 12 vols. Lond. S. Prowett. 1825 — '27.

Cumberland, John. (Pub.) British theatre. With remarks, biographical and critical, by George Daniel. Printed from the acting copies, as performed at the Theatres Royal. 41 vols. Lond. 1829. *For contents, see* Peabody Institute Library Catalogue. Baltimore, 1883. Part I., pp. 848, 849.

Cumberland, John. (Pub.) Minor theatre. With remarks, biographical and critical, by George Daniel. Printed from the acting copies, as performed at the metropolitan minor theatres. 15 vols. Lond. n. d. *For contents, see* Peabody Institute Library Catalogue. Baltimore. 1883. Part I., pp. 849, 850.

White, Thomas. Old English drama. 4 vols. Lond. 1830. Hurst. 2 vols. 1830.

Collier, J. P. Five old plays, forming a supplement to the collections of Dodsley and others. Edin. and Lond. Roxburghe Club. 1833.

Child, Francis J. Four old plays. Cambridge, Mass. 1848.

British drama: a collection of tragedies, comedies, operas and farces. 2 vols. Philadelphia. 1853.

Doubtful plays of W. Shakespeare. Tauchnitz edition. Leipzig. 1869.

Keltie, John S. Works of the British dramatists. Edin. 1870. Lond. Simpkin.

Maidment and Logan, Dramatists of the Restoration. 14 vols. Edin. and Lond. Sotheran. 1872 — '79.

Dodsley's Old plays. (Hazlitt's Dodsley). Now first chronologically arranged, revised and enlarged, with the notes of all the commentators, and new notes by W. Carew Hazlitt. 15 vols. Lond. Reeves and Turner. 1874 — '76. 157 / 6.

Simpson, R. School of Shakspere. 2 vols. Lond. Chatto. 1878.

Bullen, A. H. Old English plays. 4 vols. Lond. Nimmo. 1882.

Bullen, A. H. Old English plays. New series. 3 vols. Lond. Nimmo. 1887.

Fitzgibbon, H. M. Famous Elizabethan plays. Lond. W. H. Allen. 1889.

Thayer, William Roscoe. The best Elizabethan plays. 1 vol. Boston. Ginn. 1890.

GENERAL INDEX TO COLLECTIONS.

(BY TITLES OF PLAYS).

Abra-mule. Best Eng. plays, *5.
Abroad and at home. London stage, 4.
Absent man. Farces, 1792, 6.
Actæon and Diana. Chetwood.
Adopted child. Inchbald, Farces, 6. London stage, 1.
Adventures of five hours. Best Eng. plays, 8; Dodsley, 1744, 12; Dodsley, 1780, 12; Scott, Anc. Br. dr., 3; Collier's Dodsley, 12; Hazlitt's Dodsley, 15.
Albertus Wallenstein. Old Eng. dr., 2.
Albina. Bell, 1797, 29.
Albion queens. Bell, 1797, 22.
Albovine. Maidment and L., Davenant, 1.
Albumazar. Dodsley, 1744, 9; Dodsley, 1780, 7; Scott, Anc. Br. dr., 2; Collier's Dodsley, 7; Hazlitt's Dodsley, 11.
Alchymist. Bell, 1797, 1; Scott, Mod. Br. dr., 3; Keltie, 1870; Thayer, 1890.
Alexander and Campaspe. *See* Campaspe.
Alexander the Great. Inchbald, Br. th., 6; Lond. th., 1; Oxberry, 3; London stage, 1; Brit. dr., 1853, 2.
All fools. Dodsley, 1780, 4; Scott, Anc. Br. dr., 2; Collier's Dodsley, 4.
All for love. Best Eng. plays, 3; New Eng. th., 8; Bell, 1797, 16; Inchbald, Br. th., 6; Scott, Mod. Br. dr., 1; London th., 1; London stage, 3; Brit. dr., 1853, 2.
All in the wrong. Bell, 1797, 12; Inchbald, Br. th., 15; London th., 1; Oxberry, 20; London stage, 2.
All mistaken. Dodsley, 1744, 12; Hazlitt's Dodsley, 15.
All the world's a stage. Bell's suppl., 4; Inchbald, Farces, 4; London stage, 1; Brit. dr., 1853, 2; Farces, 1792, 4.
Alzira. Bell, 1797, 7; Brit. dr., 1853, 2.
Ambitious statesman. Maidment and L., Crowne, 3.
Ambitious step-mother. Bell, 1797, 25.
Amends for ladies. White, Old Eng. dr., 2; Five old plays, (Collier's); Hazlitt's Dodsley, 11.
Amintas. Farces, 1792, 6.
Amphitryon. Best Eng. plays, 4; New Eng. th., 9; Bell, 1797, 21.
Anatomist. Bell's suppl., 1; Farces, 1792, 1.
Andromana. Dodsley, 1744, 11; Dodsley, 1780, 11; Scott, Anc. Br. dr., 3; Hazlitt's Dodsley, 14.
Andronicus Comnenius. Maidment and L., Wilson.
Animal magnetism. London stage, 4.
Antiquary. Dodsley, 1744, 7; Dodsley, 1780, 10; Scott, Anc. Br. dr., 3; Collier's Dodsley, 10; Hazlitt's Dodsley, 13; Maidment and L., Marmion.
Antonio and Mellida. Dilke, Old Eng. plays, 2; Keltie, 1870.
Antonio's revenge. Keltie, 1870.
Antony and Cleopatra. Inchbald, Br. th., 4.
Appearance is against them. London stage, 4.

---
* The final number denotes the vol. of the collection.

Appius and Virginia. Dilke, Old Eng. pl., 5; Collier's Dodsley, 12; Hazlitt's Dodsley, 4.
Apprentice. Bell's suppl., 1; Inchbald, Farces, 3; Scott, Mod. Br. dr., 5; London th., 1; London stage, 4; Brit. dr., 1853, 1; Farces, 1792, 1.
Arden of Feversham. Scott, Mod. Br. dr., 2; London stage, 2; Brit. dr., 1853, 1.
Artaxerxes. Oxberry, 22.
As you like it. Inchbald, Br. th., 3; Oxberry, 7.
Aurenge-zebe. Best Eng. plays, 3.
Author. Bell's suppl., 3; Inchbald, Farces, 7; Scott, Mod. Br. dr., 5; Farces, 1792, 3.

Ball. Old Eng. dr., 1.
Bank note. Inchbald, Mod. th., 9.
Barbarossa. New Eng. th., 8; Bell, 1797, 26; Inchbald, Br. th., 15; Scott, Mod. Br. dr., 2; London stage, 2; British dr., 1853, 1.
Barnaby Brittle. Farces, 1792, 5.
Bashful man. London stage, 4.
Battle of Hastings. Bell, 1797, 6.
Battle of Hexham. Inchbald, Br. th., 20.
Beaux' stratagem. Best Eng. plays, 10; New Eng. th., 5; Bell, 1797, 10; Inchbald, Br. th., 8; Scott, Mod. Br. dr., 4; London th., 1; Oxberry, 7; London stage, 2; Brit. dr., 1853, 1.
Beggar's opera. Bell, 1797, 11; Inchbald, Br. th., 12; Scott, Mod. Br. dr., 5; London th., 1; Oxberry, 2; London stage, 1; Brit. dr., 1853, 1.
Belles' stratagem. Inchbald, Br. th., 19; London th., 1; Oxberry, 6; London stage, 2; Br. dr., 1853, 1.
Belphegor. Maidment and L., Wilson.
Bertram. Oxberry, 22.
Bethsabe. Keltie, 1870.
Better late than never. London stage, 3.
Bird in a cage. Dodsley, 1744, 9; Dodsley, 1780, 8; Scott, Anc. Br. dr., 1.
Birth-day. Inchbald, Farces, 2.
Birth of Merlin. Doubtful plays. Tauchnitz.
Blind boy. Inchbald, Farces, 1.
Blue beard. Oxberry, 21.
Blue devils. Oxberry, 15.
Blurt, master constable. Chetwood.
Boadicea. Bell, 1797, 2; Scott, Mod. Br. dr., 2.
Boarding school. Farces, 1792, 5.
Bold stroke for a husband. Inchbald, Br. th., 19; London stage, 3.
Bold stroke for a wife. New Eng. th., 1; Bell, 1797, 12; Inchbald, Br. th., 11; Scott, Mod. Br. dr., 4; London th., 2; Oxberry, 7; London stage, 1; Brit. dr., 1853, 1.
Bondman. Scott, Mod. Br. dr., 1.
Bon ton; or high life above stairs. Bell's suppl., 4; Inchbald, Farces, 5; Scott, Mod. Br. dr., 5: Oxberry, 15; London stage, 3; Brit. dr., 1853, 1; Farces, 1792, 4.
Bonduca. Bell, 1797, 33; Scott, Mod. Br. dr., 1.
Box lobby challenge. Inchbald, Mod. th., 5.
Braganza. London stage, 4; Inchbald, Mod. th., 6.
Bride. Bullen, n. s., 2.
Britannia triumphans. Maidment and L., Davenant, 2.
Broken heart. Scott, Mod. Br. dr., 1; White, Old Eng. dr., 2.

Brothers. Keltie, 1870. By Shirley.
Brothers. By Young. Bell, 1797, 30; Scott, Mod. Br. dr., 2.
Brothers. New Eng. th., 12 (?); Bell, 1797, 12, (Cumberland); Inchbald, Br. th., 18, (Cumberland); Scott, Mod. Br. dr., 4, (Cumberland); Lond. th., 1; London stage, 2; Brit. dr., 1853, 2.
Bucks have at ye all. Bell's suppl., 4; Farces, 1792, 4.
Busiris. Bell, 1797, 20.
Bussy d'Ambois. Dilke, Old Eng. pl., 3.
Busy body. New Eng. th., 1; Bell, 1797, 16; Inchbald, Br. th., 11; Scott, Mod. Br. dr., 4; London th., 2; Oxberry, 6; London stage, 2.

Caligula. Maidment and L., Crowne, 4.
Calisto. Maidment and L., Crowne, 1.
Calisto and Meliboea. Hazlitt's Dodsley, 1.
Cambises. Hawkins, 1; Hazlitt's Dodsley, 4.
Campaspe. Dodsley, 1744, 2; Dodsley, 1780, 2; Scott, Anc. Br. dr., 1; Collier's Dodsley, 2; Keltie, 1870.
Candlemas day. Hawkins, 1.
Captain. (Heywood). Bullen, 1882, 4.
Captain O'Blunder. Bell's suppl., 3; Farces, 1792, 3.
Captain T. Stukely. Simpson's School, 1.
Captain Underwit. Bullen, 1882, 2.
Caractacus. Bell, 1797, 31; Scott, Mod. Br. dr., 2.
Careless husband. Best. Eng. plays, 9; New Eng. th., 7; Bell, 1797, 8; Inchbald, Br. th., 9; Scott, Mod. Br. dr., 3; London stage, 3; Brit. dr., 1853, 2.
Carmelite. Bell, 1797, 16; London stage, 4; Inchbald, Mod. th., 5.
Castle of Andalusia. Inchbald, Br. th., 22.
Castle of Sorrento. London stage, 4.
Castle spectre. Oxberry, 4; London stage, 1.
Cato. New Eng. th., 10; Bell, 1797, 3; Inchbald, Br. th., 8; Scott, Mod. Br. dr., 1; London th., 3; Oxberry, 17; London stage, 2; Brit. dr., 1853, 1.
Challenge for beauty. Dilke, Old Eng. pl., 6.
Chances. Best Eng. plays, 6; New Eng. th., 11; Bell, 1797, 11; Inchbald, Br. th., 6; Scott, Mod. Br. dr., 3; London stage, 4; Brit. dr., 1853, 2.
Changeling. Dilke, Old Eng. plays, 4.
Chaplet. Bell's suppl., 1; Farces, 1792, 1.
Chapter of accidents. Bell, 1797, 34; London th., 2; Oxberry, 18; London stage, 2; Inchbald, Mod. th., 9.
Charles I. Bell, 1797, 19; Scott, Mod. Br. dr., 2.
Charles VIII. of France. Maidment and L., Crowne, 1.
Cheats. Maidment and L., Wilson.
Cheats of Scapin. Scott, Mod. Br. dr., 5; London stage, 4.
Chichevache and Bycome. Collier's Dodsley, 12.
Child of nature. Inchbald, Farces, 1; London stage, 2.
Choleric man. Bell, 1797, 4.
Chrononhotonthologos. Bell's suppl., 2; Farces, 1792, 2; London stage, 3; Scott. Mod. Br. dr., 5.
Citizen. Bell's suppl., 3; Inchbald, Farces, 4; Scott, Mod. Br. dr., 5; London th., 2; Oxberry, 11; London stage, 1; Farces, 1792, 3.
City madam. Dodsley, 1744, 8.
City match. Dodsley, 1744, 10; Dodsley, 1780, 9; Scott, Anc. Br. dr., 2; Collier's Dodsley, 9; Hazlitt's Dodsley, 13.
City nightcap. Dodsley, 1744, 9; Dodsley, 1780, 11; Scott, Anc. Br. dr., 3; Collier's Dodsley, 11; Hazlitt's Dodsley, 13; Bullen, n. s., 3.

City politicks. Maidment and L., Crowne, 2.
City wives' confederacy. Brit. dr., 1853, 2.
Clandestine marriage. Bell, 1797, 14; Inchbald, Br. th., 10; Scott, Mod. Br. dr., 4; London th., 2; Oxberry, 5; London stage, 1; Brit. dr., 1853, 1.
Cleone. Bell, 1797, 5; Scott, Mod. Br. dr., 2.
— Cleonice. Bell, 1797, 24.
Comedy of errors. Inchbald, Br. th., 1.
Commissary. Bell's suppl., 4; Scott, Mod. Br. dr., 5; Farces, 1792, 4.
Committee. New Eng. th., 5; Bell, 1797, 20; Scott, Mod. Br. dr., 3.
Comus. Bell, 1797, 1; Bell's suppl., 4, (Coleman's); Inchbald, Farces, 7, (Coleman's); Scott, Mod. Br. dr., 5, (Coleman's); Scott, Mod. Br. dr., 2, (Milton's); London th., 2, (Coleman's); London stage, 2; Brit. dr., 1853, 2; Farces, 1792, 4.
Confederacy. New Eng. th., 11; Bell, 1797, 22; Scott, Mod. Br. dr., 3; London th., 2; Oxberry, 12; London stage, 3.
Conflict of conscience. Hazlitt's Dodsley, 6.
Conscious lovers. New Eng. th., 1; Bell, 1797, 13; Inchbald, Br. th., 12; Scott, Mod. Br. dr., 4; London th., 2; London stage, 2.
Constant couple. Best Eng. plays, 10; New Eng. th., 9; Bell, 1797, 16; Inchbald, Br. th., 8; Scott, Mod. Br. dr., 4; London th., 3; London stage, 2.
Contention betw. liberality and prodigality. Hazlitt's Dodsley, 8.
Contrivances. Bell's suppl., 4; Scott, Mod. Br. dr., 5; London stage, 4; Farces, 1792, 4.
Cooper. Farces, 1792, 6.
Coriolanus. Inchbald, Br. th., 5; Oxberry, 8.
Cornelia. Dodsley, 1744, 11; Dodsley, 1780, 2; Hazlitt's Dodsley, 5.
Costlie whore. Bullen, 1882, 4.
Count of Narbonne. Inchbald, Br. th., 20; London th., 3; London stage, 3.
Countess of Salisbury. Bell, 1797, 18; Inchbald, Br. th., 16; Scott, Mod. Br. dr., 2.
Country girl. Bell, 1797, 13; Inchbald, Br. th., 16; Scott, Mod. Br. dr., 3; London th., 3; Oxberry, 8; London stage, 1; Brit. dr., 1853, 1.
Country lasses. Bell, 1797, 9.
Country wife. New Eng. th., 11.
Country wit. Maidment and L., Crowne, 3.
Covent garden. Bullen, n. s., 1.
—Creusa. Bell, 1797, 34.
Critic. Inchbald, Farces, 3; Scott, Mod. Br. dr., 5; London th., 3; Oxberry, 9; London stage, 1; Brit. dr., 1853, 1.
Cross purposes. London stage, 2; Farces, 1792, 6.
Crowne for a conquerour. Bullen, n. s., 3.
Cruel brother. Maidment and L., Davenant, 1.
Cunning man. Bell's suppl., 2; Farces, 1792, 2.
Cure for the heart. Inchbald, Br. th., 25.
Curfew. London stage, 4.
Cymbeline. Inchbald, Br. th., 4; Oxberry, 12.
Cymon. Bell, 1797, 23; Bell's suppl., 3; London th., 3; London stage, 3; Farces, 1792, 3.
Cyrus. Bell, 1797, 24.

Damon and Phillida. Farces, 1792, 5.
Damon and Pithias. Dodsley, 1744, 1; Dodsley, 1780, 1; Scott, Anc. Br. dr., 1; Collier's Dodsley, 1; Hazlitt's Dodsley, 4.
— Daphne and Amintor. Farces, 1792, 5.

Darius. Maidment and L., Crowne, 3.
David and Bethsabe. Hawkins, 2.
De Montfort. Inchbald, Br. th., 24.
Deaf and dumb. Oxberry, 6; London stage, 1.
Deaf lover. London stage, 3.
Death of Robert, Earl of Huntington. Five old plays, (Collier); Hazlitt's Dodsley, 8.
Delinquent. Inchbald, Mod. th., 2.
Desert Island. Farces, 1792, 5.
Deserted daughter. Inchbald, Br. th., 24; London stage, 3.
Deserter. Bell's suppl., 4; Inchbald, Farces, 2; Oxberry, 11; London stage, 1; Farces, 1792, 4.
Destruction of Jerusalem, Parts 1 and 2. Maidment and L., Crowne, 2.
Deuce is in him. Bell's suppl., 1; Inchbald, Farces, 6; Scott, Mod. Br. dr., 5; London stage, 3; Brit. dr., 1853, 1; Farces, 1792, 1.
Devil to pay. Bell's suppl., 2; Inchbald, Farces, 5; Scott, Mod. Br. dr., 5; London th., 3; Oxberry, 21; London stage, 1; Brit. dr., 1853, 1; Farces, 1792, 2.
Devil upon two sticks. Scott, Mod. Br. dr., 5.
Dick of Devonshire. Bullen, 1882, 2.
Dido, queen of Carthage. Old Eng. dr., 2.
Discovery. Bell, 1797, 5.
Disobedient child. Hazlitt's Dodsley, 2.
Distracted emperor. Bullen, 1882, 3.
Distracted state. Maidment and L., Tatham.
Distresses. Maidment and L., Davenant, 4.
Distrest mother. New Eng. th., 6; Bell, 1797, 6; Inchbald, Br. th., 7; Scott, Mod. Br. dr., 1; London th., 4; Oxberry, 5; London stage, 4; Brit. dr., 1853, 2.
Doctor and the apothecary. Inchbald, Farces, 6; London stage, 2; Brit. dr., 1853, 1.
Doctor Faustus. Dilke, Old Eng. pl., 1; White, Old Eng. dr., 4. (*See also* Faustus).
Dr. Last in his chariot. Scott, Mod. Br. dr., 5; Farces, 1792, 5.
Don Sebastian. Scott, Mod. Br. dr., 1.
Double dealer. Best Eng. plays, 7; New Eng. th., 9; Bell, 1797, 28; Scott, Mod. Br. dr., 3; London th., 3; London stage, 4.
Double gallant. New Eng. th., 9; Bell, 1797, 10; London th., 3.
Douglas. New Eng. th., 10; Bell, 1797, 3; Inchbald, Br. th., 16; Scott, Mod. Br. dr., 2; London th., 4; Oxberry, 12; Brit. dr., 1853, 1.
Downfall of the Earl of Huntington. Five old plays, (Collier's); Hazlitt's Dodsley, 8.
Dragon of Wantley. London stage, 2; Farces, 1792, 5.
Dramatist. Inchbald, Br. th., 20.
Drummer. New Eng. th., 7; Bell, 1797, 22; Scott, Mod. Br. dr., 4; Br. dr., 1853, 2.
Duchess of Malfi. Keltie, 1870; Thayer, 1890.
Duenna. Inchbald, Br. th., 19; Oxberry, 2; London stage, 1; Brit. dr., 1853, 2.
Duke and no duke. Farces, 1792, 5.
Duke of Milan. London th., 4; London stage, 2, Keltie, 1870.
Dumb knight. Dodsley, 1744, 6; Dodsley, 1780, 4; Scott, Anc. Br. dr., 2; Collier's Dodsley, 4; Hazlitt's Dodsley, 10.
Dumb lady. Maidment and L., Lacy.

Duplicity. London stage, 4; Inchbald, Mod. th., 4.
Earl of Essex. New Eng. th., 8; Bell, 1797, 6; Inchbald, Br. th., 22; Scott, Mod. Br. dr., 2; London th., 4; London stage, 3; Brit. dr., 1853, 2.
Earl of Warwick. Bell, 1797, 17; Inchbald, Br. th., 19; Scott, Mod. Br. dr., 2; London th., 4; London stage, 3.
Eastward hoe. Dodsley, 1744, 4; Dodsley, 1780, 4; Scott, Anc. Br. dr., 2; Collier's Dodsley, 4.
Edgar and Emmeline. Bell's suppl., 4; Inchbald, Farces, 6; Farces, 1792, 4.
Edward and Eleonora. Bell, 1797, 32.
Edward I. Collier's Dodsley, 11; White, Old Eng. dr., 4.
Edward II. Dodsley, 1744, 2; Dodsley, 1780, 2; Scott, An. Br. dr., 1; Collier's Dodsley, 2; Keltie, 1870.
Edward III. Doubtful plays. Tauchnitz.
Edward IV. Heywood. Sh. soc., '42.
Edward the Black Prince. Bell, 1797, 9; Inchbald, Br. th., 14; London th., 4; London stage, 4.
Elfrida. Bell, 1797, 34; Scott, Mod. Br. dr., 2.
Ella Rosenburg. Inchbald, Farces, 1.
Elvira. Dodsley, 1744, 12; Dodsley, 1780, 12; Scott, Anc. Br. dr., 3; Collier's Dodsley, 12; Hazlitt's Dodsley, 15.
Endymion; or the Man in the moon. Dilke, Old Eng. pl., 2.
England preserved. Inchbald, Mod. th., 8.
English friar. Maidment and L., Crowne, 4.
English merchant. Inchbald, Mod. th., 9.
English traveller. Dilke, Old Eng. pl., 6.
Englishman in Paris. Bell's suppl., 3; Scott, Mod. Br. dr., 5; Farces, 1792, 3.
Englishman returned from Paris. Bell's suppl., 3; Scott, Mod. Br. dr., 5; Farces, 1792, 3.
Englishmen for my money. White, Old Eng. dr., 1; Hazlitt's Dodsley, 10.
Entertainment at Rutland house. Maidment and L., Davenant, 3.
Ephesian matron. Farces, 1792, 6.
Eurydice. Bell, 1797, 26.
Evadne. Oxberry, 14.
Everie woman in her humor. Bullen, 1882, 4.
Every man. Hawkins, 1; Hazlitt's Dodsley, 1.
Every man in his humour. New Eng. th., 5; Bell, 1797, 4; Inchbald, Br. th., 5; Scott, Mod. Br. dr., 3; London th., 4; Oxberry, 16; London stage, 3; Brit. dr., 1853, 2; Keltie, 1870.
Every one has his fault. Inchbald, Br. th., 23; Oxberry, 16; London stage, 2.

Fair Apostate. Scott, Mod. Br. dr., 2.
Fair Em. Chetwood; Simpson's school, 2.
Fair favorite. Maidment and L., Davenant, 4.
Fair penitent. New Eng. th., 2; Bell, 1797, 3; Inchbald, Br. th., 10; Scott, Mod. Br. dr., 1; London th., 5; Oxberry, 21; London stage, 2; Brit. dr., 1853, 1.
Fair quaker of Deal. Bell, 1797, 14.
Fall of man. See State of innocence.
False delicacy. Bell, 1797, 30.
False impressions. London stage, 4; Inchbald, Mod. th., 5.
False one. Scott, Mod. Br. dr. 1.
Falstaff's wedding. Bell, 1797, 31; Scott, Mod. Br. dr., 4.
Farm house. Inchbald, Farces, 6; London stage, 2.

Farmer. Inchbald, Farces, 2.
Farmer's wife. London th., 5; London stage, 4.
Fashionable levities. Inchbald, Mod. th., 10.
Fashionable lover. Bell, 1797, 18; London th., 4; London stage, 2.
Fatal Curiosity. Bell, 1797, 23; Inchbald, Br. th., 11; Scott, Mod. Br. dr., 2; London stage, 3; Br. dr., 1853, 1.
Fatal dowry. Scott, Mod. Br. dr., 1.
Faustus. (Marlowe). Keltie, 1870.
Ferrex and Porrex. Dodsley, 1744, 2; Hawkins, 2; Dodsley, 1780, 1; Scott, Anc. Br. dr., 1; Collier's Dodsley, 1.
Fine Companion. Maidment and L., Marmion.
First floor. Inchbald, Farces, 6; London stage, 3; Br. dr., 1853, 2.
First love. Inchbald, Br. th., 18; London stage, 3.
Flora; or Hob in the well, Bell's suppl., 4; Inchbald, Farces, 5; Farces, 1792, 4.
Florizel and Perdita. Bell's suppl., 1; Farces, 1792, 1.
Follies of a day. Oxberry, 13; London stage, 2.
Folly as it flies. Inchbald, Mod. th., 2.
Fountainbleau. Inchbald, Br. th., 22.
Fortune's fool. Inchbald, Mod. th., 2.
Fortune's frolic. London th., 5; Oxberry, 13; London stage, 2; Brit. dr., 1853, 1.
Foundling. Bell, 1797, 11; Inchbald, Br. th., 14; London stage, 3.
Four P's. Dodsley, 1744, 1; Dodsley, 1780, 1; Scott, Anc. Br. dr., 1; Collier's Dodsley, 1; Hazlitt's Dodsley, 1.
Four prentises of London. Dodsley, 1780, 6; Scott, Anc. Br. dr., 3; Collier's Dodsley, 6.
Friar Bacon and Friar Bungay. Collier's Dodsley, 8; Keltie, 1870.
Fugitive. Inchbald, Mod. th., 8.
Fuimus Troes. Dodsley, 1744, 3; Dodsley, 1780, 7; Collier's Dodsley, 7.
Funeral. Best Eng. plays, 10; New Eng. th., 7; Bell, 1797, 27; Scott, Mod. Br. dr., 4.

Gamester. Dodsley, 1744, 9; New Eng. th., 4; Dodsley, 1780, 9; Bell, 1797, 10; Inchbald, Br. th., 14, (Moore); Scott, Anc. Br. dr., 2, (Shirley); Scott, Mod. Br. dr., 2, (Moore); London th., 5, (Moore); Oxberry, 18, (Moore); London stage, 1; Brit. dr., 1853, 1.
Gamesters. Bell, 1797, 6.
Gammer Gurton's needle. Dodsley, 1744, 1; Hawkins, 1; Dodsley, 1780, 2; Scott, Anc. Br. dr., 1; Collier's Dodsley, 2; White, Old Eng. dr., 1; Hazlitt's Dodsley, 3.
Gentle shepherd. Bell, 1797, 25.
George à Green. Dodsley, 1744, 1; Dodsley, 1780, 3; Scott, Anc. Br. dr., 1; Collier's Dodsley, 3.
George Barnwell. New Eng. th., 6; Bell, 1797, 14; Inchbald, Br. th., 11; Scott, Mod. Br. dr., 2; Oxberry, 17; London stage, 2; Br. dr., 1853, 1.
Ghost, fr. Mrs. Centlivre's 'Man bewitched.' Farces, 1792, 6.
Giovanni in London. London stage, 3.
Goblins. Dodsley, 1744, 7; Dodsley, 1780, 10; Collier's Dodsley, 10.
God's promises. Dodsley, 1744, 1; Dodsley, 1780, 1; Collier's Dodsley, 1; Hazlitt's Dodsley, 1.
Golden pippin. Bell's suppl., 3; Farces, 1792, 3.
Good-natured man. Bell, 1797, 17; Inchbald, Br. th., 17; Scott, Mod. Br. dr., 4; London th., 5; London stage, 2.
Gorboduc. *See* Ferrex and Porrex.

Great mogul. *See* Aurenge-zebe.
Grecian daughter. New Eng. th., 12; Bell, 1797, 4; Inchbald, Br. th., 15; Scott, Mod. Br. dr., 2; London th., 5; Oxberry, 14; London stage, 3; Br. dr., 1853, 1.
Green's Tu quoque. Dodsley, 1744, 3; Dodsley, 1780, 7; Scott, Anc. Br. dr., 2; Collier's Dodsley, 7; Hazlitt's Dodsley, 11.
Grim, the collier of Croydon. Gratiae th., Dodsley, 1744, 5; Dodsley, 1780, 11; Scott, Anc. Br. dr., 3; Collier's Dodsley, 11; Hazlitt's Dodsley, 8.
Guardian. Dodsley, 1744, 8; Bell's suppl., 1; Inchbald, Farces, 4; Scott, Mod. Br. dr., 5; London th., 5; London stage, 3; Br. dr., 1853, 1; Farces, 1792, 1.
Gustavus Vasa. Bell, 1797, 32; Inchbald, Br. th., 7; Scott, Mod. Br. dr., 2; London stage, 3; Brit. dr., 1853, 1.
Guy Mannering, Oxberry, 12.

Hamlet. Best Eng. plays, 1; Inchbald, Br. th., 1; Oxberry, 3.
Hannibal and Scipio. Bullen, n. s., 1.
Hartford bridge. Inchbald, Farces, 3.
Haunted tower. London stage, 2.
He's much to blame. London stage, 4; Inchbald, Mod. th., 4.
He would be a soldier. London stage, 3; Br. dr., 1853, 2; Inchbald, Mod. th., 8.
He would if he could. Farces, 1792, 5.
Heir. Dodsley, 1744, 7; Dodsley, 1780, 8; Scott, Anc. Br. dr., 1; Collier's Dodsley, 8; Hazlitt's Dodsley, 11.
Heir at law. Inchbald, Br. th., 21.
Heiress. Inchbald, Br. th., 22; London stage, 3.
Henry II. Bell, 1797, 28; Inchbald, Mod. th., 9.
Henry IV. Pt. 1. Best Eng. plays, 2; Inchbald, Br. th., 2; Oxberry, 14.
Henry IV. Part 2. Inchbald, Br. th., 2.
Henry V. Six old plays, 2; Inchbald, Br. th., 2; Oxberry, 18.
Henry VIII. Inchbald, Br. th., 3; Oxberry, 19.
Hero and Leander. London stage, 3; Br. dr., 1853, 1.
Hickscorner. Hazlitt's Dodsley, 1. (*See* Hycke-scorner).
High life below stairs. Bell's suppl., 1; Inchbald, Farces, 5; Scott, Mod. Br. dr., 5; London th., 6; Oxberry, 15; London stage, 1; Brit. dr., 1853, 2; Farces, 1792, 1.
Highland reel. Inchbald, Farces, 2.
Histrio-mastix. Simpson's school, 2.
Hit or miss. London th., 6.
Hog hath' lost its pearl. Dodsley, 1744, 3; Dodsley, 1780, 6; Scott, Anc. Br. dr., 3; Collier's Dodsley, 6; Hazlitt's Dodsley, 11.
Holland's leaguer. Maidment and L., Marmion.
Honest thieves. Oxberry, 9; London stage, 1.
Honest whore. Dodsley, 1744, 3; Dodsley, 1780, 3; Scott, Anc. Br. dr., 1; Collier's Dodsley, 3.
Honey moon. Inchbald, Br. th., 25.
Horace, Prologue to. Maidment and L., Crowne, 1.
How a man may choose a good wife fr. a bad. Old Eng. dr., 1; Hazlitt's Dodsley, 9.
How to grow rich. Inchbald, Mod. th., 1.
Hycke-scorner. Hawkins, 1. (*See* Hickscorner).
Hypocrite. Bell, 1797, 21; Scott, Mod. Br. dr., 4; London th., 5; Oxberry, 1; London stage, 1; Brit. dr., 1853, 1.

I'll tell you what. Inchbald, Mod. th., 7.
Imposters. Inchbald, Mod. th., 6.
Inconstant. New Eng. th., 9; Bell, 1797, 32; Inchbald, Br. th., 8; Scott, Mod. Br. dr., 4; London th., 6; Oxberry, 10; London stage, 1; Brit. dr., 1853, 1.
Indian emperor. Best Eng. plays, 4.
Inkle and Yariko. Inchbald, Br. th., 20; Br. dr., 1853, 2.
Interlude of youth. Hazlitt's Dodsley, 2.
Interludes of the four elements. Hazlitt's Dodsley, 1.
Intriguing chambermaid. Bell's suppl., 3; Scott, Mod. Br. dr., 5; Brit. dr., 1853, 2; Farces, 1792, 3.
Irene. Bell, 1797, 25; Scott, Mod. Br. dr., 2.
Irish widow. Inchbald, Farces, 5; Scott, Mod. Br. dr., 5; London th., 6; London stage, 3; Br. dr., 1853, 1; Farces, 1792, 5.
Irishman in London. Inchbald, Farces, 2.
Iron chest. Inchbald, Br. th., 21.
Is he jealous? Oxberry, 3.
Isabella. Bell, 1797, 5; Inchbald, Br. th., 7; Scott, Mod. Br. dr., 1; London th., 6; Oxberry, 21; London stage, 2; Br. dr., 1853, 1.

Jacke Drums entertainement. Simpson's school, 2.
Jack Jugler. Child, Four old plays; Hazlitt's Dodsley, 2.
Jack Straw. Hazlitt's Dodsley, 5.
Jacob and Esau. Hazlitt's Dodsley, 2,
Jane Gray, Lady. New Eng. th., 8; Bell, 1797, 15; Inchbald, Br. th., 10; Scott, Mod. Br. dr., 1; London th., 7; London stage, 3.
Jane Shore. New Eng. th., 4; Bell, 1797, 3; Inchbald, Br. th., 10; Scott, Mod. Br. dr., 1; London th., 6; Oxberry, 8; London stage, 1; Brit. dr., 1853, 1.
Jealous wife. Bell, 1797, 20; Inchbald, Br. th., 16; Scott, Mod. Br. dr., 4; London th., 6; Oxberry, 1; London stage, 1; Br. dr., 1853, 1.
Jeronymo. Dodsley, 1780, 3; Scott, Anc. Br. dr., 1; Collier's Dodsley, 3; Hazlitt's Dodsley, 4.
Jew. Inchbald, Br. th., 18, (Cumberland); London stage, 1.
Jew and the doctor. Inchbald, Farces, 2.
Jew of Malta. Dodsley, 1780, 8; Scott, Anc. Br. dr., 1; Collier's Dodsley, 8; Thayer, 1800.
Jocasta. Child, Four old plays.
John (King). Six old plays, 2; Inchbald, Br. th., 1; Oxberry, 7.
John (King) and Matilda. Bullen, n. s., 3.
John Bull. Br. th., 21.
Jovial crew. Dodsley, 1744, 6; Dodsley, 1780, 10; Scott, Anc. Br. dr., 3; Collier's Dodsley, 10.
Juliana. Maidment and L., Crowne, 1.
Julius Cæsar. Best Eng. plays, 1; Inchbald, Br. th., 4; Oxberry, 16.
Just Italian. Maidment and L., Davenant, 1.

Katharine and Petruchio. Bell's suppl., 3; Inchbald, Farces, 4; Farces, 1792, 3.
Kenilworth. Oxberry, 19.
Key to the rehearsal. Scott, Mod. Br. dr., 3.
King and no king. Scott, Mod. Br. dr., 1; Keltie, 1870.
Knack to know a knave. Hazlitt's Dodsley, 6.
Knight of the burning pestle. Keltie, 1870; Fitzgibbon, 1889.
Knights. Bell's suppl., 1; Scott, Mod. Br. dr., 5; Farces, 1792, 1.
Know your own mind. Inchbald, Br. th., 15; Oxberry, 14; London stage, 2.

Lady Alimony. Hazlitt's Dodsley, 14.
Lady mother. Bullen, 1882, 2.
Lady's last stake. Bell, 1797, 24.
Lady's privilege. Old Eng. dr., 2.
Lady's trial. Keltie, 1870.
Lame lover. Scott, Mod. Br. dr., 5; Brit. dr., 1853, 2; Farces, 1792, 6.
Laugh when you can. Inchbald, Mod. th., 2.
Law against lovers. Maidment and L., Davenant, 5.
Law of Lombardy. London stage, 4; Inchbald, Mod. th., 6.
Lear (King.) Inchbald, Br. th., 4; Oxberry, 10, 17
Leir (King.) Six old plays, 2.
Lethe. Bell's suppl., 1; Scott, Mod. Br. dr., 5; Farces, 1792, 1.
Lie of a day. Inchbald, Mod. th., 10.
Life. Inchbald, Mod. th., 1.
Life and death of Thomas Lord Cromwell. Scott, Anc. Br. dr., 1.
Like will to like. Hazlitt's Dodsley, 3.
Lilliput. Farces, 1792, 6.
Lingua. Dodsley, 1744, 5; Dodsley, 1780, 5; Scott, Anc. Br. dr., 2; Collier's Dodsley, 5; Hazlitt's Dodsley, 9.
Lionel and Clarissa. Bell, 1797, 21; Inchbald, Br. th., 17; London th., 6; Oxberry, 2; London stage, 1; Brit. dr., 1853, 2.
Lock and key. Inchbald, Farces, 3.
Locrine. Doubtful plays of Sh. Tauchnitz.
Lodviska. Inchbald, Farces, 7; Oxberry, 20; London stage, 2.
London chanticleers. Hazlitt's Dodsley, 12.
London maid. Gratiae th.
London merchant. London th., 5.
London prodigal. Scott Anc. Br. dr., 1; Doubtful plays of Sh. Tauchnitz.
London's glory. Maidment and L., Tatham.
Look about you. Hazlitt's Dodsley, 7.
Lord of the manor. London th., 7; London stage, 2.
Lost lady. Dodsley, 1744, 10; Hazlitt's Dodsley, 12.
Lottery. Bell's suppl., 2; Farces, 1792, 2.
Love a la mode. Inchbald, Farces, 1; Scott, Mod. Br. dr., 5; Oxberry, 21; London stage, 3.
Love and empire. See Abra-mule.
Love and honour. Maidment and L., Davenant, 3.
Love crowns the end. Maidment and L., Tatham.
Love for love. Best Eng. plays, 7; New Eng. th., 5; Bell, 1797, 1; Inchbald, Br. th., 13; Scott, Mod. Br. dr., 3; London th., 6; London stage, 3; Br. dr., 1853, 2.
Love in a village. Bell, 1797, 13; Inchbald, Br. th., 17; Scott, Mod. Br. dr. 5; London th., 7; Oxberry, 2; London stage, 1; Brit. dr., 1853, 2.
Love laughs at locksmiths. Oxberry, 13.
Love makes a man. New Eng. th., 7; Bell, 1797, 7; Inchbald, Br. th., 9; Scott, Mod. Br. dr., 3; London stage, 3.
Love-sick king. Chetwood.
Love will find out the way. Dodsley, 1744, 12.
Love's last shift. Best Eng. plays, 9.
Love's mistress, or Queen's masque. Old Eng. dr., 2.
Lover's melancholy. White, Old Eng. dr., 4.
Lovers' quarrels. London stage, 3.
Lovers' vows. Inchbald, Br. th., 23; London stage, 3.
Lucius Junius Brutus. Bell, 1797, 31.

Lust's dominion. Dilke, Old Eng. pl., 1; Hazlitt's Dodsley, 14.
Lusty Juventus. Hawkins, 1; Hazlitt's Dodsley, 2.
Lyar. Bell's suppl., 2; Inchbald, Farces, 5, (Foote): Scott, Mod. Br. dr., 5. (Foote); Oxberry, 15; London stage, 2; Brit. dr., 1853, 1; Farces, 1792. 2.
Lying varlet. Bell's suppl., 2; Inchbald, Farces, 4; Scott, Mod. Br. dr., 5; London th., 7; Oxberry, 11; London stage, 1; Brit. dr., 1853, 1; Farces, 1792, 2.

Macbeth. Best Eng. plays, 1; Inchbald, Br. th., 4; Oxberry, 14; Maidment and L., Davenant, 5.
Mad couple. See All mistaken.
Mad world, my masters. Dodsley, 1744, 5; Dodsley, 1780, 5; Scott, Anc. Br. dr., 2; Collier's Dodsley, 5.
Magpie. Oxberry, 11.
Mahomet. New Eng. th., 8; Bell, 1797, 23; Inchbald, Br. th., 13; Scott, Mod. Br. dr., 2; London th., 8; London stage, 4; Brit. dr., 1853, 2.
Maid of Bath. Scott, Mod. Br. dr., 5.
Maid of the mill. Bell, 1797, 8; Inchbald, Br. th., 17; Scott, Mod. Br. dr., 5; London th., 7; Oxberry, 2; London stage, 1.
Maid of the oaks. Inchbald, Farces, 6; Scott, Mod. Br. dr., 5; London th., 7; London stage, 3; Farces, 1792, 6.
Maid's tragedy. Scott, Mod. Br. dr., 1.
Malcontent. Dodsley, 1744, 4; Dodsley, 1780, 4; Scott, Anc. Br. dr., 2; Collier's Dodsley, 4.
Male coquette. Scott, Mod. Br. dr., 5.
Man of mode. Best Eng. plays, 6.
Man of the world. Bell, 1797, 27; Inchbald, Br. th., 14; London th., 7; Oxberry, 16; London stage, 1; Brit. dr., 1853, 1.
Man's the master. Maidment and L., Davenant, 5.
Mariamne. Bell, 1797, 26; Scott, Mod. Br. dr., 2.
Marriage broker. Gratiae th.
Marriage night. Dodsley, 1744, 10; Hazlitt's Dodsley, 15.
Marriage of wit and science. Hazlitt's Dodsley, 2. See also Moral play of wit and science.
Married beau. Maidment and L., Crowne, 4.
Martyr'd souldier. Bullen, 1882, 1.
Mary, Queen of Scots. Inchbald, Mod. th., 8.
Masque. Maidment and L., Cokayne.
Match at midnight. Dodsley, 1744, 6; Dodsley, 1780, 7; Scott, Anc. Br. dr., 2; Collier's Dodsley, 7; Hazlitt's Dodsley, 13.
Match in Newgate. See Revenge.
Matilda. Scott, Mod. Br. dr., 2; Inchbald, Mod. th., 8.
Matrimony. Inchbald, Farces, 1.
May day. Dilke, Old Eng. pl., 4; Farces, 1792, 6.
Maydes metamorphosis. Bullen, 1882, 1.
Mayor of Garrat. Bell's suppl., 2; Inchbald, Farces, 5; Scott, Mod. Br. dr., 5; London th., 7; Oxberry, 9; London stage, 1; Br. dr., 1853, 1; Farces, 1792, 2.
Mayor of Quinborough. Dodsley, 1744, 11; Dodsley, 1780, 11; Scott, Anc. Br. dr., 3; Collier's Dodsley, 11.
Measure for measure. Inchbald, Br. th., 3; Oxberry, 16.
Medea. New Eng. th., 12; Bell, 1797, 6.
Menaecmi. Six old plays, 1.

Merchant of Bruges. London th., 7; London stage, 4.
Merchant of Venice. Inchbald, Br. th., 2; Oxberry, 10.
Merope. New Eng. th., 4; Bell, 1797, 23.
Merry devil of Edmonton. Dodsley, 1744, 11; Dodsley, 1780, 5; Scott, Anc. Br.
  dr., 2; Collier's Dodsley, 5; Hazlitt's Dodsley, 10.
Merry wives of Windsor. Best Eng. plays, 2; Inchbald, Br. th., 3; Oxberry, 8.
Microcosmus. Dodsley, 1744, 5; Dodsley, 1780, 9; Scott, Anc. Br. dr., 2; Collier's Dodsley, 9; Bullen, n. s., 2.
Midas. Bell's suppl., 2; Inchbald, Farces, 7; Scott, Mod. Br. dr., 5; Dilke, Old
  Eng. pl., 1; London th., 8; Oxberry, 15; London stage, 1; Brit. dr.,
  1853, 1; Farces, 1792, 2.
Midnight hour. Inchbald, Farces, 1; Oxberry, 13; London stage, 1.
Miller of Mansfield. Bell's suppl., 3; Inchbald, Farces, 7; Scott, Mod. Br. dr., 5;
  London stage, 4; Farces, 1792, 3.
Minor. New Eng. th., 11; Bell, 1797, 2; Inchbald, Farces, 5; Scott, Mod. Br.
  dr., 5; Farces, 1792, 5.
Miser. New Eng. th., 1; Bell, 1797, 11; Scott, Mod. Br. dr., 4; London th., 8;
  Oxberry, 11; London stage, 1.
Miseries of inforst marriage. Dodsley, 1780, 5; Scott, Anc. Br. dr., 2; Collier's
  Dodsley, 5; Hazlitt's Dodsley, 9.
Misfortunes of Arthur. Five old plays, (Collier); Hazlitt's Dodsley, 4.
Miss in her teens. Bell's suppl., 1; Inchbald, Farces, 4; Scott, Mod. Br. dr., 5;
  London th., 8; London stage, 2; Brit. dr., 1853, 2; Farces, 1792, 1.
Mistake. Bell, 1797, 25; Scott, Mod. Br. dr., 3.
Mock doctor. Bell's suppl., 1; Inchbald, Farces, 5; Scott, Mod. Br. dr., 5:
  London th., 8; London stage, 2; Brit. dr., 1853, 1; Farces, 1792, 1.
Mogul tale. London stage, 4.
Monsieur d'Olive. Dilke, Old Eng. pl., 3.
Monsieur Tonson. London stage, 3.
More dissemblers besides women. Dilke, Old Eng. pl., 4.
Mother Bombie. Dilke, Old Eng. pl., 1.
Mountaineers. Inchbald, Br. th., 21.
Mourning bride. Best Eng. plays, 8; New Eng. th., 4; Bell, 1797, 19; Inchbald, Br. th., 13; Scott, Mod. Br. dr., 1; London th., 8; London stage,
  4; Brit. dr., 1853, 1.
Mucedorus. Hazlitt's Dodsley, 7.
Much ado about nothing. Inchbald, Br. th., 2; Oxberry, 18.
Muses' looking glass. Dodsley, 1744, 6; Dodsley, 1780, 9; Scott. Anc. Br. dr., 2;
  Collier's Dodsley, 9.
Musical lady. Bell's suppl., 2; Farces, 1792, 2.
Mustapha. Dodsley, 1744, 2.
My spouse and I. London th., 7; London stage, 4.
Mysterious husband. London stage, 3; Inchbald, Mod. th., 5.

Natural son. Bell, 1797, 20; Inchbald, Mod. th., 5.
Neck or nothing. Bell's suppl., 2; Scott, Mod. Br. dr., 5; Farces, 1792, 2.
Nero. Bullen, 1882, 1.
Netly abbey. Inchbald, Farces, 3.
New custom. Dodsley, 1744, 1; Dodsley, 1780, 1; Collier's Dodsley, 1; Hazlitt's Dodsley, 3.
New juror. Best Eng. plays, 9.
New tricke to cheat the devill. Bullen, n. s., 3.

New way to pay old debts. Inchbald, Br. th., 6; Scott, Mod. Br. dr., 3; London th., 8; Oxberry, 1; London stage, 2; Br. dr., 1853, 1; Keltie, 1870; Fitzgibbon, 1889.
New wonder, a woman never vext. Dilke, Old Eng. pl., 5; Hazlitt's Dodsley, 12.
News from Plymouth. Maidment and L., Davenant, 4.
Next door neighbors. Inchbald, Mod. th., 7.
Nice wanton. Hazlitt's Dodsley, 2.
No song, no supper. London stage, 4.
Noble souldier. Bullen, 1882, 1.
Nobody and somebody. Simpson's School, 1.
Notoriety. Inchbald, Mod. th., 1.

Obstinate lady. Maidment and L., Cokayne.
Oedipus. Best Eng. plays, 3; Bell, 1797, 15.
Old bachelour. Best Eng. plays, 7; New Eng. th., 3; Bell, 1797, 28; Scott, Mod. Br. dr., 3.
Old couple. Dodsley, 1744, 7; Dodsley, 1780, 10; Scott, Anc. Br. dr., 3; Collier's Dodsley, 10; Hazlitt's Dodsley, 12.
Old Fortunatus. Dilke, Old Eng. pl., 3.
Old maid. Bell's suppl., 2 : Inchbald, Farces, 7; Scott, Mod. Br. dr., 5; Farces, 1792, 2.
Old troop. Maidment and L., Lacy.
Orators. Bell's suppl., 4; Scott, Mod. Br. dr., 5; Farces, 1792, 4.
Ordinary. Dodsley, 1744, 10; Dodsley, 1780, 10; Scott, Anc. Br. dr., 3; Collier's Dodsley, 10; Hazlitt's Dodsley, 12.
Oroonoko. Best Eng. plays, 5; New Eng. th., 6; Bell, 1797, 19; Inchbald, Br. th., 7; Scott, Mod. Br. dr., 1; London th., 8; London stage, 2; Br. dr., 1853, 1.
Orphan. Best Eng. plays, 5; New Eng. th., 2; Bell, 1797, 9; Inchbald, Br. th., 12; Scott, Mod. Br. dr., 1; London th., 8; London stage, 3; Br. dr., 1853, 1.
Orphan of China. Bell, 1797, 24; Scott, Mod. Br. dr., 2; London th., 8; London stage, 2; Brit. dr., 1853, 2.
Othello. Best Eng. plays, 1; Inchbald, Br. th., 5; Oxberry, 5.
Ovid's tragedy. Maidment and L., Cokayne.

Padlock. Bell's suppl., 3; Inchbald, Farces, 4; Scott, Mod. Br. dr., 5; London th. 9; Oxberry, 21; London stage, 1; Br. dr., 1853, 1; Farces, 1792, 3.
Panel. London stage, 4.
Parasitaster. Dilke, Old Eng. pl., 2.
Pardoner and Frere. Child, Four old plays; Hazlitt's Dodsley, 1.
Parson's wedding. Dodsley, 1744, 9; Dodsley, 1780, 11; Scott, An. Br. dr., 3; Collier's Dodsley, 11; Hazlitt's Dodsley, 14.
Pasquil and Katherine. *See* Jacke Drums, etc.
Patron. Bell's suppl., 4; Scott, Mod. Br. dr., 5; Farces, 1792, 4.
Paul and Virginia. London stage, 4.
Peep behind the curtain. Scott, Mod. Br. dr., 5.
Percy. Brit. dr., 1853, 1; Inchbald, Mod. th., 7.
Pericles. Bell, 1797, 29.
Perkin Warbeck. Fitzgibbon, 1889.
Phaedra and Hippolitus. Best Eng. plays, 8; New Eng. th., 2; Bell, 1797, 28.
Philaster. Bell, 1797, 18; Scott, Mod. Br. dr., 1; Keltie, 1870; Thayer, 1890.
Picture. Dodsley, 1744, 8.

Pinner of Wakefield. *See* George à Green.
Pizarro. Oxberry, 20; London stage, 1; Brit. dr., 1853, 2.
Plain dealer. Best Eng. plays, 8; Bell, 1797, 23; Scott, Mod. Br. dr., 3.
Platonic lovers. Maidment and L., Davenant, 2.
Play house to be let. Maidment and L., Davenant, 4.
Point of honour. Inchbald, Br. th., 24.
Polly Honeycombe. Bell's suppl., 3; London th., 9; London stage, 2: Farces, 1792, 3.
Poor gentleman. Inchbald, Br. th., 21.
Poor soldier. Inchbald, Farces, 2.
Prince d' Amour. Maidment and L., Davenant, 1.
Prisoner at large. Inchbald, Farces, 2.
Prodigal Son. Simpson's School, 2.
Projectors. Maidment and L., Wilson.
Promos and Cassandra. Six old plays, 1.
Provoked husband. New Eng. th., 7; Bell, 1797, 18; Inchbald, Br. th., 9; Scott, Mod. Br. dr., 3; London th., 9; Oxberry, 5; London stage, 2; Br. dr., 1853, 2.
Provoked wife. Best Eng. plays, 9; New Eng. th., 3; Bell, 1797, 27; Inchbald, Br. th., 9; Scott, Mod. Br. dr., 3; London stage, 3; Brit. dr., 1853, 2.
Puritan. Scott, Anc. Br. dr., 1.
Purse. London stage, 4.

Quaker. Inchbald, Farces, 4; London th., 9; Oxberry, 11; London stage, 1; Br. dr., 1853, 1.
Queen of Arragon. Dodsley, 1744, 10; Dodsley, 1780, 9; Collier's Dodsley, 9; Hazlitt's Dodsley, 13.

Rage. Inchbald, Mod. th., 1.
Raising the wind. Inchbald, Farces, 1.
Ralph Royster Doyster. White, Old Eng. dr., 1; Hazlitt's Dodsley, 3.
Ram alley; or Merry tricks. Dodsley, 1780, 5; Scott, Anc. Br. dr., 2; Collier's Dodsley, 5; Hazlitt's Dodsley, 10.
Ramah Droog. Inchbald, Mod. th., 6.
Rape of Lucrece. Old Eng. dr., 1.
Rare triumphs of love and fortune. Hazlitt's Dodsley, 6.
Rebellion. Hazlitt's Dodsley, 14.
Recruiting officer. Best Eng. plays, 10; New Eng. th., 3; Bell, 1797, 13; Inchbald, Br. th., 8; Scott, Mod. Br. dr., 4; London th., 10; Oxberry, 6; London stage; Br. dr., 1853, 2.
Recruiting sergeant. London th., 10; London stage, 3; Brit. dr., 1853, 1; Farces, 1792, 6.
Refusal. Bell, 1797, 2; London th., 9.
Register-office. Bell's suppl., 3; Inchbald, Farces, 3; London stage, 4; Farces, 1792, 3.
Regulus. Maidment and L., Crowne, 4.
Rehearsal. Best. Eng. plays, 6; Bell, 1797, 29; Scott, Mod. Br. dr., 3; Farces 1792, 6.
Relapse. Bell, 1797, 26.
Reprisal. Bell's suppl., 2; Farces, 1792, 2.
Return fr. Parnassus. Hawkins, 3; Scott, Anc. Br. dr., 1; Hazlitt's Dodsley, 9.
Revenge. (Young.) Inchbald, Br. th., 12; Scott, Mod. Br. dr., 2; London th., 9; London stage, 1; Br. dr., 1853, 1.

Revenge, or Match in Newgate. Dodsley, 1744, 12; New Eng. th., 2; Bell. 1797, 8.
Revenger's tragedy. Dodsley, 1744, 4; Dodsley, 1780, 4; Scott, Anc. Br. dr., 2; Collier's Dodsley, 4; Hazlitt's Dodsley, 10.
Review. Oxberry, 13.
Rich and poor. Oxberry, 19.
Richard Coeur de Lion. Inchbald, Farces, 6; London th., 10; London stage, 3.
Richard III. (King). Inchbald, Br. th., 1; Oxberry, 3.
Rival candidates. Bell's suppl., 4; Farces, 1792, 4.
Rivals. Inchbald, Br. th., 19; Scott, Mod. Br. dr., 4; London th., 9; Oxberry, 1; London stage, 1; Brit. dr., 1853, 1.
Rivals. Maidment and L., Davenant, 5.
Rival queens. New Eng. th., 4; Bell, 1797, 1; Scott, Mod. Br. dr., 1.
Road to ruin. Inchbald, Br. th., 24; Oxberry, 7; London stage, 1.
Roaring girl, or Moll Cut-purse. Dodsley, 1780, 6; Scott, Anc. Br. dr., 2; Collier's Dodsley, 6.
Rob Roy. Oxberry, 10.
Roland for an Oliver. Oxberry, 22.
Roman father. New Eng. th., 12; Bell, 1797, 3; Inchbald, Br. th., 14; Scott, Mod. Br. dr., 2; London th., 9; London stage, 3; Brit. dr., 1853, 2.
Romance of an hour. Farces, 1792, 5.
Romeo and Juliet. Inchbald, Br. th., 1; Oxberry, 6.
Romp. London stage, 4; Farces, 1792, 6.
Rosina. Inchbald, Farces, 3; Scott, Mod. Br. dr., 5; London th., 9; Oxberry, 9; London stage, 2.
Royal convert. Bell, 1797, 27.
Royal king and loyal subject. Dilke, Old Eng. pl., 6.
Rugantino. Oxberry, 9.
Rule a wife and have a wife. New Eng. th., 3; Bell, 1797, 8; Inchbald, Br. th., 6; Scott, Mod. Br. dr., 3; London th., 10; Oxberry, 10; London stage, 1; Brit. dr., 1853, 2.
Rump. Maidment and L., Tatham; (also, Character of the Rump).

St. Patrick for Ireland. Chetwood.
Salmacida Spolia. Chetwood; Maidment and L., Davenant, 2.
Samson Agonistes. Bell, 1797, 34.
Satiro-mastix. Hawkins, 3.
Sauny the Scot. Maidment and L., Lacy.
Scape-goat. London stage, 4.
School for arrogance. London stage, 4; Inchbald, Mod. th., 4.
School for authors. Inchbald, Farces, 7.
School for guardians. Bell, 1797, 33.
School for lovers. Bell, 1797, 7.
School for prejudice. Inchbald, Mod. th., 4.
School for rakes. Bell, 1797, 30.
School for scandal. London stage, 4; Brit. dr., 1853, 2.
School for wives. Bell, 1797, 7; London stage, 4; Inchbald, Mod. th., 9.
School of reform. Inchbald, Br. th., 25.
Scotch figgaries. Maidment and L., Tatham.
Second maiden's tragedy. Old Eng. dr., 1; Hazlitt's Dodsley, 10.
Secrets worth knowing. Inchbald, Mod. th., 3.
Seduction. London stage, 4; Inchbald, Mod. th., 4.
Seven champions of Christendom. White, Old Eng. dr., 3.

She stoops to conquer. Bell, 1797, 9; Inchbald, Br. th., 17; Scott, Mod. Br. dr., 4; London th., 10; Oxberry, 4; London stage, 1.
She wou'd and she wou'd not. Bell, 1797, 5; Inchbald, Br. th., 9; Scott, Mod. Br. dr., 3; London th., 10; London stage, 3.
She wou'd if she cou'd. Best Eng. plays, 6.
Shepherd's holiday. Dodsley, 1744, 7; Hazlitt's Dodsley, 12.
Shipwreck. Oxberry, 9.
Shoemaker's holiday. Fitzgibbon, 1889.
Siege. Maidment and L., Davenant, 4.
Siege of Belgrade. London stage, 4.
Siege of Damascus. New Eng. th., 10; Bell, 1797, 12; Inchbald, Br. th., 10; Scott, Mod. Br. dr., 1; London th., 10; London stage, 3; Brit. dr., 1853, 2.
Siege of Rhodes. Maidment and L., Davenant, 3.
Silent woman. White, Old Eng. dr., 3; Keltie, 1870; Fitzgibbon, 1889.
Sir Courtly Nice. Maidment and L., Crowne, 3.
Sir Gyles Goosecappe. Bullen, 1882, 3.
Sir Harry Wildair. Bell, 1797, 31; Scott, Mod. Br. dr., 4.
Sir Hercules Buffoon. Maidment and L., Lacy.
Sir John Cockle at court. Scott, Mod. Br. dr., 5.
Sir John Oldcastle. Scott, Anc. Br. dr., 1.
Sir John Van Olden. Barnwell; Bullen, 1882, 2.
Soldier's daughter. Oxberry, 5; London stage, 1.
Soliman and Perseda. Hawkins, 2; Hazlitt's Dodsley, 5.
Spanish fryar. Best Eng. plays, 3; New Eng. th., 3; Bell, 1797, 2; Scott, Mod. Br. dr., 3.
Spanish gipsy. Dilke, Old Eng. pl., 4.
Spanish tragedy. Dodsley, 1744, 2; Hawkins, 2; Dodsley, 1780, 3; Scott, Anc. Br. dr., 1; Collier's Dodsley, 3; Hazlitts' Dodsley, 5.
Speculation. Inchbald, Mod. th., 2.
Speed the plough. Inchbald, Br. th., 25.
Spirit of contradiction. Bell's suppl., 4; Farces, 1792, 4.
Spoiled child. Oxberry, 15; London stage, 4.
Spring's glory. Bullen, n. s., 2.
State of innocence. Best Eng. plays, 4.
Stranger. Inchbald, Br. th., 24; London stage, 3.
Such things are. Inchbald, Br. th., 23; London stage, 1.
Sultan. Bell's suppl., 1; Inchbald, Farces, 3; Scott, Mod. Br. dr., 5; London th., 10; London stage, 3; Farces, 1792, 1.
Summer's last will and testament. Hazlitt's Dodsley, 8.
Supposes. Hawkins, 3.
Surrender of Calais. Inchbald, Br. th., 20.
Suspicious husband. New Eng. th., 1; Bell, 1797, 4; Inchbald, Br. th., 13; Scott, Mod. Br. dr., 4; London th., 10; Oxberry, 8; London stage, 2; Br. dr., 1853, 1.
Sylvester Daggerwood. Oxberry, 21.

Tailors. London stage, 4.
Tale of mystery. London stage, 2.
Tamerlane. New Eng. th., 6; Bell, 1797, 22; Inchbald, Br. th., 10; Scott, Mod. Br. dr., 1; London th., 11; Oxberry, 20; London stage, 3; Brit. dr., 1853, 2.

Taming of a shrew. Six old plays, 1.
Tancred and Gismunda. Dodsley, 1744, 11; Dodsley, 1780, 2; Collier's Dodsley, 2; Hazlitt's Dodsley, 7.
Tancred and Sigismunde. New Eng. th., 2; Bell, 1797, 14; Inchbald, Br. th., 13; Scott, Mod. Br. dr., 2; London th., 11; London stage, 4; Brit. dr., 1853, 1.
Taste. Bell's suppl., 1; Scott, Mod. Br. dr., 5; Farces, 1792, 1.
Tempest. Best Eng. plays, 2; Inchbald, Br. th., 5; Oxberry, 17; Maidment and L., Davenant, 5.
Temple of love. Maidment and L., Davenant, 1.
Tender husband. Bell, 1797, 20; Scott, Mod. Br. dr., 4; Lon. th., 11; London stage, 3; Brit. dr., 1853, 2.
Theatrical candidates. Farces, 1792, 6.
Theodosius. New Eng. th., 10; Bell, 1797, 10; Scott, Mod. Br. dr., 1.
— Thersites. Child, Four old plays; Hazlitt's Dodsley, 1; Roxburghe club.
Thierry and Theodoret. Scott, Mod. Br. dr., 1.
Thomas, Lord Cromwell. Doubtful plays of Sh. Tauchnitz.
Thomas and Sally. Bell's suppl., 2; London stage, 4; Farces, 1792, 2.
— Thracian wonder. Dilke, Old Eng. pl., 6.
Three ladies of London. Hazlitt's Dodsley, 6.
Three lords and ladies of London. Hazlitt's Dodsley, 6.
Three weeks after marriage. Bell's suppl., 4; Inchbald, Farces, 4; Scott, Mod. Br. dr., 5; London th., 11; Oxberry, 9; London stage, 1; Br. dr., 1853, 1; Farces, 1792, 4.
— Thyestes. Maidment and L., Crowne, 2.
Timanthes. Bell, 1797, 34.
Time's a tell-tale. Inchbald, Mod. th., 10.
Timon of Athens. Best Eng. plays, 2.
'Tis a pity she's a whore. Dodsley, 1744, 5; Dodsley, 1780, 8; White, Old Eng. dr., 2.
Tobacconist. London th., 11; Oxberry, 13; London stage, 2.
To marry or not to marry. Inchbald, Br. th., 23.
Tom Thumb. Inchbald, Farces, 6; Scott, Mod. Br. dr., 5; London stage, 2; Br. dr., 1853, 1.
Too late to call back yesterday. Bullen, n. s., 3.
Totenham court. Bullen, n. s., 1.
Toyshop. Bell's suppl., 3; Farces, 1792, 3.
Traitor. Keltie, 1870.
Trappolin. Maidment and L., Cokayne.
Travellers. Oxberry, 17.
Trial of treasure. Hazlitt's Dodsley, 3.
Trick to catch the old one. Dilke, Old Eng. pl., 5; White, Old Eng. dr., 3.
Trick you trick. Farces, 1792, 5.
Trip to Scotland. Farces, 1792, 6.
Trip to Scarborough. London th., 11; Oxberry, 20; London stage, 2; Inchbald, Mod. th., 7.
True Trojans. Hazlitt's Dodsley, 12.
Tryall of chevalry. Bullen, 1882, 3.
Turnpike gate. Inchbald, Farces, 3.
Twelfth night. Inchbald, Br. th., 5; Oxberry, 12.
Twenty per cent. London th., 11.
Twin rivals. Bell, 1797, 32.
— Twins. Bell's suppl., 4; Farces, 1792, 4.
Two angry women of Abington. Hazlitt's Dodsley, 7.

Two gentlemen of Verona. Oxberry, 17.
Two misers. Scott, Mod. Br. dr., 5; London th., 11; London stage, 3.
Two noble kinsmen. Scott, Mod. Br. dr., 1; Fitzgibbon, 1889; Thayer, 1890.
Two strings to your bow. Inchbald, Farces, 2; London stage, 3.

Unfortunate lovers. Maidment and L., Davenant, 3.
Unfortunate mother. Bullen, n. s., 2.
Unnatural combat. Dodsley, 1744, 8.
Upholsterer. Bell's suppl., 1; Scott, Mod. Br. dr., 5; Farces, 1792, 1.

Venice preserved. Best Eng. pl., 5; New Eng. th., 6; Bell, 1797, 15; Inchbald, Br. th., 12; Scott, Mod. Br. dr., 1; London th., 11; Oxberry, 4; London stage, 2.
Village lawyer. London stage, 4.
Virgin unmask'd. Bell's suppl., 2; London th., 11; Farces, 1792, 2.
Virgin-martyr. Keltie, 1870.
Vision unmasked. London stage, 3.
Volpone. Best Eng. plays, 4; Scott, Mod. Br. dr., 3; White, Old Eng. dr., 1.
Votary of wealth. London stage, 4; Inchbald, Mod. th., 3.

Wallace. Oxberry, 18.
Warning for faire women. Simpson's school, 2.
Waterman. Inchbald, Farces, 7; London stage, 4; Farces, 1792, 6.
Way of the world. Best Eng. pl., 7; New Eng. th., 5; Bell, 1797, 33; Scott, Mod. Br. dr., 3; London th., 12; London stage, 4.
Way to get married. Inchbald, Br. th., 25.
Way to keep him. Bell, 1797, 17; Inchbald, Br. th., 15; Scott, Mod. Br. dr., 4; London th., 12; Oxberry, 3; London stage, 1; Brit. dr., 1853, 2.
Way to pay old debts. Dodsley, 1744, 8.
Ways and means. Inchbald, Farces, 7; London stage, 3; Brit. dr., 1853, 1.
Wedding day. Inchbald, Farces, 1; Oxberry, 21; London stage, 2.
Werter. Inchbald, Mod. th., 3.
West Indian. Bell, 1797, 19; Inchbald, Br. th., 18; Scott, Mod. Br. dr., 4; London th., 12; Oxberry, 1; London stage, 1; Brit. dr., 1853, 2.
What d'ye call it? Farces, 1792, 5.
What is she? Inchbald, Mod. th., 10.
What next? London th., 12; London stage, 4.
What you will. Dilke, Old Eng. pl., 2.
Wheel of fortune. Inchbald, Br. th., 18; London stage, 1.
Which is the man? London th., 12; London stage, 2; Inchbald, Mod. th., 10.
White devil. Dodsley, 1744, 3; Dodsley, 1780, 6; Scott, Anc. Br. dr., 3; Collier's Dodsley, 6.
Who's the dupe? Inchbald, Farces, 1; Oxberry, 11; London stage, 1; Brit. dr., 1853, 2.
Who wants a guinea? Inchbald, Mod. th., 3.
Widow. Dodsley, 1744, 6; Dodsley, 1780, 12; Collier's Dodsley, 12.
Widow's tears. Dodsley, 1744, 4; Dodsley, 1780, 6; Collier's Dodsley, 6.
Wife of two husbands. Inchbald, Mod. th., 6.
Wild oats. Inchbald, Br. th., 22.
Will. Inchbald, Mod. th., 1.

Will Summer's last will and testament. Collier's Dodsley, 9. *See also* Summer's last will, etc.
Wily beguiled. Hawkins, 3; Hazlitt's Dodsley, 9.
Winter's tale. Inchbald, Br. th., 3; Oxberry, 19.
Wisdom of Dr. Dodypoll. Bullen, 1882, 3.
Wise man of the east. Inchbald, Mod. th., 7.
Wits. Dodsley, 1780, 8; Scott, Anc. Br. dr., 1; Collier's Dodsley, 8; Maidment and L., Davenant, 2.
Wives as they were. Inchbald, Br. th., 23; London stage, 2.
Woman is a weathercock. White, Old Eng. dr., 2; Five old plays. (Collier's); Hazlitt's Dodsley, 11.
Woman killed with kindness. Dodsley, 1744, 4; Dodsley, 1780, 7; Scott, Anc. Br. dr., 2; Collier's Dodsley, 7; Keltie, 1870.
Women beware women. Dilke, Old Eng. pl., 5; White, Old Eng. dr., 3.
Wonder. New Eng. th., 11; Bell, 1797, 21; Inchbald, Br. th., 11; Scott. Mod. Br. dr., 4; Oxberry, 4; London stage, 2; Brit. dr., 1853, 1.
Wonder, a woman keeps a secret. London th., 12.
Wonder of a kingdom. Dilke, Old Eng. pl., 3.
Wood daemon. Oxberry, 19.
Woodman. London stage, 4.
Woodman's hut. Oxberry, 4.
Word to the wise. Bell, 1797, 30.
Worlde and the chylde. Collier's Dodsley, 12; Hazlitt's Dodsley, 1.
Wounds of civil war. Collier's Dodsley, 8; Hazlitt's Dodsley, 7.

Ximina. Bell, 1797, 15; Brit. dr., 1853, 2.

Yarrington's Two tragedies in one. Bullen, 1882, 4.
Yorkshire tragedy. Scott, Anc. Br. dr., 1; Doubtful plays of Sh. Tauchnitz.

Zara. New Eng. th., 10; Bell, 1797, 17; Inchbald, Br. th., 7; Scott, Mod. Br. dr., 2; London th., 12; London stage, 4; Brit. dr., 1853, 2.
Zenobia. Bell, 1797, 33; Scott, Mod. Br. dr., 2.
Zorinski. Inchbald, Mod. th., 3.

AUTHORS, PLAYS, AND REFERENCES.

PRE-ELIZABETHAN DRAMA.

DRAMATISTS.

Anonymous.
Bale.
HEYWOOD, JOHN.
Lyndsay.
Medwall.
Redford.
Skelton.
Wever.

NOTE.—The plan of arrangement is, in general, to group under an author's name, first, plays in chronological order; second, accessible publications containing them; third, critical references. The second division is introduced by ✠; the third by †. Starred plays may be found in the Index.

ANONYMOUS.

*Calisto and Meliboea. Circ. 1530.
*Hycke-Scorner. Circ. 1530.
*Lusty Juventus. Temp. Edw. VI.
Marriage of Wit and Wisdom. Temp. Edw. VI.
Nature of the Four Elements, Pr. by Rastell, 1519; Percy Soc., 23; Pollard, Miracle plays, (extract).
*New Custom. Temp. Edw. VI. (Eliz. revise). Pr. by Rastell, 1573.
*Nice Wanton. Temp. Edw. VI. S. R., 1560.
Of Gentleness and Nobility. Circ. 1530, (perhaps by Rastell).
*Rare Triumphs of Love and Fortune. Pr. 1589.
*Solyman and Perseda. S. R., 1592.
*Thersites. Acted 1537. Percy Soc., 22, (ed. Halliwell); Roxburghe Club, Two Interludes, 1820.
Wealth and Health. Temp. Edw. VI.

BALE (Bishop) JOHN. Temp. Edw. VI.

Kynge Johan. Acted between 1558—'63; probably revised from earlier form. (Bale's religious plays, acc. to Fleay, date before 1538).
✠ Camden Soc. pub. 1838, ed. Collier.
Pollard, Eng. Miracle Plays, (extracts).
† Jusserand, Le Théâtre en Angleterre, (ch. 5).
Klein. Geschichte des Englischen Drama's.

HEYWOOD, JOHN. 1497?—1580?

A Mery Playe betweene the Pardoner and the Frere, the Curate, and neybour Pratte. 1533.
A Mery Playe betweene Johan Johan, the Husbande; Tyb, his Wyfe; and Syr Jhan, the Preest. 1533.
*The Play called the Foure P's, a newe and a very mery interlude of a Palmer, a Pardoner, a Potycary, and a Pedlar. 1543—'47?
Of Wit and Folly. (Dialogue).
Play of Love. (Semi-dramatic).
Play of the Wether. (Semi-dramatic). 1533.

✠A Dialogue of Wit and Folly; w. memoir and account of works, by Fairholt. Percy Soc., 20.
Pardoner and Frere. (Extracts) Pollard, Eng. Miracle Plays.
Description of a most noble Ladye. (Queen Mary of England). Lyric. Tottel's Misc., 1557. Arber Reprints.
Ballads. Harl. Misc. (Ed. Park). 10: 255—9.
The Willow Garland. Ballad. Sh. Soc. Pub. 1844. 1: 44—46.
Proverbs and Epigrams. 1562. Spenser Soc. 1867. (Also ed. w. introd. by Julian Sharman. Lond. 1874).
The Spider and the Flie. 1556. Spenser Soc. 1894.
Witticisms. Camden Remains. Ed. 1674, pp. 378—9.
† Dict. Nat. Biog. (Ward).
Herford, C. H. Studies in the Lit. Relations of Eng. and Ger. in the Sixteenth Cent.
Jusserand. Le Théâtre en Angleterre.
Klein. Geschichte des Englischen Drama's.
Madden, (Sir) F. Privy Purse Expenses of the Princess Mary, w. notes, 1831.
Puttenham, Geo. Of Poets and Poesie. Bk. 1, ch. 31. (Arber Reprints, 7).
Stow. Annals; ed. 1617. p. 617.
Symonds. Shakespeare's Predecessors.
Walpole. Royal and Noble Authors.

LYNDSAY, SIR DAVID. 1490—1555.

Ane Satyre of the Thrie Estaitis. 1535—'40.
✠Works; ed. Small, Hall and Murray. Early Eng. Text Soc. 1865—'69. (Not yet completed).
Poetical Works; ed. Laing. 3 v. (w. bibliog.) Edin. Paterson. 1879. 63/.
Best Works. Scottish Poets of Sixteenth Cent.; ed. Eyre-Todd. Glasgow. 1891—'93. 3/6.
† Aschenberg. Leben u. Werke. Leipzig. Fock. 1891.
Irving, D. Lives of Scottish Poets. 2 v. Edin. 1804.
Jusserand. Le Théâtre en Angleterre. (ch. 5).
Kissel, I. Das Sprichwort bei. d. Mittel-schott·; Dichter Lyndsay. Diss. Leipzig. Fock. 1891.
Lindsay, Lord A. W. C. Lives of the Lindsays. 3 vol. Lond. 1849.
Lives of Scottish Poets. 3 v. 1: pt. 2. (Society of Ancient Scots). Lond. 1822.
Tytler, P. F. Lives of Scottish Worthies. 3 v. Lond. 1831—'33.
· Walker, Hugh. Three Centuries of Scottish Lit. 2 v. Glasgow. MacLehose. 1893. 10/.
Wilson, Jas. Grant. Poets and Poetry of Scotland. 2 v. N. Y. Harper. 1876.

MEDWALL, HENRY. Fl. 1486.

Nature. Circ. 1490. (Probably pr. by Rastell, 1510—'20).
Of the Finding of Truth, carried away by Ignorance and Hypocrisy. Acted before Henry VIII., Christmas, 1516. (Not extant. Contained a fool).
† Collier. Dram. Poetry. 1: 69; 2: 217—24.
Jusserand. Le Théâtre en Angleterre. (ch. 3).

REDFORD, JHON. Fl. 1540.

Wyt and Science. Circ. 1545. Sh. Soc. Pub. 1848. (Ed. Halliwell).

SKELTON, JOHN. 1460—1529.

Magnyfycence. 1515—'23.

✱Poet. Works of John Skelton; ed. Dyce. 2 v. 1843.
† Chasles, V. E. P. Du Mouvement sensualiste avant la Reforme. (Rev. d. Deux Mondes, 1842, 29: 724).
Disraeli. Curiosities of Lit.
Dublin Univ. Rev., 1866; 68: 603; 1877; 89: 640.
Jonson, Ben. Fortunate Isles.
Jusserand. Le Théâtre en Angleterre. (Ch. 3).
Monday, Anthony. Downfall of Robert, Earl of Huntingdon.
Quart. Rev. 1844; 73: 510.
Retro. Rev. 1882; 6: 337.

WEVER, R. Temp. Edward VI.

✱Lusty Juventus.
† Symonds. Shakspere's Predecessors.

ELIZABETHAN DRAMA.

DRAMATISTS.

Anonymous.
Barclay.
Brandon.
Chettle.
DEKKER.
Drayton.
Edwardes.
Fulwell.
Gascoigne.
Golding.
Gosson.
GREENE.
Hathway.
Haughton.
Heywood, Jasper.
Hughes.
Ingelend.
Kempe.
Kyd.
Legge.
LYLY.
Lodge.
Lupton.
MARLOWE.
MARSTON.
Monday.

Nash.
Neville, Alex.
Newton.
Norton.
Nuce.
PEELE.
Percy.
Porter.
Preston.
Sackville.
SHAKSPEARE.
Sidney.
Smith, Wentworth.
Still.
Studley.
Tarlton.
Udall.
Wager.
Wapul.
Whetstone.
Wilmot.
Wilson, Robt. (Senior).
Wilson, Robt. (Junior).
Woodes.
?Yarrington.

ANONYMOUS.

Albion Knight. Circ. 1560. Pr. 1565. Sh. Soc. Pub. 1844.
*Appius and Virginia. By R. B. (Fleay queries Richard Bower). S. R. 1568.
*Arden of Feversham. Pr. 1592. Delius' Pseudo-Sh. Dramen.
*Charlimayne. (Distracted Emperor). Acted 1589?
Common Conditions. S. R. 1576.
*Contention between Liberality and Prodigality. 1602.
?Contention betwixt the Two Famous Houses of York and Lancaster. 1594. (2 Henry VI.) Hazlitt's. Sh. Libr.
Cradle of Security. (Not extant). Circ. 1570. (Willis, R. Mount Tabor. 1639).
Cyprian Conqueror; or, The Faithless Relict. MS. (Brit. Mus. MS. Sloane. 3709).
*King Darius. 1565.
Deadman's Fortune. (Plot only extant). 1593?
Demetrius and Marina; or, The Imperial Impostor and the Unhappy Heroine. MS.
Diana's Grove; or, The Faithful Genius. MS.
*Edward III. Pr. 1596. Delius' Pseudo-Sh. Dramen.
*Fair Em; or, The Miller's Daughter of Manchester. Acted 1590. Pr. 1631. Attributed by Fleay to Rob. Wilson.
(Tragedy of) Gismond of Salern. Acted 1568. Ed. Israel Gollancz. Lond. Nutt. 1893. 12/6. (Tudor Libr.)
Godly Queen Hester. 1561. Collier. Hist. Eng. Drama. (Extracts).
Grobiana's Nuptials. MS. (Bodl. 30).
*Famous Victories of Henry the Fifth. Before 1588. Pr. 1594. Jusserand. Le Théâtre en Angleterre. (Ch. 7).
*Histriomastix; or, The Player Whipt. Before 1599.
How to Choose a Good Wife from a Bad. Pr. 1602. (Ascribed in MS. note to "Joshua Cooke," otherwise unknown).
*Impatient Poverty. S. R. 1560.
*Jack Drum's Entertainment; or, The Comedy of Pasquil and Katherine. Acted circ. 1600.
*Jack Juggler. Circ. 1560. Roxburghe Club. Two Interludes. 1820.
*Knack to Know a Knave. Acted 1592.
Larum for London; or, The Siege of Antwerp. S. R. 1600.
*King Leir and his Three Daughters. Pr. 1594. Hazlitt's Sh. Libr.
*(Life and Death of) Jack Straw, a Notable Rebel. 1587.
*(Life and Death of) Captain Thomas Stukely. S. R. 1600.
*(Life and Death of) Thomas, Lord Cromwell. Pr. 1602. Sh.'s Doubtful Plays. Tauchnitz.
*Locrine. S. R. 1594.
*Look About You. 1600.
Love's Changelings Changed. (Founded on Sidney's Arcadia). MS. (Eg. MSS. 1994).
*Lust's Dominion; or, The Lascivious Queen. (Perhaps identical with Spanish Moor's Trag.) Pr. 1657, as Marlowe's.
Maid's Metamorphosis. 1600.
*Marriage of Wit and Science. (Wit and Will). Acted 1568. Sh. Soc. Pub. 1846.
*Misfortunes of Arthur. 1587. Jusserand. Le Théâtre en Angleterre. (Ch. 6).
Misogonus. 1559? Fleay. Hist. of the Stage, pp. 58, 60; and Collier, Hist. Eng. Dr. Poetry, 2: 464—481.

*Mucedorus. Before 1598. Wagner, Wilhelm. Fresh Conjectures on Text (called out by Warnke and Proesholdt's critical text), Sh. Jahrbuch, 14.

Narcissus, a Twelfth-Night Merriment, ed. Margaret L. Lee; w. introd. and notes. (Pr. fr. orig. MS. 1602). Lond. Nutt. 1893. 7/6.

*Nobody and Somebody. Pr. 1606. Probably Elizabethan. Gosse: Jacobean Poets.

Orestes. Acted circ. 1568.

Pelopidarum Secunda. MS. (Harl. 5110).

*Pilgrimage to Parnassus, with the two parts of Return from Parnassus. 1597—1601. Oxford. Clar. Press. 1886. 8/6.

*Rare Triumphs of Love and Fortune. Acted 1582. Pr. 1589.

*Return from Parnassus. Acted 1602. Pr. 1606. (Arber Reprint).

Richard II. 1591? 11 copies pr. by Halliwell. (Eg. MS. 1994).

True Tragedy of Richard, Duke of York. Circ. 1590. Hazlitt's Sh. Libr. Sh. Soc. Pub. 1844.

Robin Conscience. Pr. 1573.

True History of George Scanderbage. Acted 1600?

First Part of the Tragical Reign of Selimus. 1594. Swinburne. Study of Shakespeare. pp. 30, 31.

Seven Deadly Sins. 2 pts. (Fleay identifies with the Five Plays in One and The Three Plays in One. 1585).

Sir Clyomon and Sir Clamydes. Circ. 1570. Pr. in Bullen's Peele.

*Sir John Oldcastle. 1600.

Sir Thomas More. 1596. Sh. Soc. Pub. 1844. Ed. Dyce.

*Spanish Moor's Tragedy. (See Lust's Dominion).

Sylla Dictator. (Catiline). Acted 1588.

Taming of a Shrew. 1594. Sh. Soc. Pub. 1844.

*Tancred and Gismunda. Acted 1568. Pr. 1592.

Tell Tale. MS. (Dulwich MSS.)

*Three Ladies of London. By R. W. (Fleay conjectures Rob. Wilson). Pr. 1584.

*Three Lords and Ladies of London. By R. W. Pr. 1590.

Tom Tiler and his Wife. Pr. 1563.

*Timon. 1601. Repr. Dyce. Sh. Soc. Pub. 1842.

*Trial of Treasure. Pr. 1566. Percy Soc. 28. Ed. Halliwell.

*Troublesome Reign of King John. 2 pts. Pr. 1591. Hazlitt's Sh. Libr.

*True Chronicle Hist. of King Leir and His Three Daughters. 1593.

*Warning for Fair Women. Pr. 1599. Jusserand. Le Théâtre en Angleterre. (Ch. 7).

Weakest goeth to the Wall. S. R. 1600.

Whimsies of Senor Hidalgo. MS. (Harl. 5152).

*Wily Beguiled. Circ. 1597. Fleay. Biog. Chron. Eng. Dr.

*Wisdom of Doctor Doddypol. Pr. 1600.

Wizzard. MS. (Brit. Mus. MSS. Addit. 10, 306).

BARCLAY, (Sir) WILLIAM. 1677.

*The Lost Lady. Pr. 1638.

BRANDON, SAMUEL. 16th Century.

Virtuous Octavia. 1598.

† Dict. Nat. Biog.

Fleay. Biog. Chron. Eng. Dr.

Jusserand. Le Théâtre en Angleterre. (Ch. 6).

CHETTLE, HENRY. 1562—1605?

Plays wr. by Chettle alone.

    Woman's Tragedy. July, 1598.
    'Tis No Deceit to Deceive the Deceiver. Nov., 1598.
    Troy's Revenge, with the Tragedy of Polyphemus. Feb., 1599.
    Sir Placidas. Apr., 1599.
    Damon and Pythias. Feb., Mar., Apr., 1600.
    Wooing of Death. May, 1600.
    All is not Gold that Glisters. Mar., Apr., 1601.
    Life of Cardinal Wolsey. June, July, Aug., 1601.
    Tobias. May, June, 1602.
    Danish Tragedy. July, 1602.
    Robin Goodfellow. Sept., 1602. (Forgery?)
    Tragedy of Hoffman. Dec., 1602. Jan., 1603.
    London Florentine, pt 2. Mar., 1603.
        (Of the above only Tragedy of Hoffman is extant).

Wr. in collaboration.

    Second Part of Robin Hood. Feb., 1598. (With Monday).
    "A book wherein is a part of a Welshman." Mar., 1598. (With Drayton).
    Famous Wars of Henry I. Mar., 1598. (With Drayton and Dekker).
    Earl Goodwin and his Three Sons, pt. 1. Mar., 1598. (With Drayton, Dekker and Wilson).
    Pierce of Exton. Apr., 1598. (With Drayton, Dekker and Wilson).
    Earl Goodwin and his Three Sons, pt. 2. Apr., 1598. (With Drayton, Dekker and Wilson).
    Black Batman of the North, pt. 1. May, 1598. (With Drayton, Dekker and Wilson).
    Black Batman of the North, pt. 2. June, 1598. (With Wilson).
    Richard Cordelion's Funeral. June, 1598. (With Monday, Drayton and Wilson).
    Conquest of Brute, with First Finding of the Bath. July, Aug., Sept., 1598. (With Day).
    Hot Anger Soon Cold. Aug., 1598. (With Jonson and Porter).
    Chance Medley. Aug., 1598. (With Drayton, Monday and Wilson).
    Catiline's Conspiracy. Aug., 1598. (With Wilson).
    First Part of Robin Hood. Nov., 1598. (Wr. by Monday. "Mended" by Chettle).
    Spencers. Mar., 1599. (With Porter).
    Troilus and Cressida. Apr., 1599. (With Dekker).
    Agamemnon. May, 1599. (With Dekker).
    Stepmother's Tragedy. July, 1599. (With Dekker).
    Robert II., King of Scots. Sept., 1599. (With Dekker, Jonson and "Other Jentelman)."
    Orphans' Tragedy. Nov., 1599. (With Day and Haughton).
    Patient Grisel. Dec., 1599. (With Dekker and Haughton).
    Arcadian Virgin. Dec., 1599. (With Haughton).
    Seven Wise Masters. Mar., 1600. (With Dekker, Haughton and Day).
    Golden Ass and Cupid and Psyche. Apr., 1600. (With Dekker and Day).
    Blind Beggar of Bethnal Green. May, 1600. (With Day).
    Sebastian, King of Portugal. Apr., May, 1601. (With Dekker).
    First Part of Cardinal Wolsey. Oct., Nov., 1601. (With Drayton, Monday and Smith).

Too Good to be True. Nov., 1601. Jan., 1602. (With Hathway and Smith).
Proud Woman of Antwerp. Jan., 1602. (Wr. by Haughton and Day; "Mended" by Chettle).
Love parts Friendship. May, 1602. (With Wentworth Smith).
Femelanco. Sept., 1602. (With Robinson).
Lady Jane, pt. 1. Oct., 1602. (With Dekker, Heywood, Smith and Webster).
Christmas comes but once a Year. Nov., 1602. (With Dekker, Heywood, and Webster).
London Florentine, pt. 1. Dec., 1602. (With Heywood).
Shore's Wife. May, 1603. (With Day).

[Of the above only the two parts of Robin Hood, Patient Grisel and Blind Beggar of Bethnal Green are extant; but for Lady Jane, see Webster's Sir Thomas Wyat].

✠ *Downfall of Robert, Earl of Huntington (=First Part of Robin Hood). Lond. 1601.
*Death of Robert, Earl of Huntington (=Second Part of Robin Hood). Lond. 1601.
Pleasant Comedie of Patient Grissill. Lond. 1603. Repr. Sh. Soc. Pub. 1841; ed. Herm. Vernhagen. Erlangen. Junge. 1893. 2 m.
Blind Beggar of Bethnal Green. Lond. 1659. Repr. in Bullen's Day. 1880.
Kind-Hart's Dreame. Lond. 1593. Ed. Edw. F. Rimbault. Lond. 1841. Percy Soc., 5. 1842. Ingleby. Sh. Allusion Books. 1874.
Pierce Plainnes' Seaven Yere's Prentiship. 1595. (Unique copy in Bodleian Libr.)
England's Mourning Garment. Lond. 1603. Harl. Misc. 1744. Ingleby. Sh. Allusion Books. 1874.
Englande's Mourning Garment. Somes, J. "Baron Somes." Order and Proceedings at the Funerall of Eliz. Apr. 28, 1603. Third Collection of Scarce and Valuable Tracts, 1. 1751.
Tragedy of Hoffman; or, A Revenge for a Father. 1631. Repr., w. emendations, by H. B(arrett) L(eonard). 1851.
Tragedy of Hoffman, hrsg. v. R. Ackermann (after Brit. Mus. 1631 ed.) Bambg. Uhlenhuth. 1894. 1 m.
Mad Pranks and Merry Jests of Robin Goodfellow. Repr. fr. ed. of 1628. W. introd. by Collier. Lond. 1841. Percy Soc., 2.
† Delius. Chettle's Hoffman u. Sh.'s Hamlet. Sh. Jahrbuch 9, 1874.
Harvey, Gabriel. Pierce's Supererogation. 1593. Repr. 1814. (Brydges. Archaica, 2).
Henslowe. Diary.
Ingleby. Sh. Allusion Books, pt. 1., pp. 7—21.
Nash, Th. Have with you to Saffron Walden. 1596.

DEKKER, THOMAS. 1567?—1632?

(Classed with Elizabethans rather than Jacobeans, because his style is of the earlier period).

Extant Plays, with pub. dates.

*Shoemaker's Holiday. 1600.
*Old Fortunatus. 1600.
*Satiro-mastix; or, The Untrussing of the Humorous Poet. [Ben Jonson]. 1602.
Patient Grisel. (*See* Chettle).
*Magnificent Entertainment given to King James. Masque. 1604.
*Honest Whore. 1604.
*Second Part of the Honest Whore. 1630.
Westward Ho. 1607.

Northward Ho. 1607.
Whore of Babylon. 1607.
*Roaring Girl. 1611. (With Middleton).
If it be not Good, the Devil is in it. 1612.
Troia Nova Triumphans. Pageant. 1612.
*Virgin Martyr. 1622. (With Massinger).
Britannia's Honor. Pageant. 1628.
London's Tempe. Pageant. 1629.
Match Me in London. 1631.
*Noble Spanish Soldier. 1634. (*See* Samuel Rowley).
*Wonder of a Kingdom. 1636.
Sun's Darling. "Moral Masque." 1634. (With Ford).
Witch of Edmonton. 1658. (With Ford and Rowley).
(For Dekker's lost plays and non-dram. works, see Bullen's article in Dict. Nat. Biog. and Fleay's Biog. Chron.)

✠ Dram. Works now first collected, w. illus. notes and memoir. 4 v. Lond. Pearson. 1873. 73/6.
Works; ed. Bullen. 4 v. Lond. Nimmo. 1887. 30/.
Selections; ed. w. introd. and notes, E. Rhys. Lond. Vizetelly. 1887. 2/6. (Mermaid Series).
Patient Grissil; a comedy. Repr. fr. the black letter ed. of 1603, w. introd. and notes. Sh. Soc. Pub. 1841.
Troia-nova Triumphans. London Triumphing; London Tempe, or the Field of Happiness. (Percy Soc., 10). Fairholt. Lord Mayor's Pageants.
Grosart. Huth Libr. Non-Dram. Works.
Seven Deadly Sins of London. 1606. Lond. 1879. Arber. Eng. Scholar's Libr., 7. Collier. Illustr. of Old Eng. Lit., 2.
Dreams. Repr. fr. the ed. of 1620; ed. Halliwell. Lond. 1860.
Gull's Hornbook. Lond. 1609. Repr. w. illus. notes by Dr. John Nott. Bristol. 1812. (Hindley, C. Old Book Collectors' Miscel., 2).
Knight's Conjuring; Done in Earnest, Discovered in Jest. Ed. E. F. Rimbault. Lond. 1842. (Percy Soc., 5).

† Bodenstedt. Shakespeare's Zeitgenossen.
Gosse. Jacobean Poets.
Hazlitt. Dram. Lit. of the Age of Eliz.
Henslowe. Diary.
Jonson, Ben. Poetaster. (Demetrius=Dekker).
Jusserand. Eng. Novel in the Time of Shakespeare.
Kuplin, P. Ueber den Dramatischen Vers T. Dekker's. Halle diss. 1893.
Retro. Rev. 11. 1825.
Shakspere and Jonson. Dramatic, versus Wit-Combats. Auxiliary Forces. Appendix. 1864.
Swinburne. Nineteenth Cent. Jan., 1887. Study of Shakespeare, p. 143.
Symonds, J. A. Acad. 35 : 137.
Whipple. Essays and Reviews.

DRAYTON, MICHAEL. 1563—1631.

This distinguished poet wrote for Henslowe's theatres twenty-four plays, usually working in collaboration (with Chettle, Dekker, Hathway, Middleton, Monday, Smith, Webster, Wilson); but there is no certainty that any dramatic work of his is now extant.

✠ Collected Poems. (Incomplete). 4 v. 1748; 1753.
Poly-Olbion; ed. Richard Hooper. 3 v. 1876. Entire works in preparation.
Selections; ed. Bullen. 1883.

Drayton's Rarer Works; ed. Collier. Roxburghe Club. 1856.
Facsimile Reprints of Early Editions. Spenser Soc.
† Anderson, Brit. Poets, 3.
Athen. 1883, 1: 470.
Bell. Lit. and Sci. Men., 1: 1.
Chalmers. Eng. Poets, 4.
Dict. Nat. Biog. (Bullen).
Disraeli. Amenities of Lit., 2: 248.
Dub. Univ. Rev. 94: 56.
Fleay. Biog. Chron. Eng. Drama. (24 pp.)
Gosse. Jacobean Poets.
Hazlitt. Dram. Lit. of the Age of Eliz.
Henslowe. Diary. 1598—1603.
Jameson, (Mrs.) Loves of the Poets.

EDWARDES, RICHARD. 1523—'66.

*Damon and Pythias. Acted 1564.
Palaemon and Arcyte. 2 pts. Acted 1566. (Not extant).
† Collier. Hist. Eng. Dram. Poetry, 1: 183—4; 2: 389—93.
Fleay. Biog. Chron. Eng. Drama.
Fleay. Hist. of the Stage, pp. 58, 60.
Meres. Palladis Tamia. 1598.
Paradyse of Daynty Devises. 1576.
Puttenham. Arte of Eng. Poesie. 1589. (Arber Reprint).
Webbe. Discourse of Eng. Poetry. 1586. (Arber Reprint).

FULWELL, ULPIAN. Fl. 1575.

*Like will to Like, quoth the Devil to the Collier. S. R. 1568.
† Dict. Nat. Biog.

GASCOIGNE, GEORGE. 1525?—'77.

*Supposes. Tr. fr. Ariosto. Acted 1566.
*Jocasta. Tr. fr. Euripides. Acted 1566.
Glass of Government. Pr. 1575.
Princely Pleasures at the Court of Kenilworth. Pageant. Pr. 1576.
Tale of Hemetes the Hermit. Pageant. (Wr. in English, Latin, Italian and French). Presented 1575.
Mask for Viscount Montacute. Pr. 1573.
‡Collected Works; ed. Abel Jeffes. 1587.
Poems; ed. W. C. Hazlitt. Roxburghe Libr. 1868—'9.
Ancient Crit. Essays; ed. Haslewood. 1815.
Arber Reprints.
    Certayne notes of instruction concerning the making of verse or ryme in English. 1575.
    Steele Glas. (Blank Verse Satire).
    Complaynt of Philomene. An Elegie. 1576.
† Fleay. Biog. Chron. Eng. Drama. (7 pp.)
Harvey. Foure Letters. 1592. (*See under* Greene).
Herford. Lit. Relations of England and Germany.
Klein. Geschichte des Englischen Drama's.
Puttenham. Arte of Eng. Poesie. 1589. (Arber Reprint).

Webbe. Discourse of Eng. Poetrie. 1586. (Arber Reprint).
Whetstons, Geo. A Remembrance of the wel imployed life, and godly end of George Gaskoigne, Esquire, who deceased at Stalmford in Lincoln shire, the 7 of October, 1577. Unique. Bodleian. (Arber Reprint).

GOLDING, ARTHUR. 1536?—1605?
(Translator of Ovid's Metamorphoses).

Beza's Tragedy of Abraham's Sacrifice. Translation. 1575.
† Dict. Nat. Biog.

GOSSON, STEPHEN. 1555—1624.

Catiline's Conspiracies.
Captain Mario.
Praise at Parting.
[These plays, non-extant, were written before 1580].
School of Abuse, containing a pleasant invective against Poets, Pipers. Players, Jesters, and such like Caterpillars of a Commonwealth. 1579. Repr. in Somes' Tracts. 1810, 3: 552—74. Sh. Soc. Pub. 1841. ed. Collier. Arber Reprints. 1868.
Plays confuted in Five Actions, proving they are not to be suffered in a Christian Commonweal by the way both the Cavils of Thomas Lodge and the "Play of Plays" written in their Defence and other Objections of Players' Friends are truly set down and directly answered. 1582. See Hazlitt. Stage under Tudor and Stuart Princes. 1869.
† Jusserand. Le Théâtre en Angleterre. (Ch. 6).
Tarlton. Horse-load of Fools. (q. v.) (Goose' Son=Gosson).

GREENE, ROBERT. 1560?—'92.

Alphonsus, King of Arragon. (Perhaps earliest written). Pr. 1599.
Orlando Furioso. Pr. 1594.
Looking Glass for London and England. (With Lodge). Pr. 1594.
*Friar Bacon and Friar Bungay. Pr. 1594.
James the Fourth. S. R. 1594.
*George à Greene, the Pinner of Wakefield. Pr. 1595.
Non-Dram. Works.
Mamillia. 1583.
Mirror of Modesty. 1584.
Gividonius, the Card of Fancy. 1584.
Arbasto, the Anatomy of Fortune. 1584.
Morando, the Tritameron of Love. 1584.
Planetomachia. 1585.
Farewell to Folly. S. R. 1587.
Penelope's Web. 1587.
Euphues, his Censure to Philautus. 1587.
Perimedes the Blacksmith. 1588.
Pandosto, the Triumph of Time. 1588.
Alcida, Greene's Metamorphosis. S. R. 1588.
The Spanish Masquerade. 1589.
Menaphon. 1589.
Ciceronis Amor. 1589.
Greene's Orpharion. 1590.

Cornucopia, or, The Royal Exchange. 1590.
Greene's Mourning Garment. 1590.
Greene's Never Too Late; or, A Powder of Experience. 1590.
Francesco's Fortunes. 1590.
Maiden's Dream. 1591.
Notable Discovery of Cozenage. 1591.
Conycatching. Second Part. 1591.
Conycatching. Third Part. 1592.
He and She Coneycatcher. 1592.
Nascimur pro Patria. 1592.
Black Book's Messenger. 1592.
Philomela. 1592.
Quip for an Upstart Courtier. 1592.
Groatsworth of Wit, bought with a Million of Repentance. 1592.
Repentance of Robert Greene. 1592.
Greene's Vision, written at the instant of his Death and containing a penitent Passion for the Folly of his Pen. 1592.
Plays and Poems; ed. Dyce. 2 v. 1831. 1 v. 1858. (With Peele).
Complete Works; ed. Grosart. 15 v. 1881—'6. (Huth Libr.) (Vol. I. contains Storojenko's memoir tr. fr. the Russian).
Friar Bacon and Friar Bungay, ed. Ward. Oxford. Clar. Press. 1882. 5/6. (With Marlowe's Faustus).
Poems; ed. Bell. Bohn. 1846.
Mirror of Modesty. Repr. Collier. 1866. Illustrations of Old Eng. Lit.
Perimedes the Blacksmith. Repr. Collier. 1867? . Misc. Tracts, 1.
Pandosto. Collier's Sh. Libr., 1. Hazlitt's Sh. Libr., 4. Harl. Misc., 5. 1744. (*Also* " Thieves falling out).''
Groatsworth of Wit; ed. Ingleby. Sh. Allusion Books. 1874.
Menaphon. Arber Reprints.
Arcadia; or, Menaphon. Lond. 1814. Brydges. Archaica, 1.
Philomena; the Lady Fitzwater's Nightingale. Lond. 1814. Brydges. Archaica, 1.
Maiden's Dream. (19 pp.) Sh. Soc. Pub., 2.
Quip for an Upstart Courtier. Repr. Collier. 1867? Misc. Tracts.
Bernhardi, W. Leben und Schriften.
Boas. Shakspere and his Predecessors.
Bodenstedt. Shakespeare's Vorläufer. Shakespeare's Zeitgenossen, 3.
Conrad. Greene als Dramatiker. Sh. Jahrbuch, 29; 30. 1894.
Creizenach, W. Zu Greene's James the Fourth. Anglia 8 : 419—423.
Delius. Pandosto u. Winters's Tale. Sh. Jahrbuch, 15. 1880.
Harvey, G. Foure letters and certain sonnets; especially touching Rob. Greene and other parties by him abused. 1592. (Works, 1 : Huth Libr.) Same in Brydges. Archaica, 2. Same in Collier. Misc. Tracts, 5.
Herman, E. Sh. wider Green, Marlowe u. Nash. (*In his* Sh. Studien, 2).
Jeaffreson, J. C. Novels and Novelists, 1. 21 pp.
Jusserand. Eng. Novel in Time of Shakespeare. N. Y. & Lond. 1890. pp. 150—192.
Knaut, K. Ueber die metrik R. Greene's. Halle diss. 1890. 63 pp. (W. Wilke. Engl. Studien, 16 : 297-99).
Lowell. Early Eug. Dramatists.
Mertius, O. Robert Greene and the play of George à Greene, the Pinner of Wakefield. Breslau. Lindner. 1885. Inaug. diss. (Max Koch. Engl. Studien, 10 : 122—23).

Rowlands, Samuel. 'Tis Merrie when Gossips Meete. 1602. (Preface).
Simpson. School of Shakespeare. 2: 339. ("Mr. Simpson's account of Robert Greene and his prose works is the best I know."—Furnival).
Symonds. Shakspere's Predecessors in the Eng. Drama. pp. 540—563.
Thom. Eng. Prose Romances. Famous Hist. of Friar Bacon.
Thynn. Introd. to Debate between Pride and Lowliness. Sh. Soc. Pub. 1841.

HATHWAY, RICHARD. Fl. 1600.

Life and Death of Arthur. 1598.
Valentine and Orson. 1598. (With Monday).
*Sir John Oldcastle, 2 pts. 1599. (With Drayton, Monday, Wilson).
Owen Tudor. 1600. (With Drayton, Monday, Wilson).
Fair Constance of Rome, pt. 1. 1600. (With Drayton, Monday, Wilson).
Fair Constance of Rome, pt. 2. 1600. (With Chettle and Day).
*Hannibal and Scipio. 1601. (With Rankens).
Scogan and Skelton. 1601. (With Rankens).
Conquest of Spain by John à Gaunt. 1601. (With Rankens).
Six Clothiers, pt. 1. 1601. (With Haughton and Smith).
Six Clothiers, pt. 2. 1601. (With Haughton and Smith).
Too Good to be True; or, the Northern Man. 1601. (With Chettle and Smith).
As Merry as May Be. 1602. (With Day and Smith).
Bosse of Billingsgate. 1603. (With Day).
Black Dog of Newgate, pt. 1. 1602. (With Day, Smith, etc.)
Unfortunate General. 1603. (With Day, Smith, etc.)
Black Dog of Newgate, pt. 2. 1603. (With Day, Smith, etc.)
[Of Hathway's plays only the first part of Sir John Oldcastle is known to be extant].
† Bodenham. Belvidére. 1600. (Commend. Verses).
Halliwell-Phillips. Outlines of the Life of Shakespeare. 7th ed. 2: 183.
Henslowe. Diary.

HAUGHTON, WILLIAM. Fl. 1598.
(Harton, Haulton, Hawton, "Yonge Horton.")

*Englishmen for my Money; or, A Woman will have her Will. Acted 1598. Pr. 1616.
Poor Man's Paradise. Wr. 1599.
Patient Grissell. Wr. 1599. (With Chettle and Dekker).
Cox of Collumpton. Wr. 1599. (With Day).
Tragedy of Merry. Wr. 1599. (With Day).
Spanish Moor's Tragedy. Wr. 1600. (With Dekker and Day). (Perhaps identical with Lust's Dominion).
Seven Wise Masters. Wr. 1600. (With Chettle, Dekker, Day).
Devil and his Dame. Wr. 1600.
English Fugitives. Wr. 1600.
Strange News out of Poland. Wr. 1600. (With "Pett.")
Indies. Wr. 1600.
Robin Hood's Pen'orths. Wr. 1600.
Blind Beggar of Bethnal Green, pts. 2 and 3. 1601. (With Day and Chettle).
Conquest of the West Indies. 1601. (With Day and Wentworth Smith).
Six Yeomen of the West. 1601. (With Day).

Proud Woman of Antwerp. 1601.
Second Part of Thomas Dough. 1601. (With Day).
Six Clothiers, pt. 1 and 2. 1601. (With Hathway).
Cartwright. 1602.
As Merry as May Be. 1602. (With Day, Hathway, Smith).
[Of Haughton's independent plays only the first is known to be extant; of his plays in collaboration, only Patient Grissell and Blind Beggar of Bethnal Green—see under Chettle and Day].
† Alleyn Papers, pp. XXVII., 23, 25. Sh. Soc. Pub. 1843.
Bullen. Day's Dram. Works. Preface. (*See* Day).
Dict. Nat. Biog. (Bullen).
Fleay. Biog. Chron. Eng. Drama.
Henslowe. Diary.
Swinburne. Study of Shakespeare, p. 127.

HEYWOOD, JASPER. 1535—'98.

Seneca's Tragedies. (Translations).
Troas. 1559.
*Thyestes. 1560.
Hercules Fureus. 1561.
✠Newton, Th. Seneca's Tragedies. 1581 ; 1591.
† Dict. Nat. Biog.
Symonds. Shakspere's Predecessors.
Ward. Eng. Dr. Lit.

HUGHES, THOMAS. Fl. 1587.

*Misfortunes of Arthur. 1587.
† Klein. Geschichte des Englischen Drama's.

INGELEND, TH. Fl. 1550.

*Disobedient Child. Acted 1560.
✠Percy Soc. 23, 1848. (Ed. Halliwell).
† Jusserand. Le Théâtre en Angleterre. (Ch. 3).

KEMPE, WILLIAM. Fl. 1600.

Nine Daies Wonder. 1600. (Dedication to Anne Fitton). Ed. Dyce. Camden Soc. Arber Reprints.
As Actor.
  Romeo and Juliet. Q$_2$ (1599). Q$_3$ (1609). Act 4 : Scene 5. (Kempe as Peter).
  Much Ado about Nothing. Q. (1600). F. (1623). Act 4 : Scene 2. (Kempe as Dogberry).
† Academy, July 5, 1884.
  An Almond for a Parrot. 1589. (Dedication to Kempe).
  Collier. Memoirs of the Principal Actors in the Plays of Shakespeare. Sh. Soc. Pub. 1848. pp. 89—119.
  Day. Travels of the Three Eng. Brothers, q. v.
  Dict. Nat. Biog.
  Fleay. Biog. Chron. Eng. Drama.
  Griffiths. Evenings with Shakspere.
  Henslowe. Diary.

Heywood. Apology for Actors.
Jahrbuch. (Sh.), 22. 1887.
Knack to Know a Knave. *See* Index.
Nicholson, B. Kempe and the Play of Hamlet. Sh. Soc. Trans., 1: 1. 1880—'82.
Return from Parnassus. Arber Reprint.
Sat. Rev. April 17, 1886.
Tyler, Th. Shakespeare's Sonnets, pp. 76—78. Lond. Nutt. 1890.
Wily Beguiled. *See* Index. (Will Cricket perhaps=Kempe. *See* Fleay: Biog. Chron. Eng. Drama under Peele).

KYD, THOMAS. 1557?—'95?

*Spanish Tragedy. S. R. 1592.
*Jeronymo. pt. 1. Pr. 1605.
*Cornelia. (Tr. fr. French of Garnier). S. R. 1593.
Truethe of the most wicked and secret Murthering of John Brewen, Goldsmith, of London, committed by his owne wife. (Pamphlet). S. R. 1592. Repr. in Collier's Illustrations of Early Eng. Popular Lit. 1863.
† Boas. Shakspere and his Predecessors.
Dict. Nat. Biog. (Sidney Lee).
Fleay. Biog. Chron. Eng. Drama.
Klein. Geschichte des Englischen Drama's.
Lamb. Specimens of Eng. Dram. Poets.
Markscheffel, K. T. Kyd's Tragödien. Jahresb. d. realgymn. zu. Weimar. 1886—'87. Progr. (Max. Koch, Engl. Studien, 15: 120—21).
Ritzenfeldt. Der Gebrauch des Pronomens, Artikels u. Verbs bei Th. Kyd im Vergleiche zu dem Gebrauch bei Shakespeare. Kiel. 1889.
Sarrazin, G. Die entstehung Hamlet tragödie, 1. Shakespeare's Hamlet u. T. Kyd. (Anglia, 12: 143—157).
Der Corambus—Hamlet u. T. Kyd. (Anglia, 13: 117—124).
Die Modernisierung der Sage. (Anglia, 14: 322—345).
Der Verfasser von Soliman and Perseda. (Engl. Studien, 15: 250—63).
T. Kyd u. sein Kreis, Berlin. E. Felber. 1892. (E. Koeppel. Engl. Studien, 18: 125—133).
Worp. Die Fabel der Spanish Tragedy.' Sh. Jahrbuch, 29; 30. 1894.

LEGGE, THOMAS. 1535—1607.

Destruction of Jerusalem. 1577. (Not extant).
Richardus Tertius. (Latin). 1579. Ed. Barron Field. Sh. Soc. Pub. 1844.
Ed. Hazlitt, Sh.'s Libr., 5. 1875.
† Nash. Have with you to Saffron Walden. 1596.
Nichols. Progresses of Queen Eliz.

LODGE, THOMAS. 1558?—1625.

*Wounds of Civil War. 1587?
Looking-glass for London and England. Before 1590. (With Greene). Repr. in Greene's Dram. Works; ed. Dyce. 1831.
Non-Dram. Works.
Defence of Stage Plays. 1580. Sh. Soc. Pub. 1853. (In reply to Gosson's School of Abuse, 1579).

Alarum against Usurers. 1584. Sh. Soc. Pub. 1853. (In reply to Gosson's Playes confuted in five Actions. 1582).
Delectable Historie of Forbonius and Prisceria. (Romance). 1584. Repr. Sh. Soc. Pub. 1853.
Scillaes Metamorphosis. (Poem). 1589. Repr. S. W. Singer. Chiswick. 1819.
Rosalynde. (Romance). 1590. Repr. Waldron, 1802; in Collier's Sh. Libr. 1843; in Hazlitt's Sh. Libr. 1875; in Cassell's Nat. Libr. 1886; in Halliwell's fo. ed. Sh. v. 6.
History of Robert, Duke of Normandy. (Hist. Romance). 1591.
Catharos. (Prose discussion). '1591.
Euphues Shadow. 1592.
Phillis. (Poem). 1593.
Life and Death of William Longbeard. (Hist. Romance). 1593. Repr. in Collier's Illus. Old Eng. Lit. 2. 1860.
A Fig for Momus. (Satires, eclogues and epistles). 1595. Repr. Sir Alex. Boswell at Auchinleck Press, 1817.
Divil Conjured. (Moral Conference). 1596.
Margarite of America. (Romance). 1596.
Wits Miserie and World's Madnesse. (Essay). 1596.
?Prosopopoeia. (Relig. tract). 1596.
Josephus' Works. Translation. 1602.
Treatise of the Plague. (Medical). 1603.
Seneca's Works. Translation. 1614.
The Poor Man's Talent. (Popular medical treatise). Wr. circ. 1622. First pr. 1881. (Hunterian Club).
Du Bartas. Translation. 1625.
✠ Works, (exc. trans. of Josephus, Seneca and Du Bartas). Repr. Hunterian Club, Glasgow, 1878—'82.
† Arber. English Garner.
Boas. Shakspere and his Predecessors.
Buckhan, J. Poet-Lore, 3: 601.
Carl, R. Ueber T. Lodge's Leben u. Werke. Eine kritische Untersuchung im Auschluss an Davis Laing. (Anglia, 10: 235—288). Halle. 1887.
Delius, N. Lodge's Rosalynde and Shakespeare's As You Like It. Jahrbuch, 6: 226—249.
England's Helicon. 1600. Repr. Bullen. Lond. Nimmo. 1887. 30/.
Gosse. Seventeenth Cent. Studies. 40 pp. (Introd. to Hunterian ed. of Lodge's Works).
Ingleby, C. M. Was Thomas Lodge an Actor? 1868. Notes and Queries, 6th ser., 11: 107, 415.
Jusserand. Eng. Novel in the Time of Shakespeare.
Klein. Geschichte des Englischen Drama's.
Notes and Queries. 3d ser., 1: 202; 5th ser., 1: 21—23.
Saintsbury. Elizabethan Literature.
Stone, W. G. Shakspere's As You Like It and Lodge's Rosalynde compared. Sh. Soc. Pub. 1884. 1: 277—293.
Symonds. Predecessors of Shakspere.

LYLY, (Lilly) JOHN. 1554?—1606.

*Alexander and Campaspe. Pr. 1584.
Sapho and Phao. Pr. 1584.
*Endimion. Pr. 1591.

Gallathea. Pr. 1592.
*Mydas. Pr. 1592.
*Mother Bombie. Pr. 1594.
Woman in the Moone. Pr. 1597.
Love's Metamorphosis. Pr. 1601.

Non-Dram. Works.

 Euphues. 1579. Arber Reprints. Lond. 1868. Ed. Landmann. Heilbronn. 1887.
 Pap with a Hatchet. 1589. Repr. Petheram. Puritan Discipline Tracts. 1844. Saintsbury. Eliz. and Jac. Pamphlets.
✠ Six Court Comedies. (Endimion, Campaspe, Sapho and Phao, Gallathea, Mydas, Mother Bombie). 1632.
 Dram. Works; ed. Fairholt. 2 v. Lond. Smith. 1858.
 Endimion; ed. Geo. P. Baker, w. introd. and bibliog. N. Y. Holt. 1894. 85c.
† Arber Reprints. Eng. Scholar's Libr. 8. (List of Martin Marprelate books).
 Boas. Shakspere and his Predecessors.
 Bodenstedt. Shakespeare's Zeitgenossen.
 Child, C. G. John Lyly and Euphuism. Leipzig. Deichert. 1894. 2 m.
 Fleay. Biog. Chron. Eng. Drama. (Also Sh. Soc. Pub. 4. 1887).
 Furière. Projets de Mariage de la Reine Elizabeth. Paris. Levy. 1882.
 Goodlet, John. Engl. Studien, 5. (Shakspere's Debt to John Lilly).
 Halpin, N. J. Oberon's Vision in Mid. Night's Dream, illus. by comp. w. Lyly's Endimion. Sh. Soc. Pub. 1843.
 Hart, J. M. Euphuism. Repr. fr. Trans. of Ohio Colleges, 1889.
 Hazlitt. Dram. Lit. of the Age of Eliz.
 Hense. Lilly u. Sh. in ihren Verhältniss zum klassischen Alterthum. Sh. Jahrbuch, 7. 1872. John Lilly u. Sh. Jahrbuch, 8. 1873.
 Jusserand. Eng. Novel in the Time of Shakespeare.
 Klein. Geschichte des Englischen Drama's.
 Landmann. Shakspere and Euphuism. Sh. Soc. Pub. 1880—'85. Pt. 2; pp. 241—76. Der Euphuismus. Diss. Giessen. 1881.
 Lee, Sidney. Huon of Bordeaux. Early Eng. Text Soc. 1883—'88. Pt. 4; pp. 785 sq.
 Morley. Quart. Rev. Apr., 1861. (Euphuism).
 Raleigh, Walter. Eng. Novel. N. Y. Scribner, 1896. $1.25.
 Rushton. Shakespeare's Euphuism. Lond. Longmans. 1871.
 Sat. Rev. May 29, 1869.
 Steinhäuser, Karl. John Lyly als Dramatiker. Halle diss. 1884.
 Symonds. Shakspere's Predecessors.

LUPTON, THOMAS. Fl. 1575.

 All for Money. Pr. 1577. Repr. in Collier's Lit. of Sixteenth and Seventeenth Centuries Illustrated. 1851.

MARLOWE, CHRISTOPHER. 1564—'93.

*Tamburlaine. 2 parts. 1587? Qs. 1590; 1592; 1605—6.
*Dr. Faustus. 1588? Qs. 1604; 1609; 1611; 1616; 1619; 1620; 1624; 1631; 1663.
*Jew of Malta. Before 1588. Q. 1633. (Ed. Th. Heywood).
*Edward II. 1591? Qs. 1594; 1598; 1604; 1612; 1622.
 Massacre at Paris. 1593? Q. n. d.
*Dido. Q. 1594? (With Nash).

Non-Dram. Works.
- Epigrams and Elegies. (Trans. of Ovid's Amores). Circ. 1597. (Notes and Queries; 3rd Ser., 12: 436).
- First Book of Lucan. (Pharsalia). 1600. Repr. Percy, in Specimens of Blank Verse before Milton.
- Hero and Leander. First two sestiads. (Completed by Chapman). Qs. 1598; 1606; 1613; 1617; 1629; 1637. Repr. in Bridges' Restituta, 1814. (Notes and Queries. 6th Ser., 11: 305, 352; 12: 15). Ed. Singer. 1821. (No. 12 of Select Early Eng. Poets). Ed. Ricketts and Shannon. Lond. Mathews and Lane. 1894. 35/.
- Song: "Come live with me and be my love." The Passionate Pilgrim. 1599. England's Helicon. 1600.
- "I walked along a stream for pureness rare." England's Parnassus. 1600.
- ✠ Works; w. memoir by Robinson. 3 v. Lond. Pickering. 1826.
- Works; ed. Dyce. 3 v. 1850. (1 v. 1858). Lond. Routledge. n. d. 7/6.
- Works; ed. Cunningham. 1870?
- Works; ed. Bullen. 3 v. Lond. Nimmo. 1888. ea. 7/6.
- Best Plays; ed. Havelock Ellis, w. introd. by Symonds. (Mermaid Series). Lond. Vizetelly. 1887. 2/6.
- Selected Works; ed. Pinkerton. (Canterbury Poets). Lond. Scott. 1885. 1/.
- Poems; ed. Bell. (Annotated Ed. of the Eng. Poets). 1854.
- Marlowe's Werke. Historische kritische Ausgabe von H. Breymann and Albrecht Wagner. Heilbronn. Henninger. 1885. (L. Kellner. Engl. Studien, 9: 297—301). (Dr. Faustus and Jew of Malta. Engl. Studien, 14: 137—42).
- Works; trans. into French by Rabbe, w. introd. by Richepin. 2 v. Paris. 1885.
- Selected Works; trans. into German, in Bodenstedt's Sh.'s Zeitgenossen und ihre Werke, 3. 1860.
- Tamburlaine; ed. Hales and Jerram. 1877. (Lond. Series of Eng. Classics).
- Tamburlaine; ed. Albrecht Wagner. Heilbronn. Henninger. 1885. 4 m.
- Marlowe. Tragical History of Dr. Faustus. Greene, Honorable History of Friar Bungay; ed. Ward. Oxford. Clar. Press. 1887. 6/6. (H. Breymann, Engl. Studien, 12: 443—450).
- Faustus. (Morley. Univ. Libr.) Lond. Routledge. 1883. 1/.
- Faustus; ed. Wagner. Lond. 1885.
- Faustus; ed. Breymann. Heilbronn. 1889. (Qs. of 1604 and 1616 pr. on opp. pp.)
- Jew of Malta; ed. Oxberry. 1818.
- Edward II.; ed. Wagner. Hamburg. 1871.
- Edward II.; ed. Fleay. 1877. (Collier's School and Coll. Classics).
- Edward II.; ed. Tancock. Oxford. Clar. Press. 1887. 3/6.
- Edward II.; ed. w. introd. and notes. McLaughlin. N. Y. Holt. 1895. 70c.
- † Acad. Oct. 20, 1883. (Tamburlaine).
- Beard, Thomas. Theatre of God's Judgments. 1597. p. 148.
- Boas. Shakspere and his Predecessors.
- Breymann, H. Engl. Studien, 5: 56—66. 1881—'82. (Faustus. Reply to Albers in Sh. Jahrbuch für Rom. u. Eng. Lit.)
- Broughton, Jas. Gentlemen's Mag., 1800, pt. 1. (Five papers).
- Courtney, W. L. Studies at Leisure. "On Kit Marlowe's Death." Lond. Chapman. 1892. 6/. (Univ. Rev. 1890, 6: 356).
- Delius. Marlowe's Faustus und seine Quelle. Bielefeld. 1881.

Dowden, (Prof.) Edward. Transcripts and Studies. "Marlowe." Lond. Paul. 1887. 12/. (Fortn. Rev., 1870).
Drayton. Epistle * * of Poets and Poetry. 1627.
Düntzner. Anglia. 1: 44.
Faligan, Ernest. De Marlovianis Fabulis. Lat. Thesis. Paris, 1887.
Fischer, Otto. Zur Charakteristik der Dramen Marlowe's. München. 1889.
Fleay. Biog. Chron Eng. Drama. (Sh. Soc. Trans., 2. 1885).
Frankel, L. Zum stoffe von Marlowe's Tamburlaine. (Engl. Studien, 16: 459—462).
Friedrich, J. Didodramen des Dolce, Jodelle und Marlowe in ihren Verhältniss zu einander und zu Vergil's Eneid. Kempton. 1888.
Genée, (Dr.) Rudolph. Sh. Soc. Trans. 1875—76. Collation of Edward II. Q. 1594, w. Dyce's text, 1850.
Hazlitt. Dram. of the Age of Eliz.
Heinemann, Wm. An essay towards a bibliog. of Marlowe's Faustus. Repr. fr. the Bibliographer. 1884.
Herford. Lit. Relations of Eng. and Germany.
Hermann, E. Shakspeare wider Robert Greene, Marlowe and Nash. 91 pp. *In his* Sh. Studien, 2: 3, p. 598.
Hertzberg. Sh. u. seine Vorläufer. Sh. Jahrbuch, 15. 1880.
Horne, R. H. Death of Marlowe, a tragedy. 39 pp. Marlowe's Works; ed. Bullen, 3: 315.
Ingram, J. H. Univ. Rev. 1889. 4: 382.
Kellner. Die Quelle von Marlowe's Jew of Malta. Engl. Studien, 10: 80—110.
Klein. Geschichte des Englischen Drama's.
Klose, R. Die unterschiede zwischen dem Casseler texte v. Marlowe's Edward II. u. dem von 1598; ed. Wagner. (Engl. Studien, 5: 242—'45).
Lamb. Specimens of Eng. Dram. Poetry.
Lee, Jane. Sh. Soc. Trans., 2. 1875—'76. "On the Authorship of 2 & 3 Henry VI."
Lewis, J. G. Christopher Marlowe; his life and works. Canterbury. 1890.
Lowell. Old Eng. Dramatists.
Meissner. Die Englischen Comödianten * * in Oesterreich.
Meres. Palladis Tamia. 1598.
Mommsen, C. I. T. Marlowe und Shakespeare. Frankfurt. 1886.
Pröscholdt, L. Eine collation der aeltesten quarto von Marlowe's Dr. Faustus. Anglia, 3: 88—96. (Breymann, H. Zu L. Pröscholdt's Collation of Marlowe's Faustus. Anglia, 4: 288—91).
Return from Parnassus. (*See* Index).
Reviews. Fraser, 47: 221; Cornh., 30: 329; Every Sat., 9: 670; 17: 340; Ecl. Mo., 76: 241; Blackwood, 1: 388, (Faustus); 2:21, (Edward II.); 2: 260, (Jew of Malta).
Schroeer, K. J. Zu Marlowe's Faustus. (Anglia, 5: 134—36).
Swinburne. A Study of Shakespeare, p. 26—65, *passim*.
Swinburne. Poems and Ballads; Second Series. "In the Bay." Lond. Chatto. 1889.
Symonds. Shakspere's Predecessors.
Ulrici. Ch. Marlowe u. Sh.'s Verhältniss zu ihm. Sh. Jahrbuch, 1. 1865.
Vaughan, Wm. Golden Grove. 1600.
Verity. Marlowe's Influence on Shakespeare. 1886.
Wagner, Max. The Eng. dram. blank verse before Marlowe. Th. 1. Progr.-abhandl. Ostern. 1881. (J. Schupper, Engl. Studien, 5; 457—8). Th. 2. Ostern. 1882. (Engl. Studien, 8: 393).

Wagner, Wilhelm. Emendationen u. Bemerkungen zu Marlowe. Sh. Jahrbuch. 11.

MARSTON, JOHN. 1575?—1634.

* Antonio and Mellida. 1602.
* Antonio's Revenge. 1602.
* Malcontent. 1604.
* Eastward Ho. 1605. (Revived at Drury Lane 1751 as The Prentices, and 1775, as Old City Manners).
  Dutch Courtesan. 1605. (Revived by Betterton in 1680 as The Revenge; or, A Match in Newgate, wh. was itself adapted by Bullock, 1715, as A Woman's Revenge).
* Parasitaster; or, The Fawn. 1606.
  Wonder of Women; or, The Tragedy of Sophonisba. 1606.
* What You Will. 1607.
  ?Insatiate Countess. 1613.

Non-Dram. Works.

Metamorphosis of Pigmalion's Image. And certain Satires. 1598.
Scourge of Villainy. Three Books of Satires. 1598.
✠ Tragedies and Comedies. 1 v. 1633.
Works; ed. Halliwell. 3 v. Lond. Smith. 1855. 15/.
Poems; ed. Grosart. 2 v. Manchester. 1879. (51 copies pr.)
Selections; ed. Sharp. (Canterbury Poets). Lond. Scott. 1885. 2/6.
Works; ed. Bullen. 3 v. Lond. Nimmo. 1887. ea. 7/6.
† Athen. 1887, 2: 190.
Bodenstedt. Sh.'s Zeitgenossen u. ihre Werke.
Chester, Robert. Love's Martyr. 1601. (Poem by Marston appended).
Deighton, K. Marston's Works, Conjectural Readings. 1893.
Disraeli. Quarrels of Authors.
Gosse. Jacobean Poets.
Griffiths, L. M. Poet-Lore, 2: 280; 360; 414.
Hazlitt. Dram. Lit. of Age of Eliz.
Henslowe. Diary. Sept. 28, 1599.
Hogarth. Prints: The Industrious and Idle Prentice. (Drawn, perhaps, from Eastward Ho).
Horne. New Spirit of the Age.
Jonson. Conversations with Drummond of Hawthornden. Poetaster. (Crispinus a caricature of Marston). Sejanus. (Commend. Verses by Marston).
Lamb. Specimens of Eng. Dram. Poets.
Meres. Palladis Tamia.
Retro. Rev. 1822, 6: 113.
Return from Parnassus. (*See* Index).
Scholten, V. Metrische Untersuchungen zu Marston's Trauerspielen. Halle diss. 1886. 1/6.
Shakespeare and Jonson. Dramatic, versus Wit Combats.
Stoddard, R. H. Dial, 8: 79.
Swinburne. Nineteenth Cent. Oct., 1888, 24: 531.
Weever, John. Epigrams. 1599.
W. I. Whipping of the Satire. 1601.

MONDAY, ANTHONY. 1553—1633.

[Dram. career mainly 1584—1602].

Fidele and Fortunio. 1584. (Now extant)
John a Kent and John à Cumber. 1594? (Notes and Queries, 1st ser., 4: 55, 83).
Mother Redcap. 1597.
*Downfall of Robert, Earl of Huntingdon. 1598. (With Chettle).
*Death of Robert, Earl of Huntingdon. 1598. ((With Chettle).
Richard Cour de Lion's Funeral. 1598. (With Chettle, Drayton, Wilson).
Valentine and Orson. 1598. (With Hathway).
Chance Medley. 1598. (With Chettle?, Drayton, Wilson).
*Sir John Oldcastle, 2 parts. 1599. (With Drayton, Hathway, Wilson).
Owen Tudor. 1599? (With Drayton, Hathway, Wilson).
Fair Constance of Rome. 1600. (With Dekker, Drayton, Hathway).
Rising of Cardinal Wolsey. 1601. (With Chettle, Drayton, Smith).
Jeptha. 1602. (With Dekker).
Cæsar's Fall. 1602. (With Drayton, Middleton, Webster, Dekker?)
Two Harpies. 1602. (With Dekker, Drayton, Middleton, Webster).
Widow's Charm. 1602.
Set at Tennis. 1602.

[Of the above only four, John a Kent and John a Cumber, the two Robin Hood Plays and the first part of Sir John Oldcastle are extant].

Lord Mayor's Pageants.

 Triumphs of re-united Britannia. 1605. (Nichols. Progresses of James I., 1: 564—76).
 Camp-bell; or, the Ironmongers Faire Field. 1609.
 Chrysothriambos; The Triumphs of Gold. 1611.
 Himatia-Poleos; Triumphs of Old Drapery. 1614.
 Metropolis Coronata; Triumphs of Ancient Drapery. 1615. (Nichols. Progresses of James I., 3: 107—18).
 Chrysanaleia, the Golden Fishing; or, the Honour of Fishmongers. 1616. (Re-prod. in folio by J. Gough Nichols, w. 12 colored plates by Henry Shaw. Lond. 1844. 2nd ed., 1869. See also Nichols. Progresses of James I., 3: 195—207).
 Siderothriambos; or, Steel and Iron Triumphing. 1618.
 Triumphs of the Golden Fleece. 1623.

[All in the Brit. Museum, except Chrysothriambos, wh. is in the Duke of Devonshire's collection].

[For his translations of French romances, Palladino, Palmerin, Palmendos, Gerileon, Amadis de Gaule, etc., and for his many miscellaneous works, see Dict. Nat. Biog. (Seccombe).]

✣ John à Kent and John à Cumber; ed. w. introd. and notes. Collier. Sh. Soc. Pub. 1846.
† Arber. An Eng. Garner.
 Brydges. Censura Literaria and Restituta.
 Chettle. Kind-Harte's Dream. 1592. Percy Soc. 1841.
 Cohn. Shakespeare in Germany, 1865, p. 47.
 Collier. John à Kent and John à Cumber. Introd. Sh. Soc. Pub. 1851.
  Memoirs of Actors, p. 111. Sh. Soc. Pub. 1846.
 Copley, Anthony. Wits, Fits and Fancies, 1614, p. 134.
 Cunningham. Extracts fr. Accounts of the Revels at Court. Sh. Soc. Pub. 1842.
 Drake. Shakespeare and his Time, 1: 234—5; 2: 237.
 Fairholt. Lord Mayor's Pageants. Introd. p. 38. Percy Soc. 1843.

Gifford. Jonson's Works. 1816, 6: 325.
Henslowe. Diary, pp. 106, 118, 158, 163, 171, 235.
Huth. Ancient Ballads and Broadsides, 1867, p. 370.
Jonson. Case is Altered. 1599. (Antonio Balladino=Monday).
Kempe. Nine Daies Wonder. 1600. Camden Soc. *Also* Arber Reprints.
Marston. Histrio-mastix. 1598?
Meres. Palladis Tamia.
Middleton. Triumphs of Truth. 1613.
Nichols. Progresses of James I.
Nichols, J. Gough. Lord Mayor's Pageants, p. 102.
Notes and Queries. (For specific references, *see* Dict. Nat. Biog.)
(Pound, Thomas)? True Report of the Death and Martyrdom of M. Campion. 1581. (Cf. Monday's Brief Answer, 1582).
Simpson, Richard. Edmund Campion. A Biography. Lond. 1867.
Webbe. Discourse of Eng. Poetry. 1586. Arber Reprints.

NASH, THOMAS. 1567—1601.

*Dido. Acted 1591. Pr. 1594. (With Marlowe).
*Summer's Last Will and Testament. Acted 1592.
Isle of Dogs. 1597. (Not extant).
Prose Works.
Anatomy of Absurdities. 1588.
Address to the Gentlemen Students of both Universities. (Prefixed to Greene's Menaphon). 1589.
Pasquil of England; A Countercuff for Martin Junior. Aug., 1589.
Pasquil of England; His Return and Meeting with Marforius. Oct., 1589.
?Mirror for Martinists. Dec., 1589.
Pasquil's Apology. July, 1590.
Astrological Prognostications for 1591 by Thomas Scarlet. 1590.
Address before Sidney's Astrophel and Stella. 1591.
Pierce Penniless, his Supplication to the Devil. 1592.
Apology of Pierce Penniless; or, Strange News of the Intercepting Certain Letters. 1592.
Christ's Tears over Jerusalem. 1593.
Terrors of the Night; or, A Discourse of Apparitions. 1593.
Unfortunate Traveller; or, the Life of Jack Wilton. 1593.
Have with you to Saffron Walden. Pr. 1596.
Nash's Lenten Stuff. (Praise of the Red Herring). 1599.
✠ Complete Works; ed. Grosart. 6 v. Lond. 1883—'85. (Huth Libr.)
Anatomy of Absurdity. Repr. Collier; Illus. of Old Eng. Lit., v. 3., 1866.
Pierce Penniless, his Supplication to the Devil. Repr. Collier. Sh. Soc. Pub. 1842. *Also in his* Misc. Tracts. 6. 1868.
Apology of Pierce Penniless; or, Strange News of the Intercepting Certain Letters. Repr. Collier. Misc. Tracts, 2.
Christ's Tears over Jerusalem. Repr. Bridges. Archaica, 1. 1815.
Unfortunate Traveller; or, The Life of Jack Wilton; ed. Gosse. Cheswick Press Reprints. 1892.
Have with you to Saffron Walden. Repr. Collier. Misc. Tracts, 9.
Nash's Lenten Stuff. Repr. Harl. Misc. *Also* ed. C. Hindley, Old Book Collect. Misc., 1.
† Anon. Return of the Knight of the Post from Hell with the Devil's Answer to the Supplication of Piers Penniless. 1606. (Cf. Dekker's News from Hell brought by the Devil's Carrier. 1606).

Arber. Eng. Garner, 1: 467.
Arber, Edward. Introductory Sketch to the Martin Marprelate Controversy. 1588—'90. (Arber Reprints).
C. H. (Henry Chettle)? Piers Plainness' Seven Years Prenticeship. 1595.
Clerke, Wm. Polimanteia. 1595.
Dekker. News from Hell. 1606.
Dict. Nat. Biog. (Sidney Lee). (Cf. arts. on Greene, Gabriel Harvey, Richard Harvey, Lyly and Marlowe).
Disraeli. Calamities of Authors. Quarrels of Authors.
Dowland. Second Book of Songs. 1600. "If floods of tears could cleanse my follies past." (See Sh. Soc. Pub., 1: 76—9; 2: 62—4).
Ecl. Mo., 30: 224.
Fitzgeffrey, Chas. Affaniae. 1601. (Cenotaphia).
Fleay. Shakspere and Puritanism. Anglia, 7: 223.
Grosart. Harvey's Works, 3: 43. (Portrait of Nash).
Harvey, Gabriel. Works; ed. Grosart. 3 v. 1884—5. (Huth Libr). Four Letters and Certain Sonnets touching R. Greene, 1592. New Letters of Notable Contents. 1593. Trimming of Th. Nash. 1597.
Herford. Lit. Relations of Eng. and Germany.
Herman, E. Sh. wider Greene, Marlowe u. Nash. (In his Sh. Studien, 2).
Jusserand. Eng. Novel in Time of Eliz.
Henslowe. Diary.
Maskell, William. Martin Marprelate Controversy. Lond. 1845.
Meres. Palladis Tamia.
Notes and Queries. 2nd ser., 4: 320.
Raleigh, Walter. Eng. Novel. N. Y. Scribner. 1896. $1.25.
Retro. Rev. 1828; 1853.
Return from Parnassus. See Index.
Scott, T. J. Poems attr. to Nash, in Dowland Ayres, 1600. Sh. Soc. Trans., 2. 1845.
Taylor, John. (The Water-Poet). Differing Worships * * or Tom Nash his Ghost (the old Martin queller) newly roused. 1640. Crop-ear Curried; or, Tom Nash his Ghost. 1644.

NEVILLE, ALEX. 1544—1614.

*Trans. of Seneca's Œdipus. 1560. (See Newton).
† Gascoigne. Flowers of Poesy. 1572.
Googe, Barnabe. Eclogues and Sonnets. 1563. (Commend. Verses by Neville).
Notes and Queries. 1st ser., 5: 442; 3rd ser., 3: 114, 117.

NEWTON, THOMAS. 1542?—1607.

Seneca his Ten Tragedies tr. into English. 1581, (ed. Newton, who himself tr. only the Thebais. See Jasper Heywood, Alex. Neville, Nuce and Studley).
† Symonds. Shakspere's Predecessors.

NORTON, THOMAS. 1532—1584.

*Gorbodoc; or, Ferrex and Porrex. (First three acts). See Sackville. Acted 1562. Pr. 1565. Repr. W. D. Cooper. Sh. Soc. Pub. 1847. Lucy Toulmin Smith in Vollmöller's Englische Sprach—und Literaturdenkmale. 1883.
† Klein. Geschichte des Englischen Drama's.

NUCE, THOMAS.   —1617.

Trans. of Seneca's Octavia. 1561? (*See* Newton).
† Studley, John. Trans. of Seneca's Agamemnon. 1561. (Pref. Verses by Nuce).

PEELE, GEORGE. 1558?—1597?

Arraignment of Paris. 1581?
Hunting of Cupid. S. R. 1591. (Not extant, exc. fragments ed. Dyce).
*Edward I. Pr. 1593.
Battle of Alcazar. Pr. 1594.
Old Wives' Tale. Pr. 1595.
*David and Bethsabe. Pr. 1599.

Pageants.

Pageant for Lord Mayor. 1585.
Descensus Astraeae. (Lord Mayor). 1591.
Speeches to Queen Eliz. at Theobalds. 1591.

Miscellaneous Writings.

Lines to Thomas Watson. 1582.
Farewell to Norris and Drake. 1589.
Fall of Troy. 1589.
Eclogue Gratulatory to the Earl of Essex. 1589.
Polyhymnia. 1590.
Honour of the Garter. 1593.
Praise of Chastity. (Phoenix Nest, 1593).
Anglorum Feriae. 1595.

✣ Works; ed. Dyce. 3 v. Lond. Pickering. 1838. 31/6.
Peele and Greene. Works; ed. Dyce. Lond. and N. Y. Routledge. 1861.
Plays and Poems; ed. Morley. Lond. Routledge. 1887. 1/. (Morley's Univ. Libr.)
Works; ed. Bullen. 2 v. Lond. Nimmo. 1888. ea. 7/6.
† Boas. Shakspere and his Predecessors.
Fairholt. Lord Mayors' Pageants.
Fleay. Biog. Chron. Eng. Dram.
Henslowe. Diary.
Klein. Geschichte des Englischen Drama's.
Lammerhirt, R. Untersuchungen über sein Leben u. seine Werke. Rostock. 1882. 68 pp. (E. Einenkel. Anglia, 7: 3, 4).
Lond. Mag. 10: 61.
Mery Conceited Jests. (Hindley, C. Old book collect. miscel., 1. Hazlitt, W. C. Shakespeare Jest-books, 2).
Penner, E. Metrische Untersuchungen zu G. Peele. Halle diss. 1890. 44 pp. (W. Wilke, Engl. Studien, 16: 297—99).
Schelling. Modern Language Notes. Apr., 1893.
Segar. Honour, Military and Civil. 1602.
Symonds. Shakspere's Predecessors.

PERCY, WILLIAM. 1575—1648.

Arabia Sitiens. 1601. MS.
Cuckqueans. 1601. (Pr. Haslewood, Roxburghe Club, 1824).
Fairy Pastoral. (Pr. Haslewood, Roxburghe Club, 1824).

Aphrodisial; or, Sea Feast. 1602. MS.
Country's Tragedy in Vacuuum; or Cupid's Sacrifice. 1602. MS.
Necromantes; or, The Two Supposed Heads. Acted by the children of St. Paul's. Circ. 1602. MS.
Sonnets to the fairest Celia. 1594. (Repr. Brydges, 1818; Grosart, Occasional Issues, 1877; Arber, Eng. Garner, 6: 135—56).
† Barnes, Barnabe. Parthenophil. 1593. (Ded. to Percy).

HENRY PORTER. Fl. 1598.

Hot Anger Soon Cold. 1598. (With Chettle and Johnson. Not extant).
*Two Angry Women of Abington. 1598. Pr. 1599.
Spencers. 1599. (With Chettle. Not extant).
✠Two Angry Women of Abington; ed. Dyce, Percy Soc., 1841; ed. Havelock Ellis, Nero and Other Plays. 1888. (Mermaid Ser.)
† Griffith. Evenings with Shakspere. p. 246.
Henslowe. Diary.
Weever. Epigrams. 1599.

PRESTON, THOMAS. Fl. 1570.

*Cambyses. 1570?
† Fleay. Hist. of the Stage. p. 64.
Jusserand. Le Théâtre en Angleterre. (Ch. 7).

SACKVILLE, THOMAS. 1536—1608.

*Gorboduc; or, Ferrex and Porrex. (Last two acts. See Norton). Acted 1562. Pr. 1565.
✠Gorboduc; or, Ferrex and Porrex; ed. W. D. Cooper. Sh. Soc. Pub. 1847; ed. Lucy Toulmin Smith. Heilbronn. 1883. (Vollmöller, K. Eng. Sprach-u.—Literaturdenkmale des 16—18 Jahr., 1).
Works. Lond. Smith. 1859. 4/.
Works. Anderson. Brit. Poets, 1. 1793.
† Boas. Shakspere and his Predecessors.
Hazlitt. Age of Eliz.
Jahrbuch. (Sh.) Verfasser des Gorboduc, 15: 369.
Jusserand. Le Théâtre en Angleterre. (Ch. 6).
Klein. Geschichte des Englischen Drama's.
Symonds. Shakspere's Predecessors.
Ward. Eng. Dram. Lit.

SHAKESPEARE, WILLIAM. 1564—1616.

Venus and Adonis. (Poem). S. R. Apr. 18, 1593. Qs. 1593, 1594, 1596, 1599, 1602 (2), 1617, 1620.
Lucrece. (Poem). S. R. May 9, 1594. Qs. 1594, 1598, 1600, 1607, 1616.
?Titus Andronicus. (Wr. circ. 1588?) S. R. Feb. 6, 1594. Qs. 1600, 1611.
?1, 2, 3 Henry VI. (With Greene, Peele, Kyd, Marlowe? 1588—'92?) Pts. 1 and 2, S. R. Apr. 19, 1602.
Love's Labours Lost. (Wr. before 1590?) Revised for Court presentation 1598. S. R. Jan. 22, 1607. Q. 1598.
*Comedy of Errors. (Wr. before 1591?)
*Two Gentlemen of Verona. (Wr. 1590—'92?)

Midsummer Night's Dream. (Wr. 1592—'94?) Revision, perhaps, for Court performance. S. R. Oct. 8, 1600. Qs. 1600 (2).

*?Richard III. (Wr. 1592—'94?) S. R. Oct. 20, 1597. Qs. 1597, 1598, 1608 (2), 1615.

Richard II. (Wr. 1592—'94?) S. R. Aug. 29, 1597. Qs. 1597, 1598, 1608 (2), 1615.

*Romeo and Juliet. (Perhaps wr. circ. 1590 and revised circ. 1595). Qs. 1597, 1599, 1609, n. d., 1637.

*King John. (Wr. circ. 1595?)

*Merchant of Venice. (Wr. 1594—'96?) S. R. July 22, 1598. Qs. 1600 (2), 1637, 1652.

*?Taming of the Shrew. (Wr. 1596—'97?) Original authorship unknown. Revision probably by Sh.

*1 Henry IV. (Wr. 1596—'97?) S. R. Feb. 25, 1598. Qs. 1598, 1599, 1604, 1608, 1613, 1622.

*2 Henry IV. (Wr. 1596—'97?) S. R. Aug. 23, 1600. Q. 1600.

*Merry Wives of Windsor. (Wr. 1597—'98?) S. R. Jan. 18, 1602. Qs. 1602, 1619.

*Henry V. (Wr. 1598—'99?) S. R. Aug. 4, 1600. Qs. 1600, 1602, 1608.

*Much Ado about Nothing. (Wr. circ. 1599?) S. R. Aug. 4, 1600. Q. 1600.

*As You Like It. (Wr. 1599—1600?) S. R. Aug. 4, 1600.

*Twelfth Night. (Wr. circ. 1600?)

[Passionate Pilgrim]. Lyric Miscellany, including sonnets, etc., by Sh. Pr. 1599.

Sonnets. (Wr. 1595—1605?) S. R. May 20, 1609. Q. 1609.

*Julius Cæsar. (Wr. 1600—1601?)

All's Well that Ends Well. (Wr. circ. 1601?)

*Hamlet. (First draft perhaps as early as 1589. Revision 1601—1603?) S. R. July 26, 1602. Qs. 1603, 1604, 1605, 1611.

*Measure for Measure. (Wr. 1602—1604?)

Troilus and Cressida. (Wr. 1602—1609?) S. R. Feb. 7, 1603. Qs. 1609 (2).

*Othello. (Wr. circ. 1604?) S. R. Oct. 6, 1621. Q. 1622.

*King Lear. (Wr. circ. 1605?) S. R. Nov. 26, 1607. Qs. 1608 (2).

*Macbeth. (Wr. circ. 1606?)

*Antony and Cleopatra. (Wr. circ. 1607?) S. R. May 20, 1608.

*Coriolanus. (Wr. 1607—1608?)

*Timon. (Wr. 1607—1608?) Sh.'s only in part.

*Pericles. (Wr. 1607—1608?) Sh.'s only in part. S. R. May 20, 1608. Qs. 1609, 1611, 1619.

*Cymbeline. (Wr. 1608—'10?)

*Winter's Tale. (Wr. circ. 1610?)

*Tempest. (Wr. 1610—'12?)

*?Two Noble Kinsmen. (Wr. circ. 1612? With Fletcher).

*?Henry VIII. (Wr. circ. 1613? With Fletcher and possibly Massinger).

Important Editions.

> First Folio, 1623, ed. Heminge and Condell. (Containing all the above plays exc. Pericles). Repr. 1807; Booth, 1864, 52/6; reprod. in exact facsimile, ed. H. Staunton. Day, 1866, 126/; reprod. in reduced fac-simile, w. introd. J. O. Halliwell. Chatto, 1875, 7/6.
>
> Second Folio, 1632.
>
> Third Folio, 1663—'64. (Adds Pericles, London Prodigal, Thomas Lord Cromwell, Sir John Oldcastle, Puritan Widow, Locrine and the Yorkshire Tragedy).

Fourth Folio, 1685. (Repr. of Third, w. modern spelling).
Dramatic Works; ed. N. Rowe, w. introd. and notes, 6 v., 1709. (Includes the doubtful plays). Repr., 8 v., 1714.
Dramatic Works; ed. Alex. Pope, w. textual emendations, 6 v., 1725. (Rejects the doubtful plays). Repr. 1728, 1731, 1735, 1766, 1768.
Works; ed. Lewis Theobald, w. textual emendations, 7 v., 1733. (The basis of subsequent editions). Repr. 1740, 1752, 1757, 1762, 1767, 1772, 1773.
Works; ed. (Sir) Th. Hanmer, 6 v., 1744. Repr. 1747, 1750—'51, 1760, 1770—'71.
Works; ed. Wm. Warburton, 8 v., 1747. Repr. 1747.
Works; ed. (Dr.) Samuel Johnson, 8 v., 1765. Repr. 1768.
Twenty Plays; pr. from original Quartos; Geo. Steevens, 4 v., 1766.
Works; ed. Edward Capell, 10 v., 1767. (3 v. of Notes added in 1781).
Plays; w. notes by Johnson and Steevens, 10 v., 1773. Repr. 1778; repr. Isaac Reed, 1785; repr. Steevens, 15 v., 1793, w. glossary by Reed and essays by Farmer and Malone; repr. Reed, 21 v., 1803, 1813.
Plays and Poems; ed. Edmond Malone, 10 v., 1790.
Works, w. illustrations; pub. John Boydell, 9 v. fo., 1802. Bickers, 1873. 63/.
Works; ed. Alex. Chalmers, 9 v., 1805, 1809, 1823.
"1821 Variorum;" or "Boswell's Malone." (Works, w. collation of texts; ed. Malone and Jas. Boswell). 21 v., 1821.
Works; ed. Wm. Harness, 8 v., 1825.
"Aldine Edition;" ed. S. W. Singer, 10 v., 1826. Lond. Bell. 1875—'77. ea. 2/6.
Works; ed. A. J. Valpy, 15 v., 1832—'34.
"Pictorial Edition;" ed. Chas. Knight, w. illus. by Harvey, 1843. Lond. Virtue. 1888—'89; ea. 6/.
"National Edition;" ed. Chas. Knight. 6 v., 1851—'52. ea. 6/.
Works; ed. J. P. Collier, 8 v., 1842—'44. Repr. 6 v., 1858; repr. 8 v., 1875—'78. £25.
Works; ed. (Prof.) H. N. Hudson, 3 v., 1851—'56; "Expurgated Shakespeare," 23 v., Bost. 1879—'81, ea. 50c.; "Harvard Edition," 20 v. or 10 v., Bost. 1880, $25 or $20.
Works; ed. Alex. Dyce, 6 v., 1857; "Library Edition," 10 v. Lond. Sonnenschein, 1885—'86. ea. 9/. New ed. 1891.
"Illustrated Edition;" ed. Howard Staunton, w. 824 illus. by Sir John Gilbert, 3 v., 1858—'60, Routledge, 1868, 42/; "Library Edition;" 6 v., Routledge, 1889, 42/; "Edition de Luxe;" 15 v., Routledge, 1881, £6, 10/.
Works; ed. Chas. and Mary Cowden-Clarke, 4 v., 1864.
Works; ed. J. O. Halliwell, 16 v. fo., 1853—'65.
Works; ed. Richard Grant White, 12 v., 1866. Lond. Low, 1883, 3 v., 36/; 6v., 63/. Boston, Houghton, 6 v., $10.
Works; ed. (Prof.) N. Delius, (w. notes in English). 2 v. Elberfeld, 1859—'60. 1882. 16/.
"Cambridge Edition;" ed. Clark and Wright, 9 v., Macmillan, 1863—'66, £9; New ed., 9 v., Macmillan, 1891—'93, ea. 10/6, $3; "Edition de Luxe," 40 v., ea. 6/, $2; "Globe Edition," Macmillan, 3/6, $1; Select Plays (15), Clarendon Press, 1/ to 2/6 ea.
Lithographic Fac-similes of the Early Quartos, Lithog. E. W. Ashbee. 48 v., 1866—'71. £60.
"New Variorum;" ed. (Dr.) H. H. Furness. Phil. Lippincott. 1871—'96, in prog., ea. $4. (Romeo and Juliet, Macbeth, Hamlet (2), Lear, Othello, Merchant of Venice, As You Like It, Tempest, Midsummer Night's Dream, *now ready*).

"Friendly Edition;" ed. (Dr.) W. A. Rolfe. 40 v. N. Y. Harper. 1876–'84, ea. 50c.
"Leopold Edition;" Based on Text of Delius w. introd. by (Dr.) F. J. Furnivall. Lond. Cassell. 1880, 1889. 3/6.
Quarto Fac-similes; lithog. Griggs and Praetorius. 43 v. Lond. Quaritch. 1881–'90. £15, 15/.
"Irving Edition;" ed. Henry Irving and F. A. Marshall. 8 v. Lond. Blackie. 1887–'90. ea. 10/6. "Edition de Luxe," ea. 31/6.
"Bankside Edition;" ed. Appleton Morgan. 20 v. N. Y. Sh. Soc. 1888–'91. ea. $2.50.
Select Plays (20); ed. K. Deighton. (Eng. Classics). Lond. and N. Y. Macmillan. 1890–'94. ea. 1/6 to 2/6. 40c.
"Oxford Edition;" ed. W. J. Craig. Clarendon Press. N. Y. Nelson. 1891. India Paper, 10/6, $3.75. Ordinary Paper, 3/6, $1.75. "Oxford Miniature Edition." 6 v. 21/. $8.
"Temple Edition;" ed. Israel Gollancz. Lond. Dent. N. Y. Macmillan. 1894: in prog., ea. 1/, 45c.
Poems; w. memoir by Dyce. Lond. Bell. 1/6.
Songs and Sonnets; w. notes by F. F. Palgrave. Lond. Macmillan. 1879. 4/6.
Sonnets; ed. (Prof.) E. Dowden. Lond. Paul. 1881. 6/.
Sonnets; ed. T. Tyler. Lond. Nutt. 1890. 12/.
(For fuller lists of editions of complete works, of separate plays and poems, of foreign editions and translations use the references immediately below).

Bibliography.
Cohn, (Dr.) Albert. Sh.-Bibliographie. *Pub. annually in Jahrbuch, (Sh.)*
Halliwell, J. O. Brief Handlist of Books, MSS., etc., illustrative of the Life and Writings of Sh. 1859. Catalogue of the Sh.-Study Books in his Own Library. 1876. Collection of Sh. Rarities. (Calendar; ed. E. E. Baker). N. Y. Longmans. 1891. 10/6. List of Works illustr. of the Life and Writings of Sh. 1867. Shakesperiana. A Catalogue of the Early Editions of Sh.'s Plays. 1841.
Lowndes, W. T. Bibliog. of Sh. 115 pp. (*In his* Bibliographer's Manual. 1863).
Hubbard, J. M. Catalogue of the Works of Sh., orig. and trans., together with the Shakesperiana embraced in the Barton Collection of the Boston Public Library. 1880.
Lenox Library. Contributions to a Catalogue. No. 5. Works of Sh., etc. 1880.
Morgan, A. Digest Shakspearcanæ, 2 pts. (Down to 1887). N. Y. Sh. Soc. 1887. 15/.
Thimm, F. Shakespeariana fr. 1564 to 1871. (England, Germany and France). 1872. (Continued in Sh. Soc. Pub. Lond.)
Winsor, Justin. Bibliog. of orig. Quartos and Folios of Sh., with particular reference to Copies in America. 1876. Sh.'s Poems. Bibliog. of the Earlier Editions. 9 pp. (Harvard Coll. Library, Bibliog. Contrib. 1, 2).
Wyman, W. H. Bibliog. of the Bacon-Sh. Controversy. 1884.

Linguistics, etc.
Abbott, (Dr.) E. A. Sh. Grammar. Lond. Macmillan. 1873. 6/.
Adams, W. H. D. Concordance to the Plays of Sh. Lond. Routledge. 1886. 10/6.
Bartlett, John. New and Complete Concordance to Dram. Works (and Poems) of Sh. Lond. and N. Y. Macmillan. 1894. 42/. $14.00. New ed. $7.50.
Bathurst, C. Sh.'s Versification in different periods of his Life. 1857.

Browne, Geo. H. Notes on Sh.'s Versification. Boston. 1884.
Cowden-Clarke, Chas. and Mary. The Sh. Key, unlocking the Treasures of his Style. 1879.
Cowden-Clarke, Mary. Complete Concordance to Sh. Lond. Bickers. 1888. 25/.
Craik, G. L. The English of Sh. 1857.
Dyce, Alex. Glossary to Sh. 1881. (Works; ed. Dyce, v. 10).
Ellis, A. J. Early English Pronunciation, w. especial reference to Sh. and Chaucer. Early Eng. Text Soc. 1869—'75. 1889.
Fleay, F. G. Sh. Manual. Lond. Macmillan. 1876. 4/6.
Furness, (Mrs.) H. H. Concordance to Sh.'s Poems. Phil. Lippincott. 1874. $4.
Halliwell, J. O. Sh. Glossary. (*In his* Dict. of Archaic and Provincial Words, 2 v.) Lond. Smith. 1887. 15/.
Mackay, (Dr.) Chas. New Glossary of Obscure Words and Phrases in Sh. and his Contemp. Lond. Low. 1887. 21/.
Nares, A. R. Sh. Glossary. (*In his* Glossary of Words, Phrases, etc., illust. Eng. Authors; ed. Halliwell and Wright. 2 v. Lond. Reeves and Turner. 1888. 21/.)
O'Connor, Evangeline. Analytical Index to the Works of Sh. Lond. Paul. 1887. 5/.
Schmidt, (Dr.) Alex. Sh. Lexicon. 2 v. Berlin. 1886. 31/6.
Siddons, J. H. The Sh. Referee. Washington. 1886. $2.
Walker, W. S. Crit. Exam. of the Text of Sh., with remarks on the Language. 1860.

Biography.

Baynes, (Prof.) Th. Spencer. Sh. Studies. (What Sh. learned at School). Lond. Longmans. 1894. 7/6.
Beisley, Sidney. Sh.'s Garden. Lond. 1864.
Bucknill, (Dr.) J. C. The Medical Knowledge of Sh. Lond. Longmans. 1680. 7/6.
Campbell, John (Lord). Sh.'s Legal Acquirements Considered. Lond. Murray. 1859. 5/.
Drake, N. Sh. and his Times. 2 v. Lond. 1817. 30/.
Dyer, J. F. T. The Folk-lore of Sh. Lond. Griffith. 1884. 14/.
Ellacombe, Henry N. Plant-lore and Garden-craft of Sh. Exeter. Pollard. 1884. 6/6.
Elze, (Dr.) Karl. William Shakespeare, a Literary Biography, trans. Dora Schmitz. Lond. Bell. 1888. 6/.
Farmer, Richard. An Essay on the Learning of Sh. Lond. 1821.
Fleay, F. G. Chron. Hist. of Life and Work of Sh. Lond. Nimmo. 1886. 15/.
French, G. R. Shakspeareana Genealogica. Lond. 1869.
Goadby, Edwin. The England of Sh. Lond. Cassell. 1889. 2/6.
Guizot, F. P. G. Sh. and His Times. Lond. 1855.
Halliwell, J. O. Hist. Acc. of New Place, Stratford. (60 ill.) Lond. Smith. 1870. 63/.
Outlines of the Life of Sh. 2 v. London. Longmans. 1889. 21/.
Harrison, W. Description of England in Sh.'s Youth. (1577). Ed. F. J. Furnivall. Sh. Soc. Pub. 1877; 78; 81; 87. Lond. Scott. 1887. 1/.
Harting, J. E. Ornithology of Sh. Van Voorst. 1871. 12/6.
Kingsley, Chas. Miscellaneous. (Sir Walter Raleigh and his Times). Lond. and N. Y. Macmillan. 1890. 3/6.

Lee, Sidney. Stratford on Avon. Lond. 1890.
Neil, S. Crit. Biography of Sh. Lond. Houlston. 1863. 1/.
Norris, J. Parker. Portraits of Sh. Phil. Lindsay. 1885. $10.
Phipson, E. Animal Lore of Sh.'s Time. London. Paul. 1883. 9/.
Rolfe, (Dr.) W. J. Sh. the Boy. N. Y. Harper. 1896.
Rushton, Wm. L. Sh. a Lawyer. Lond. 1858.
Rye, W. B. England as seen by Foreigners in days of Eliz. and Jas. I. Lond. Smith. 1865. 15/.
Smith, Roach. Rural Life of Sh. Lond. Bell. 2/6.
Stafford, W. Compendious or Briefe Examination of certayne Complaints of divers of our Countrymen in these our Dayes, A. D. 1781. Sh. Soc. Pub. 1876.
Stubbes, Philip. Anatomie of the Abuses in Eng. in Sh.'s Youth. (1583). Sh. Soc. Pub. 1871, 1879.
Thornbury, G. W. Sh.'s England. 2 v. Lond. Longmans. 1856. 15/.
Viles, E., (and Furnivall, F. J.) The Rogues and Vagabonds of Sh.'s Youth. Sh. Soc. Pub. 1880.
Walter, Jas. Sh.'s Home and Rural Life. Lond. Longmans. 1874.
Wheler, R. Hist. and Descriptive Acc. of Birthplace of Sh. Stratford-on-Avon. 1863.
Wilder, Daniel W. Life of Sh. Bost. 1893.
Williams, (Dr.) J. L. Home and Haunts of Sh. Lond. Low. 1893. £15. N. Y. Scribner. 1893. $37.50.
Winter, W. Sh.'s England. Bost. Houghton. $1. Bost. Ticknor. 1888. 50c.
Wise, John R. Shakespeare; his Birthplace and its Neighborhood. Lond. Smith. 3/6.
Wordsworth, (Bishop) C. Sh.'s Knowledge and Use of the Bible. Lond. Smith. 1880. 7/6.

Criticism.

Anglia. (*See* Contents).
Boas, F. S. Shakspere and his Predecessors. N. Y. Scribner. 1896. $1.50.
Brink, (Prof.) Bern. ten. Shakspere: Fünf Vorlesungen. Strassburg. Trübner. 1893. 2 m.
Carlyle, Th. Heroes and Hero Worship. Lond. Chapman. (1841). 1887. 1/.
Chasles, Philarète. Etudes sur Sh. Paris. 1851.
Coleridge, Samuel Taylor. Lectures on Sh. Lond. Bell. 3/6.
Courtenay, T. P. Commentaries on the Hist. Plays of Sh. 2 v. Lond. 1840.
Daniel, P. A. Time Analysis of Sh.'s Plays. Sh. Soc. Trans. 1877—'79.
De Quincey, Th. Biographical and Historical Essays. Bost. Houghton. $1.50.
Dowden, (Prof.) E. Development of Sh.'s Mind and Art. Lond. Paul. 1880. 12. Intro. to Sh. Lond. Blackie. 1893. 2/6. N. Y. Scribner. 1893. $1. Shakspere Primer. Lond. and N. Y. Macmillan. 1877. 1/.
Elze, (Dr.) Karl. Essays on Sh. Lond. and N. Y. Macmillan. 1874. 12/. $4.
Emerson, Ralph W. Representative Men. Bost. Houghton. $1.
Englische Studien. (*See* Contents).
Faucit, Helen. (Lady Martin). Some of Sh.'s Female Characters. Lond. Blackwood. 1888. 7/6.
Furnivall, (Dr.) F. J. The Succession of Sh.'s Works. Lond. Smith. 1874.

Gervinus, G. G. Sh. Commentaries, trans. F. E. Bunnett. 2 v. Lond. Smith. 1887. 14/.
Hazlitt, Wm. Characters of Sh.'s Plays. Lond. Bohn. 1888. 1/.
Hudson, (Prof.) H. N. Shakspere: his Life, Art and Characters. 2 v. Bost. 1883. $4.
Hugo, Victor. William Shakespeare; trans. M. B. Anderson. Chicago. 1887. $2.
Ingleby, C. M. Sh. Allusion Books. Centurie of Prayse. (The above, ed. Lucy Toulmin Smith).
Jahrbuch (Sh.) 30 v. 1865 to date. (*See* Contents).
Jameson, (Mrs.) Anna. Characteristics of Sh.'s Women. Lond. Bohn. (1832) 1879. 3/6. Bost. Houghton. $1.25.
Kemble, Frances A. Notes upon some of Sh.'s Plays. Lond. Bentley. 1882. 7/6.
Kreyssig, Fr. Vorlesungen über Sh. Berlin. 1877. Shakespeare-Fragen. Leipzig. 1891.
Lewes, L. The Women of Sh.; trans. fr. the German by Helen Zimmern. N. Y. Putnam. 1894. $2.50.
Lloyd, Watkins. Essays on Sh. Lond. Bell. 1876. 2/6.
Lowell, Jas. Russell. Among my Books. Second Ser. Boston. Houghton. $2.
Moulton, Richard G. Sh. as a Dram. Artist. (Merchant of Venice, Rich. III., Macbeth, Julius Cæsar, Lear, Tempest). Clar. Press. 1889. 6/. N. Y. Macmillan. $1.50.
Pater, Walter. Appreciations. Lond. and N. Y. Macmillan. 1889. 8/6.
Ransome, (Prof.) Cyril. Short Studies of Sh.'s Plots. (Hamlet, Cæsar, Macbeth, Lear, Richard II., Othello, Coriolanus, Tempest).
Rötscher, H. F. Sh. in seinen höchsten Charactergebilden. Dresden. 1864.
Rümelin, Gustav. Shakespeare Studien. Stuttgart. 1866.
Rymer, Th. The Tragedies of the last Age considered and examined. 1678. Short View of Tragedy. 1693.
Schlegel, A. W. Lectures on Dram. Art. and Lit. Lond. Bohn. 1846. 3/6.
Shakespeare Soc. (Lond.) Publications, 1841—'53. 40 nos. (Succeeded by New Sh. Soc. Publications. 1874—'86. 47 v.
Simrock, Karl. Die Quellen d. Sh. in Novellen, Märchen u. Sagen, 2 v. Bonn. 1870. 8/. On the Plots of Sh.'s Plays; (trans.) ed. J. O. Halliwell. Sh. Soc. 5/.
Snider, Denton J. System of Sh.'s Dramas. 2 v. St. Louis. 1877.
Stapfer, Paul. Sh. and Classical Antiquity. Trans. E. J. Carey. Lond. Paul. 1880.
Stokes, Henry Paine. Chronological Order of Sh.'s Plays. Lond. 1878.
Swinburne, A. C. A Study of Sh. Lond. Chatto. 1880. 8/.
Ulrici, (Dr.) H. The Dram. Art of Sh. 2 v. Lond. Bohn. 1876. 3/6.
Warner, B. E. Eng. Hist. in Sh.'s Plays; w. bibliog., chronol. tables and index. Lond. and N. Y. Longmans. 1894. 6/.
Wendell, (Prof.) Barrett. William Shakspere. N. Y. Scribner. 1894. $1.75.
White, Richard Grant. Studies in Sh. Lond. Low. 1885. 10/6.

Miscellaneous.

Bacon, Delia. Philosophy of Sh.'s Plays Unfolded. Lond. 1857.
Boaden, Jas. An Inquiry into the Authenticity of Various Pictures and Prints—so-called Portraits of Sh. Lond. 1824.
Cohn, Albert. Sh. in Germany in the Sixteenth and Seventeenth Cent. Lond. 1865.

Collier, J. Payne. Notes and Emendations to Sh.'s Plays, fr. early MS. corrections in 1632 ed. (Forgery). Lond. Whittaker. 1853. 12/. (Ed.) Sh.'s Library. 2 v. Lond. 1843. 25/.
Donnelly, Ignatius. Sh.'s Great Cryptogram. 2 v. Lond. Low. 1888. 30/.
Douce, Francis. Illustrations of Sh. Lond. Tegg. 1839. 9/.
Green, H. Sh. and the Emblem Writers. Trübner. 1870. 31/6.
Griffith, L. M. Evenings with Sh. Bristol. 1889.
Hazlitt, W. C. Sh. Jest Books. Lond. Sotheran. 1881. 7/6. Sh. Library. 6 v. Lond. Reeves and Turner. 1875. 42/.
Ingleby, (Dr.) C. M. Complete View of the (Collier) Sh. Controversy. Lond. Nattali and Bond. 1861. 6/6.
Ireland, W. H. Misc. Papers and Legal Instruments under Hand and Seal of Sh. (Forgery). Lond. 1796. Confessions; w. particulars of his Sh. Fabrications, w. introd. R. G. White. N. Y. 1874. $2.
Lamb, Chas. and Mary. Tales from Sh. Lond. Macmillan. (1807) 1878. 4/6. Bost. Houghton. $1.
Leo, (Prof.) F. A. (Ed.) Four Chapters of North's Plutarch. (Photographed fr. ed. 1595). Trübner. 1878. 31/6.
Malone, Edw. Inquiry into Authenticity of Papers, etc., attrib. (by Ireland) to Sh. Lond. 1796.
Norris, J. Parker. Portraits of Sh. Phil. Lindsay. 1885.

SIDNEY, (Sir) PHILIP. 1554—'86.

Lady of the May. Masque. Presented to Eliz. 1578. Pr. with Arcadia, 3rd ed., 1698; repr. Nichols, Progresses of Elizabeth, 2: 94.
Defense of Poesy. (Apology for Poetry). 1583? Arber Reprint. 1868. Ed. Shuckburgh, Evelyn S. Camb. Press. 1890. 3/. N. Y. Macmillan. 1890. 90c. Ed. Cook, (Prof.) Alb. S., w. introd. and notes. Bost. Ginn. 1890. 90c.
Misc. Works; ed. Wm. Gray. Lond. Gibbings. 1893. 12/6.
Bourne, H. R. Fox. Sir Philip Sidney and the Chivalry of England. (Heroes of the Nations). N. Y. Putnam. $1.50.
Jusserand. Eng. Novel in the time of Eliz. Le Théâtre en Angleterre. (Ch. 6).
Raleigh, Walter. Eng. Novel. N. Y. Scribner. 1896. $1.25.
Symonds. Sir Philip Sidney. (Eng. Men of Letters). Lond. Macmillan. 1890. 1/.

SMITH, WENTWORTH. Fl. 1600.

Conquest of the West Indies. 1601. (With Day and Haughton).
Rising of Cardinal Wolsey. 1601. (With Chettle, Drayton, Monday).
Six Clothiers. 2 pts. 1601. (With Hathway and Haughton).
Too Good to be True. (With Chettle and Hathway).
Love parts Friendship. 1602. (With Chettle).
As Merry as May Be. 1602. (With Day and Hathway).
Albert Galles. 1602. (With Heywood).
Marshal Osric. 1602. (With Heywood)?
Two (Three) Brothers. 1602.
Lady Jane. 1602. (With Chettle, Dekker, Heywood, Webster).

Black Dog of Newgate. 2 pts. 1602—'3. (With Day, Hathway and "the other poet").
Unfortunate General. 1603.
Italian Tragedy. 1603.

[The above plays are not extant, unless Heywood's Royal King and Loyal Subject is a recast of Marshal Osric. See Fleay: Biog. Chron. Eng. Drama under Heywood. It has been suggested that Wentworth Smith may be the W. S. to whom the authorship of Locrine, Thomas Lord Cromwell and the Puritan was attributed].

† Collier. Hist. Eng. Dram. Poetry. 3: 98, 99.
Fleay. Biog. Chron. Eng. Drama.
Henslowe. Diary.
Jahrbuch. (Sh.) 27: 148.

STILL, JOHN. 1543—1607.

*Gammer Gurton's Needle. Wr. 1561? Acted 1566. Apparently pr. as Dyceon of Bedlam. 1575. (Authorship not certain).
† Boas. Shakspere and his Predecessors. p. 21—2.
Fleay. Hist. of the Stage. p. 58.
Klein. Geschichte des Englischen Drama's.
Swinburne. Study of Shakespeare. p. 24, 28.
Symonds. Shakspere's Predecessors. p. 205—208.
Ward. Eng. Dram. Lit. 1: 142, 143.

STUDLEY, JOHN. Fl. 1566.

Seneca's Tragedies. (Trans.)
  *Medea.
  Agamemnon.
  *Phædra.
  Hercules on OEta.
(See Th. Newton).

TARLTON, RICHARD. —1588.

Seven Deadly Sins. (See references below under Fleay).
Ballad on the Floods. 1570. Repr. Collier. Percy Soc., 1840; also, Sh. Soc. Pub. 1844. p. 78—84.
Horse-load of Fools. (Jig). Before 1583. Repr. Sh. Soc. Pub. 1844. (In Halliwell's Introd.) (Player Fool=Himself).
† Fleay. Biog. Chron. Eng. Drama. 2: 259; Hist. of the Stage, p. 67, 83—85; Life of Shakespeare. p. 27, 264, 296.
Fuller. Worthies of England; ed. 1811. 2: 311—12.
Halliwell, J. O. Account of Life. (Introd. to Tarlton's Jests, and News out of Purgatory. Repr. Sh. Soc. Pub. 1844).
Harvey, Gabriel. Four Letters. 1592, passim. Repr. Brydges, Archaica, 2, and Grosart, Harvey's Works, 1. (Huth Libr.)
Nash. Pierce Penniless. 1592. Collier ed., p. 36.

UDALL, NICHOLAS. 1506—'64.

*Ralph Roister Doister. Wr. before 1553? Repr. F. Marshall, 1821; W. D. Cooper, Sh. Soc. Pub. 1847; Arber Reprints, 1869. (See Index).
† Arber. Eng. Garner.
Boas. Shakspere and his Predecessors.
Fleay. Hist. of the Stage. p. 59.
Hales, J. W. The Date of the First Eng. Comedy. (Ralph Roister Doister). Engl. Studien, 18: 408—421).

Jahrbuch. (Sh.) 15: 368; 17: 274.
Jusserand. Le Théâtre en Angleterre. (Ch. 6).
Klein. Geschichte des Englischen Drama's.
Swinburne. Study of Shakespeare. p. 27, 28.
Symonds. Shakspere's Predecessors.

WAGER, W. Fl. 1575.

The Longer Thou Livest the more Fool Thou Art. Pr. 1571—'76.
† Collier. Eng. Dram. Lit. 2: 332—38.

WAPUL, GEORGE. Fl. 1575.

Tide Tarryeth no Man. Pr. 1576.
† Collier. Illustrations of Early Eng. Lit. 1863. v. 2.
Jusserand. Le Théâtre en Angleterre.

WHETSTONE, GEORGE. Fl. 1575.

*Promos and Cassandra. Pr. 1578. (Used by Sh. in Measure for Measure). (*See* Index).
† Jahrbuch. (Sh.) 13: 163.

WILMOT, ROBERT. Fl. 1568.

*Tancred and Gismunda. Presented before Eliz., 1568. Pr. 1592.

WILSON, ROBERT. (Senior). Fl. 1574.

*?Three Ladies of London. 1583? Pr. 1592.
*?Three Lords and Three Ladies of London. 1588? Pr. 1590.
Cobbler's Prophecy. Pr. 1594. (*See* Index, and Collier, Hist. Eng. Dram. Lit. 3: 247, 248).
† Fleay. Biog. Chron. Eng. Dram.
Jahrbuch. (Sh.) 29/30: 310.

WILSON, ROBERT. (Junior). —1600.

Earl Godwin, 2 pts. 1598. (With Chettle, Dekker, Drayton).
Piers of Exton. 1598. (With Chettle, Dekker, Drayton).
Black Batman of the North. 1598. (Pt. 1 with Chettle, Dekker, Drayton; pt. 2 with Chettle).
Richard Coeur de Lion's Funeral. 1598. (With Chettle, Drayton, Monday).
Madman's Morris. 1598. (With Dekker, Drayton).
Hannibal and Hermes. 1598. (With Dekker, Drayton).
Piers of Winchester. 1598. (With Dekker, Drayton).
Chance Medley. 1598. (With Dekker, Monday).
Catiline's Conspiracy. 1598. (With Chettle).
*Sir John Oldcastle, 2 pts. 1598. (With Drayton, Hathway, Monday).
[Of the above plays only the first part of Sir John Oldcastle is extant. *See* Index].
† Henslowe. Diary.

WOODES, NATHANIEL. Fl. 1581.

*Conflict of Conscience. Pr. 1581.
✠Roxburghe Club. 1851.
† Fleay. Hist. of the Stage.

?YARRINGTON, ROBERT.

?Two Tragedies in One. 1601.
† Fleay. Biog. Chron. Eng. Drama.

JACOBEAN DRAMA.

DRAMATISTS.

Alexander.
Anon.
Armin.
Barnes.
Barry.
BEAUMONT and FLETCHER.
Breton.
Brewer.
Brome, Alex.
Brome, Richard.
Brookes.
Broune.
Campion.
Carew, Eliz.
Carew, Th.
Carey.
Carlell.
Cartwright.
CHAPMAN.
Cooke, John.
Daborne.
Daniel.
Davenport.
Day.
Denham.
Drue.
Dugdale.
Field.
Fisher.
FLETCHER, JOHN.
Fletcher, Phineas.
FORD.
Forde.
Freeman.
Glapthorne.
Goffe.
Gomersal.
Gough, J.
Greville.
Habington.
Harding.
Hausted.
Hawkins.
Heming.
HEYWOOD, THOMAS.
Holiday.
Jones.

JONSON.
Killigrew, Henry.
Kirke.
Lovelace.
Machin.
Markham.
Marmion.
Mason.
MASSINGER.
May.
Mayne.
Mead.
MIDDLETON.
MILTON.
Montagu.
Nabbes.
Nevile, Robt.
Niccols.
Phillips.
Quarles.
Randolph.
Rawlins.
Richards.
Rowley, Samuel.
Rowley, William.
Rutter.
Sampson.
?Savile.
Sharpe.
Sharpham.
SHIRLEY, JAMES.
Shirley, Henry.
?Smith, William.
Squire.
Stephens.
Strode.
Suckling.
Swinhoe.
Tailor.
Taylor.
Tomkins.
TOURNEUR.
Townsend.
WEBSTER.
White.
Wilkins.
Wilson, Arthur.

ALEXANDER, WILLIAM. Earl of Stirling. (1567?—1640).

*Darius. 1604.
Croesus. 1604.
The Alexandraean. 1605.
*Julius Cæsar. 1607.
✠Works, containing the Monarchic Tragedies. Edin. 1603. Lond. 1604, 1607, 1616.
Poetical Works. 3 v. Lond. Sotheran. 1872. 30/. Glasgow. 1870.
† Anderson. Scottish Nation. 3 v. Fullarton. Edin. 1877. 60/.
Chalmers. Eng. Poets. v. 5.
Rogers, Chas. Memorials of the Earl of Stirling and the House of Alexander. 2 v. Lond. Houlston. 1877. 63/.
Walpole. Catalogue of Royal and Noble Authors. 5 v. Lond. 1758. Repr. 1806.

ANONYMOUS.

Alphonsus, Emperor of Germany. Pr. 1654. Acted at Blackfriars (revival) 1636. Att. by Moseley to Chapman and by Fleay to Peele.
*Andromana. After 1642. By "J. S." (Founded on Sidney's Arcadia). Fleay. Biog. Chron. Eng. Drama. 2: 173.
Barnavelt. Acted 1619.
Bastard. Pr. 1652. (Probably Jacobean).
Bloody Banquet. "By T. D." Pr. 1630.
*Captain Underwit. Acted 1639. Pr. by Bullen as Shirley's, but held by Fleay as identical with Cavendish's Country Captain.
*Costly Whore. 1633.
Cruel War. Pr. 1643.
*Dick of Devonshire. Claimed by Fleay for Shirley, whose Brothers was licensed in 1626, but assigned by Bullen to Heywood.
Entertainment of James I. from Edinburgh to London. T. M. 1603. Arber Reprints. Lond. and N. Y. Macmillan.
*Every Woman in her Humor. 1609.
Exchange Ware at Second Hand; viz. Band, Ruff, and Cuff. 1615.
Fair Maid of Bristow. S. R. 1605.
Fair Maid of the Exchange. 1607. See Gosse: Jacobean Poets.
Faithful Friends. Acted 1614? S. R. 1660. Pr. 1812.
Fatal Marriage; or, A Second Lucretia. MS. (Eg. MSS. 1994).
General. 1638?
*Ghost. Wr. 1640. Pr. 1653.
Honest Lawyer. S. R. 1615. By "S. S." See Fleay. Biog. Chron. Eng. Drama. 2: 173, 174.
*Lingua; or, The Combat of the Tongue and the five Senses for Superiority. 1607. (Assigned by Daniel, Fleay and Furnivall to Tomkins). See Gosse: Jacobean Poets.
*London Chanticleers. Acted 1637? Pr. 1659.
*London Prodigal. 1605.
Marcus Tullius Cicero, that famous Roman Orator, his Tragedy. Pr. 1651.
*Merry Devil of Edmonton. Pr. 1608.
*(Stately Tragedy of Claudius Tiberius) Nero. 1607.
(Tragedy of) Nero. 1624. Ed. H. P. Horne, Mermaid Series. See Gosse: Jacobean Poets.

News out of the West; or, The Character of a Mountebank. Pr. 1647.
Parricide; or, Revenge for Honour. 1654. (Claimed for Glapthorne and again for Chapman).
Pathomachia; or, The Battle of the Affections, Shadowed by a feigned Siege of the City Pathopolis. (Running Title, Love's Lodestone). 1630.
Petronius Maximus. 1619. By "W. S." See Edinb. Mag. July, 1821. v. 88.
*Puritan; or, the Widow of Watling Street. Pr. 1607.
Queen; or, The Excellency of her Sex. Pr. 1653.
Revenge for Honour. See Parricide.
Second Maiden's Tragedy. Wr. 1611. See Gosse: Jacobean Poets.
Sight and Search. Dated 1643. MS.
*Sir Giles Goosecap, Knight. 1606.
Swetnam the Woman-hater arraigned by Women. 1620. (Swetnam's Arraignment of Women. 1615). See Gosse: Jacobean Poets.
*Thracian Wonder. Acted 1617? Pr. 1661. Assigned by Kirkman to Webster and Rowley, by Fleay to Heywood.
*Trial of Chivalry. 1605.
Two Noble Ladies; or, The Converted Conjuror. 1619—'22.
Two Wise Men and all the Rest Fools. 1619.
Unfortunate Usurper. Temp. Charles I. Pr. 1663.
Usurping Tyrant. (The Second Maiden's Tragedy). Licensed 1611.
Valiant Scot. (Sir Wm. Wallace). 1637. "By J. W. gent."
Welsh Ambassador. MS. 1623.
Wit of Woman. Pr. 1604.
Work for Cutlers; or, A Merry Dialogue between Sword, Rapier, and Dagger. 1615. Reprinted, Harl. Misc. X.
*Yorkshire Tragedy. Pr. 1608.

ARMIN, ROBERT. (Reign of Jas. I.)

Two Maids of Moreclacke. 1609.
Valiant Welshman. 1615.
Nest of Ninnies. 1608. (Prose tract of autob. interest). Re-pr. fr. ed. 1608. Lond. 1842. Sh. Soc. Pub.
Italian Tailor and his Boy. 1609. (Prose tract of autob. interest).
✠Works. 1615—'19; ed. Grosart. 1800.
† Davies, John. Scourge of Folly. (Circ. 1611).
Tarlton. Jests and News out of Purgatory. 1611. "How Tarlton made Armin his adopted son to succeed him." Sh. Soc. Pub. 1844.

BARNES, BARNABY. (1569?—1609).

Divil's Charter; a Tragœdie conteining the Life and Death of Pope Alexander the Sixt. 1607.
Parthenophil and Parthenophe. Sonnets, Madrigals, Elegies and Odes. 1593. Arber Reprints. Lond. and N. Y. Macmillan.
† Bell. Lit. and Sci. Men. 2: 150. 1839.
Dowden. Academy. Sept. 2, 1876.

BARRY, LODOWICK. (Reign of James I.)

*Ram Alley. 1611.

BEAUMONT, FRANCIS. 1586—1616, and FLETCHER, JOHN. 1576—1625.

[List of works, with dates (often conjectural) of first productions, and authorship (sometimes conjectural) after Fleay.]

Woman Hater. 1607. Beaumont.
Faithful Shepherdess. 1608. Both.
Four Plays in One. 1608. Both.
Love's Cure. 1608. Both, revised by Massinger.
Scornful Lady. 1609. Both.
*Knight of the Burning Pestle. 1610. Both.
Coxcomb. 1610. Both, revised by Massinger.
Cupid's Revenge. 1610. Both, revised perhaps by Massinger, perhaps Field, perhaps Daborne.
*Philaster. 1610. Both.
*A King and No King. 1611. (Pub. 1608). Both.
*The Maid's Tragedy. 1612. Both.
Mask of the Inner Temple and Gray's Inn. 1613. Beaumont.
✠Comedies and Tragedies. 1647.
Fifty Comedies and Tragedies. 1679.
Works. 1711.
Works; ed. Theobald, Seward and Sympson. 1750.
Dramatick Works. 1778.
Dramatic Works. 1811.
Works. (Weber's ed.) Edin. 1812.
Works. (Darley's ed.) 1839.
Works; with new collation of texts, notes and life by Dyce. 11 v. Lond. Moxom. 1843—'46.
Works. (Darley's new ed.) 2 v. Lond. Routledge. 1866. ea. 10/6.
Works, ed. Bullen. Lond. Nimmo. In prep. ea. 7/6.
Best Plays, ed. w. introd. and notes by J. St. Loe Strachy. 2 v. (Mermaid Series). Lond. Vizetelly. 1877. ea. 2/6.
Selected Plays. w. introd. by J. S. Fletcher. (Canterbury Poets). Lond. Scott. 1887. 1/.
† Bibliography by A. C. Potter. No. 39 of the Harvard Lib. Bib. Contributions. Cambridge, Mass., 1890.
Boyle, R. Beaumont, Fletcher and Massinger. Engl. Studien, 5: 74—96; 7: 66—87; 8: 39—61; 9: 209—39; 10: 383—412.
C. J. A note on Cervantes and Beaumont and Fletcher. Fraser's Mag., May, 1875. 91: 592—7.
Colby, J. Rose. Some Ethical Aspects of Later Elizabethan Tragedy. (Beaumont and Fletcher). Ph. D. Thesis. Univ. of Mich. Ann Arbor, 1886.
Coleridge. Lectures on Shakespeare and Other Dramatists.
Donne, Wm. Bodham. Essays on the Drama. Lond. 1863. p. 34—66. Also in Fraser's Mag. Mar., 1850. 41: 321—32.
Dryden, John. The Grounds of Criticism in Tragedy. (In answer to Rymer). Dryden's Works, ed. Scott. Lond. 1808. 6: 243—66.
Fleay. On Metrical Tests as applied to Dramatic Poetry. Part. II. Fletcher. Beaumont, Massinger. New Sh. Soc.'s Trans. 1874. p. 51—84. Also in Fleay's Sh. Manual. Lond. 1876.
Fraser's Mag. 41: 321—32. Works of Beaumont and Fletcher.
Gosse. Jacobean Poets.
Hazlitt. Lectures on the Dram. Lit. of the Age of Eliz.

Hunt, Leigh. Beauties of Beaumont and Fletcher, "with opinions of distinguished critics, notes and preface." 1855. 2nd ed. Lond. 1862. Bohn. 3/6.
Leonhardt, B. Ueber Beaumont and Fletcher's Knight of the Burning Pestle. Annaberg. 1885. (Rev. by Max Koch in Engl. Studien, 1885—'86. 9: 361—63. Reply to Max Koch in Eng. Studien, 1888. 12: 307—313). Ueber Beziehung von Beaumont and Fletcher's Philaster, or Love lies a-Bleeding zu Shakespeare's Hamlet u. Cymbeline. (Anglia, 8: 424—47).
Lowell. Old Eng. dramatists. 1892.
Macaulay, G. C. Francis Beaumont. A Critical Study. Lond. Paul. 1883. 5/.
Mason. Comments on the Plays of Beaumont and Fletcher. 1798.
Oliphant, E. F. Works of Beaumont and Fletcher. (Engl. Studien, 14: 53—94; 15: 321—60; 16: 180—200. Also 17: 171—75; 18: 292—96. [R. Boyle].)
Saintsbury. Hist. of Eliz. Lit.
Schlegel. Lectures on Dram. Art and Lit.
Scriblerus. Explanations of some Passages in the Text of Beaumont and Fletcher. 1814.
Sh. Soc. Trans. 1880—'86. p. 579—628.
Shakspere and Jonson. Dramatic, versus Wit Combats. Auxiliary Forces. Beaumont, etc. 1864.
Swinburne. Beaumont and Fletcher. Ency. Brit., 9th ed. 3: 469—74.
Ward. Hist. of Eng. Dram. Lit.
Whipple, E. P. Beaumont and Fletcher. Atlantic Monthly. 1886. 21: 176-185. Lit. of the Age of Eliz.

BRETON, NICHOLAS. 1545?—1626?

An Olde Man's Lesson and a Young Man's Love. 1605.
"An Interlude, ed. Breton." Fleay.
Bower of Delights; ed. Grosart. Lond. Stock. 1893. 3/6. (Eliz. Libr.) See Peabody Cat.
† Dict. Nat. Biog. (6 p.)
Gosse. Jacobean Poets.
Grosart. Chertsey Worthies Libr. 2 v. 1877.

BREWER, ANTHONY. Fl. 1650.

*Country Girl. 1647. (Signed T. B., taken by Kirkman, Baker, Halliwell and Fleay for Tony Brewer. Bullen suggests the tract writer, Thomas Brewer).
*Love-sick King. 1655.
† Dict. Nat. Biog.
Fleay. Biog. Chron. Eng. Dram.

BROME, ALEX. 1620?—1666.

Cunning Lovers. Acted before 1639; pr. 1654.
Beaumont and Fletcher. Works. 1647. Commend. Verses.
† Chalmer, A. Eng. Poets, 6.
Dict. Nat. Biog.
Hazlitt, Handbook.
Walton. Angler. 2nd ed.

BROME, RICHARD. (—1652). (Dates largely conjectural).

Fault in Friendship. Licensed 1623.
Lovesick Maid. Licensed 1629.
Lovesick Court. ?
City Wit. 1629.
Damoiselle. ?
Northern Lass. 1631.
Queen's Exchange. 1631 or '32.
*Covent Garden Weeded. 1632.
Novella. 1633.
Last Lancashire Witches. 1634. (Brome's alteration of Heywood's play).
New Academy. ?
Queen and Concubine. ?
Sparagus Garden. 1635.
Mad Couple well Matched. 1636.
English Moor. ?
Antipodes. ?
Court Beggar. 1640?
*Jovial Crew; or, The Merry Beggars. 1641.
✠Five New Playes by Richard Brome, ed. Alex. Brome. (Not a kinsman). 1 v. 1653.
New Playes; (five more) by Richard Brome, ed. Alex. Brome. 1 v. 1659.
Dramatic Works. Lond. Pearson. 1873. 3 v. 31/6.
† Faust, E. K. R. R. Brome; ein Beitrag zur Geschichte der Engl. Lit. Inaug. dissert. Halle. 1887. (Max Koch. Engl. Studien, 12: 97).
(Faust). Herrig's Archiv, 82: 1.
On the Time-Poets.
Swinburne. R. Brome. Fortn. Rev. 57: 500.

BROOKES, (Dr.) SAMUEL. Fl. 1600.

Sciros. 1613.

BROUNE, WILLIAM. 1591—1643.

Inner Temple Masque. (Circe and Ulysses). Wr. circ. 1615. First pr. in Davies' ed. of Broune's Works. 3 v. Lond. 1772.
✠Works; ed. w. memoir for Roxburghe Club by William Carew Hazlitt. 2 v. 1868. For Poems, see entries in Peabody Cat.
† Bell. Lit. and Sci. Men. 2: 137.
Chalmers. Eng. Poets. 6: 225.
Gosse. Jacobean Poets. p. 151.
Ward. Eng. Poets. 2: 65.

CAMPION, (Dr.) THOMAS. —1619.

Mask. (Twelfth Night. Whitehall. Wedding of Lord Hay). 1607.
Lord's Mask. (Wedding of Count Palatine and Lady Elizabeth). Feb., 1613.
Mask. (Presented by Lord Knowles at Caversham House before the Queen), April, 1613.
Mask. (Wedding of Earl of Somerset and [divorced] Countess of Essex). Dec., 1613.
Two Books of Ayres. 1610.

Third and Fourth Books of Ayres. 1612.
A new Way of making foure parts in Counterpoint. 1613.
Observations on the Art of English Poesie. 1602. (Answered by Daniel in his Panegyrike Congratulatory, with a Defence of Ryme).
✠Works, ed. Bullen, w. introd. and notes. Lond. Nimmo. 1889. 21/. See Athen. 1889. 1: 403. Acad. 34: 340.
Lyrical Poems, ed. Ernest Rhys. Lond. Dent. 1896.
Nichols. Progresses of Elizabeth.
Nichols. Progresses of James I.
† Arber. An English Garner.
Gosse. Jacobean Poets.
Simpson, R. Life of Campion. Lond. Williams. 1867. 16/.

CAREW, [CAREY] (Lady) ELIZ. Fl. 1600.

*Mariamne, the Fair Queen of Jewry. 1613.
† Dict. Nat. Biog.
Nash. Christ's Tears over Jerusalem. Dedication.
Spenser. Faery Queene. Introd. sonnet.
Spenser. Muiopotmos. Dedication.

CAREW, THOMAS. 1598?—1639?

Coelum Britannicum. 1634. (Whitehall Masque).
✠Poems, ed. w. notes and memoir by W. C. Hazlitt. Lond. 1870. Roxburghe. Lib.
Poems and Masques; ed. J. W. Ebsworth. Lond. Reeves and T. 1893. 4/. Lib. of old authors.
Anderson. Br. Poets. v. 3.
Chalmers. Eng. Poets. v. 5.
† Nichols. Progresses of James I. 3: 224.
Quart. Rev. 4: 165. 1810.
Retro. Rev. 6: 224. 1822. Poems.

CAREY, HENRY: Viscount Falkland. 1610—'43.

*Marriage Night. 1664.

CARLELL, LODOWICK. Fl. 1629—'64.

Deserving Favorite. 1629.
Arviragus and Philicia. 2 pts. 1639.
Passionate Lover. 2 pts. 1655.
Fool would be a Favorite. 1657.
Osmond, the Great Turk.?
Heraclius, Emperor of the East. Pr. 1664.
Spartan Ladies. 1646. Not extant. (Adapt. fr. Corneille).
† Pepys. Diary.

CARTWRIGHT, (Rev.) WILLIAM. 1611—'43.

*Ordinary. Before 1635.
Lady Errant. 1635—36.

Royal Slave. 1636.
Siege; or, Love's Convert. 1637.
‡Plays and Poems. Coll. H. Moseley. 1 v. 1651. (56 copies of commend. verses prefixed).
Chalmers. Eng. Poets. v. 6.
† Choate. Wells of English.
Evelyn. Diary, ed. 1850. 1: 421.
Dunham. Lit. and Sci. Men. v. 2.
Mo. Rev. 110: 235. Life and Corresp.
Retro. Rev. 9: 160. Plays and Poems.
Ward. Eng. Poets. v. 2.

CHAPMAN, GEO. 1559?—1634. (Dates somewhat conjectural).

Blind Beggar of Alexandria. 1596.
Comedy of Humours. (Humorous Day's Mirth). 1597.
*All Fools. 1599.
*May Day. 1601.
Gentleman Usher. 1601.
Chabot. (Re-wr. by Shirley). 1604?
*Monsieur D'Olive. 1604.
*Bussy d'Ambois. 1604.
*Eastward Ho. (With Jonson and Marston). 1605.
*Widow's Tears. 1605.
*(Revenge of) Bussy d'Ambois. 1606.
Byron's Conspiracy. 1607.
Byron's Tragedy. 1608.
Cæsar and Pompey. 1608?
Mask of the Middle Temple and Lincoln's Inn. 1613.
‡Chapman's Works; ed. R. H. Shepherd. 3 v. 1. Comedies and Tragedies, w. notes and memoir. 2. Iliad and Odyssey. 3. Misc. Poems and Translations, w. crit. essay on Chapman by Swinburne. Lond. Chatto. 1873—'75. 18/.
Best Plays; ed. W. L. Phelps. (Mermaid Series). N. Y. Scribner's. 1895. $1.25.
† Acad. 35: 171.
Bodenstedt. Chapman in seinem Verhältniss zu Sh. Jahrbuch (Sh.) 1, 1865.
Choate. Wells of English.
Coleridge. Literary Remains. 1: 259—63.
Cornh. Mag. 30: 23.
Dunham. Lives of Lit. and Sci. Men. 2: 337—9.
Elste, E. Der Blankvers in den Dramen G. Chapman's. Halle diss. 1892. 63 p. (Boyle, R. Engl. Studien, 17: 274—76).
Gosse. Jacobean Poets.
Hazlitt. Dram. Lit. of the Age of Eliz.
Henslowe. Diary.
Lond. Quart. 43: 32.
Lowell. Chapman, the Dramatist. Harper's, 85: 561. Old Eng. Dramatists.
Morley. Eng. Writers. 10: 464.
On the Time-Poets.
Retro. Rev. 4: 333, 1821; 5: 317, 1822.
Shakspere and Jonson. Dramatic, versus Wit Combats. Auxiliary Forces; Beaumont, * * Chapman, etc. 1864.
Swinburne. Geo. Chapman. A Critical Essay. Lond. Chatto. 1875. 7/.
Ward. Eng. Dram. Lit.

COOKE, JOHN. Fl. 1614.

*Greene's Tu Quoque; or, The City Gallant. Lond. 1614. (W. preface by Th. Heywood).
† Gosse. Jacobean Poets.

DABORNE, (Rev.) ROBERT. (— 1628).

Christian turned Turk. 1610—'12.
Poor Man's Comfort. 1610—'12.
Machiavell and the Devil. 1613.
Arraignment of London. 1613. (With Tourneur).
Bellman of London. 1613.
Owl. 1613.
Faithful Friends. 1614.
She Saint. 1614. (The last six not published).
[For plays in collaboration, *see* Field and Massinger].
Christopher Brook. Ghost of King Richard the Third. Lond. 1615. Commend. Verses by Daborne.
Sermon on Zach. 11: 7. Lond. 1618.
† Collier. Memoirs of Edward Alleyn, Sh. Soc. Pub., 1841, p. 120—1. New Facts regarding the Life of Shakespeare, Sh. Soc. Pub., 1835, p. 40.
Correspondence with Henslowe. Variorum Sh. (Malone). Vol. 21.
Fleay. Biog. Chron. Eng. Drama. (9 p.)
Gosse. Jacobean Poets.
Henslowe. Diary.

DANIEL, SAMUEL. (1562—1619).

Cleopatra. (Never acted). 1594.
Vision of the Twelve Goddesses. (Presented at Hampton Court). Pr. 1604.
Philotas. (Acted by the Children of the Queen's Revels). Pr. 1605 and 1607.
The Queen's Arcadia. (Presented to the Queen in Christ's Church, Oxford). Pr. 1605.
Tethy's Festival; or, The Queen's Wake. (Presented at Whitehall). Pr. 1610.
Hymen's Triumph. (Presented at Somerset House at the Nuptials of Lord Roxburghe). Pr. 1615.
Panegyrike Congratulatory, with a Defence of Ryme. 1602. (In reply to Campion).
✠Whole Workes in poetrie. 1623.
Poetical Works, w. memoir. 1718.
Works, ed. Grosart. Repr. in Huth Library.
† Anderson. British Poets, v. 4.
Arber. English Garner.
Austin and Ralph. Poets-Laureate.
Chalmers. Eng. Poets, v. 3.
Choate. Wells of English.
Fleay. Biog. Chron. Eng. Drama. 15 p.
Fuller. Worthies of England.
Gosse. Jacobean Poets.
Hazlitt. Dram. Lit. of the Age of Eliz.
Jameson, Mrs. Loves of the Poets.
Jonson. Conversations with Drummond of Hawthornden. Cynthia's Revels. (Fleay identifies Hedon with Daniel).

Jusserand. Le Théâtre en Angleterre. (Ch. 6).
Macmillan's Mag. 68: 433. 1893.
Meres. Palladis Tamia.
Morley. Eng. Writers. 10: 208.
Nash. Piers Penniless.
Return from Parnassus. 1601. Arber Reprint.
Saintsbury. Daniel's Tragedies. Grosart's ed. of Daniel, v. 3.
Spenser. " Colin Clouts come home again."

DAVENPORT, ROBERT. Fl. 1623.

*City Nightcap. Licensed 1624. Pr. 1661.
*New Trick to cheat the Devil. Pr. 1639.
*King John and Matilda. Pr. 1655; 1662.
† Dunham. Lit. and Sci. Men, v. 2.
Retro. Rev. 4: 87—100. (Rev. of King John and Matilda).
Swinburne. Fortn. Rev. 54: 774.

DAY, JOHN. Fl. 1606.

Ile of Guls. Pr. 1606.
Travailes of the three English Brothers, Sir Thomas, Sir Anthony, Mr. Robert Sherley. Pr. 1607. (MS. in Athen.)
Law-Trickes; or, Who would have thought It. Pr. 1608.
Humour out of Breath. Pr. 1608. 1860 (Ed. Halliwell).
Parliament of Bees. Pr. 1641.
Blind Beggar of Bethnal Green. 1659.
⚜Works. (1607—'59), ed. Bullen, w. introd. and notes. Chiswick Press, 1881. £3, 5/.
Best Plays, ed. Arthur Symons. Lond. Vizetelly. 1888. 2/6. (Mermaid Series).
† Gosse. Works of Day. Acad. 21: 21. Jacobean Poets.
Roxburghe Club. Sherley Brothers: Lives of Sirs Thomas, Anthony, and Robert Sherley, Knts. Ed. E. P. Shirley. 1848.
Travailes of the three English Brothers. 1607. Reviewed in Fry's Bibliogr. memor. 1816. p. 345—50.

DENHAM, (Sir) JOHN. 1615—'69.

Sophy. Acted 1641. Pr. 1642.
⚜Collected Works. 1668; 1671; 1676; 1684; 1709. Repr. in Johnson's (1779), Anderson's (1793), Park's (1808), and Chalmers' (1810) Collections of Eng. Poets.
Poems and Translations: with the Sophy, a tragedy. Lond. 1709.
† Aubrey, J. Lives of Eminent Men. (In Letters written by Eminent Persons. 1813).
Gosse. Shakespeare to Pope.
Johnson. Lives of the Poets.
Marvell. Works. Ed. Grosart.
Notes and Queries. 4th Ser. 1: 532; 10: 249.
Pepys. Diary. *passim*.

DRUE, THOMAS. Fl. 1631.

Life of the Duchess of Suffolk. 1629.
† Dict. Nat. Biog. (Bullen).
Fleay. Biog. Chron. Eng. Drama.

DUGDALE, G. Fl. 1603.

Time Triumphant. King James's Coronation at Westminster, July 25, 1603; and Coronation Procession (delayed by the Plague), March 15, 1604. (Arber Reprints).

FIELD, NATHANIEL. 1587—1633.

*Woman is a Weathercock. Pr. 1612. White's Old Eng. Drama, v. 2; ed. Collier, 1829; ed. Verity, 1888. (Mermaid Series).
*Amends for Ladies. Pr. 1618. White's Old Eng. Drama, v. 2; ed. Collier, 1829; ed. Verity, 1888. (Mermaid Series).
*Fatal Dowry. 1632. (*See* Massinger and Fletcher).
Remonstrance of N. F. addressed to a Preacher in Southwark, who had been arraigning against the Players of the Globe Theatre, in the year 1616. First ed. fr. the orig. MS. (Halliwell). Lond. 1865.
† Collier. Hist. Eng. Dram. Poetry. Memoirs of Alleyn, and Alleyn Papers. Sh. Soc. Pub. 1841.
Dunham. Lit. and Sci. Men. v. 2.
Fleay. Field's Career. (Engl. Studien, 13: 28).
Gosse. Jacobean Poets.
Henslowe. Diary.

FISHER, JASPER. Fl. 1639.

*Fuimus Troes, the True Trojans. 1633.
† Dict. Nat. Biog.

FLETCHER, JOHN. 1579—1625.
(*See* Beaumont and Fletcher).

Also (by Fletcher apart from Beaumont, with dates of production, often conjectural).
Monsieur Thomas. Circ. 1609.
*Two Noble Kinsmen. Circ. 1611. (With unknown collaborator, perhaps Shakespeare).
Love's Pilgrimage. 1612. (First three acts apparently by Fletcher).
*Captain. 1613. (In part).
Honest Man's Fortune. 1613. (Perhaps with Daborne, Field, and Massinger).
Nice Valor; or, The Passionate Madman. 1613. (In part).
Nightwalker; or, The Little Thief. Before 1615. (In part).
Wit without Money. 1614.
Woman's Prize; or, The Tamer Tamed. 1615?
Beggars' Bush. Circ. 1615. (With Massinger).
*Chances. 1615.
Faithful Friends. 1616. (Perhaps mainly by Daborne).
Jeweller of Amsterdam; or, The Hague. 1616. (With Field and Massinger. Not extant).
*Bonduca. 1616. (Possibly with Field).

Valentinian. 1616.
The Bloody Brother. Circ. 1616. (With Massinger and others).
*Thierry and Theodoret. 1617? (With Massinger and others).
*Henry VIII. See Shakespeare.
Knight of Malta. 1617? (With Massinger and another).
Queen of Corinth. 1618? (With Massinger and perhaps Field).
Mad Lover. Circ. 1618.
Loyal Subject. 1618.
Humorous Lieutenant. 1619.
*Sir John van Olden Barnaveldt. 1619. (With Massinger).
Custom of the Country. 1619? (With Massinger).
Double Marriage. Circ. 1620. (With Massinger).
Little French Lawyer. Circ. 1620. (With Massinger).
*False One. Circ. 1620. (With Massinger).
Woman Pleased. Circ. 1620.
Island Princess. 1621.
Pilgrim. 1621.
Wildgoose Chase. 1621.
Prophetess. 1622. (With Massinger).
Sea Voyage. 1622. (With Massinger).
Spanish Curate. 1622. (With Massinger).
*Maid in the Mill. 1623. (With W. Rowley).
Devil of Dowgate. 1623. (Perhaps mainly by Rowley).
Wandering Lovers. 1623. (Revised by Massinger, 1634, as The Lovers' Progress).
A Wife for a Month. 1624.
*Rule a Wife and have a Wife. 1624.
Elder Brother. 1625. (Revised by Massinger, 1635, as The Orator).
Fair Maid of the Inn. 1626. (With Massinger and another).
Noble Gentleman. 1626.
A Very Woman. 1628? (Revised by Massinger. Circ. 1634).

[For bibliography, see Beaumont].

Also

† Creasy, Sir E. S. Eminent Etonians.
  Delius. On the Ascription of the Two Noble Kinsmen to Sh. and Fletcher. Sh. Jahrbuch, 13.
  Fleay. On the Chronology of the Plays of Fletcher and Massinger. (Engl. Studien, 9: 12—35). Biog. Chron. Eng. Drama.
  Hazlitt. Dram. Lit. of Age of Eliz.
  Lee. Athenæum. 1884. Jan. 19. (On Sir John van Olden Barnaveldt).
  Lowell. Beaumont and Fletcher. Harper, 85: 757.
  Simson, J. Eminent Men of Kent. G., J. & P. Fletcher.
  Swinburne. Study of Shakespeare. 73; 75, 76; 82—94.
  Symonds, J. A. In the Key of Blue and Other Prose Essays. (Some Notes on Fletcher's Valentinian). Lond. Mathews. 1893. 8/6. Also in Fortn. Rev. Sept., 1886, p. 46. Littell's Living Age: Oct., 1886, p. 71.

FLETCHER, PHINEAS. 1582—1650.

Sicelides. 1631. MS. (Brit. Mus. MS. Addit. 4453).
✠Poems, ed. w. memoir, essay and notes. Grosart. 4 v., 1869. Fuller Worthies' Libr.

† Bell. Songs fr. the Dramatists.
Chalmers. Eng. Poets. v. 6.
Gosse. Jacobean Poets.
Hazlitt. Dram. Lit. of the Age of Eliz.
Retro. Rev. 2: 341. (Purple Island).

FORD, JOHN. 1586—

An Ill Beginning has a Good End. Acted 1613. Not extant.
Witch of Edmonton. (With Dekker and W. Rowley). Acted circ. 1621. Pr. 1658.
Sun's Darling Masque. Acted 1624. Pr. 1656—7.
Fairy Knight. (With Dekker). Acted 1624. Not extant.
A Late Murther of the Son upon the Mother. (With Webster). Acted 1624. Not extant.
Bristow Merchant. (With Dekker). Acted 1624. Not extant.
*'Tis Pity She's a Whore. Acted circ. 1626. Pr. 1633.
*Lover's Melancholy. Acted 1628. Pr. 1629.
*Broken Heart. Acted circ. 1629. Pr. 1633.
Love's Sacrifice. Acted circ. 1630. Pr. 1633.
Fancies Chaste and Noble. Acted before 1636. Pr. 1638.
*Perkin Warbeck. Acted circ. 1633. Pr. 1634.
*Lady's Trial. Acted circ. 1637. Pr. 1639.
Beauty in a Trance. S. R. 1653. Not extant.
Royal Combat. S. R. 1660. Not extant.
*London Merchant. S. R. 1660. Not extant.

Non Dram. Works.

Fame's Memorial; or, The Duke of Devonshire Deceased. 1606.
Honor Triumphant; or, The Peer's Challenge. 1606. Repr. Sh. Soc. Pub. 1843.
Monarch's Meeting; or, The King of Denmark's Welcome into England. 1606.
Sir Thomas Overbury's Ghost. 1615.
Line of Life. 1620. Repr. Sh. Soc. Pub. 1843.
✠ Collected Works, ed. Weber. 1811. 2 v.
Dram. and Poetic Works, ed. Gifford. 1827. (1831), 2 v.; re-ed. Dyce. 3 v. Lond. 1869. 36/.
Dram. Works. w. Massinger. Introd. by Hartley Coleridge. 1840; 1848.
Bodenstedt. Sh.'s Zeitgenossen. 1. Webster. 2. Ford. 3. Lilly, Green and Marlowe. Berlin. 1858—'60.
Best Plays, ed. Havelock Ellis. Lond. 1888. (Mermaid Series). (*See* Spec. 62: 482).
Broken Heart; ed., w. introd. and notes, Clinton Scollard. N. Y. Holt. 1895. 50c.
† Colby, J. Rose. Some Ethical Aspects of Later Elizabethan Tragedy. (Ford). Ph. D. Thesis. Univ. of Mich. Ann Arbor. 1886.
Dunham. Lit. and Sci. Men. v. 2.
Gosse. Seventeenth Century Studies. John Webster, p. 59.
Hannemann, H. L. E. Metrische Untersuchungen zu John Ford. Halle. 1888. Diss. v. 2.
Hazlitt. Dram. Lit. of Age of Eliz.

Jeffrey, F. Ford's Dram. Works. Contrib. to the Edin. Rev. (*See also* Edin. Rev. 18: 275, 1811).
Lamb. Specimens of Dram. Poets.
Lowell. Old. Eng. Dram. Convers. on the old Poets.
Magazin Für Literatur. Dec. 8, 1895.
Malone. Essay on Shakespeare, Ford and Jonson. Malone's Sh. 1790. v. 2.
On the Time-Poets.
Reviews.
    Blackwood's Mag. 6: 409—417. (Anal. Essay on Witch of Edmonton).
    Edin. Rev. 18: 275—304. (Discussion of Weber's ed.)
    Fortn. Rev. 16: 42—63. (Criticism by Swinburne).
    Harper's Mag. 85: 942. (Criticism by Lowell).
    Quart. Rev. 6: 462—87. (Criticism of Prin. Dram. Works).
    Spec. 62: 482. (Best Plays).
Swinburne. Essays and Studies.
Thompson, Sylvanus. Memorials of John Ford.
Whipple. Essays and Reviews. Lit. of the Age of Eliz.
Wolff, Max. J. Ford ein nachahmer Shakespeare's. Heidel. diss. Heidelberg. J. Hörning. 1880. 41 pp. (Kolbing, E. Engl. Studien, 4: 479—80).

FORDE, THOMAS. Fl. 1660.

Love's Labyrinth; or, The Royal Shepherdess. Pr. 1660.
† Bailey. Life of Thomas Fuller. 1874. p. 585—6; 759.

FREEMAN, Sir RALPH. Fl. 1610—'55.

Imperiale. Pr. 1630.

GLAPTHORNE, HENRY. Fl. 1639.

*Lady Mother. Licensed 1635. (Pr. for the first time in Bullen's Old Eng. Plays. v. 2. 1883).
Hollander. Wr. circ. 1635.
*Ladies Privilege. Wr. circ. 1636.
Argalus and Parthenia. (Founded on Sidney's Arcadia). Acted circ. 1638.
Wit in a Constable. Wr. 1639.
Duchess of Fernandina. S. R. 1660. (Not extant).
*Albertus Wallenstein. 1639?
⚹Plays and Poems, w. illustr. notes and a memoir. Lond. Pearson. 1874. 2 v. 21/. (Retro. Rev. 1824. 10: 122).
† Bullen. Collection of Old Eng. Plays. 2: 101—102.
Zwickert, Max. Henry Glapthorne. (Inaug. Diss.) Halle.

GOFFE, THOMAS. 1591—1629.

Raging Turk; or Bajazet, the Second. Wr. 1615—1623. Pr. 1632.
Courageous Turk; or, Amurath the First. Wr. 1615—1623. Pr. 1633.
Orestes. Wr. 1615—1623. Pr. 1633.
Careless Shepherdess. Acted circ. 1629.
⚹Three Excellent Tragedies (Bajazet, Amurath, Orestes). Coll. by Richard Meighen. Lond. 1656.
† Gosse. Jacobean Poets.

GOMERSAL, ROBERT. 1600?—1646?

Ludovick Sforsa, Duke of Milan. Pr. 1628.
(Included in) Poems. 1633.

GOUGH, J. Fl. 1640.

Strange Discovery. 1640.

GREVILLE, (Sir) FULKE. (First Lord Brooke). 1554—1628.

*Mustapha. Pr. 1609.
Alaham. Pr. 1633.
Life of the renowned Sir Philip Sidney. 1652. (Autobiographical values).
✠ Certain Learned and Elegant Works of the Right Honorable Fulke, Lord Brooke, written in his youth and familiar exercise with Sir Philip Sidney. 1633.
Works, ed. w. memoir. introd. critical essays, etc. Grosart. Fuller Worthies' Libr. 4 v. 1870.
† Bolton, Edmund. Hypercritica. 1622. (Praises Mustapha).
Davison. Poetical Rhapsody. 1602.
Gosse. Jacobean Poets.
Hazlitt. Table Talk.

HABINGTON, WILLIAM. 1605—'54.

*Queene of Arragon. Acted 1640. (Revised at the Restoration, Samuel Butler contributing prologue and epilogue).
Non-Dramatic Works.
    Poems to Castara (his wife) 1634.
    History of Edward IV. 1640.
    Observations on History. 1641.
✠ Castara. Lond. 1870. (Arber Reprints). (Retro. Rev. 12: 274. 1825).
Hist. of Edward IV. Repr. in Kennett's Complete Hist. of Eng. 1706.
† Hallam. Lit. of Europe.
Jameson. (Mrs.) Loves of the Poets.
Johnson. Lives of the Poets.
Willmott, A. R. Lives of Eng. Sacred Poets. v. 1. 1839.

HARDING, SAMUEL. Fl. 1641.

Sicily and Naples; or, The Fatal Union. Pr. 1640.

HAUSTED, Peter. —1645.

The Rival Friends. 1632.
† Huth. Inedited Poetical Miscellanies. 1870. (Critical verses on Hausted's comedy.
Masson. Life of Milton. 1: 214, 218—19.

HAWKINS, WILLIAM. —1637.

Apollo Shroving. A Lyrical Drama. Lond. 1627.
† Dict. Nat. Biog.

HEMING, WILLIAM. Fl. 1632.
(Hemminge).

Coursing of the Hare; or, The Madcap. Acted 1633. (Not extant).
Fatal Contract. Pr. 1653. (Altered by Settle to Love and Revenge).
Jew's Tragedy. Pr. 1662.

HEYWOOD, THOMAS. —1650.

*Four Prentices of London, with The Conquest of Jerusalem. Pr. 1615. (Acted 15 or 20 years earlier).
*Edward IV. 2 pts. 1600.
If you know not me, you know nobody; or, The Troubles of Queen Elizabeth. 2 pts. 1605—6.
*Royal King and Loyal Subject. Pr. 1637. (Acted 1602?).
*Woman Killed with Kindness. Acted 1603. Pr. 1607.
Fair Maid of the Exchange. Pr. 1607.
*Rape of Lucrece. Pr. 1608.
Golden Age. Pr. 1611.
Silver Age. Acted 1612.
Brazen Age. Pr. 1613.
Fair Maid of the West. 2 pts. Acted 1617. Pr. 1631.
Captives; or, The Lost Recovered. 1624.
Iron Age. Pr. 1632.
*English Traveller. Pr. 1633.
Maidenhead Well Lost. 1634.
*Love's Mistress; or, The Queen's Masque. 1636.
*Challenge for Beauty. 1636.
Wise Woman of Hogsdon. 1638.
Fortune by Land and Sea. (With Wm. Rowley). Pr. 1655. (Wr. some 50 yrs. earlier).
Late Lancashire Witches. 1634. (With Richard Brome).

Lost Plays.

    War without Blows. 1598?
    Joan as Good as my Lady. 1599?
    The Blind eat many a Fly. 1602?
    How to Learn of a Woman to Woo. Acted 1605.
    Love's Masterpiece. S. R. 1640.
    "Alberte Galles." (With Wentworth Smith). 1602?
    Marshal Osrick. (With Wentworth Smith). 1602?
    London Florentine. (With Chettle). 1602?
    Like Quits Like. (With Chettle). 1602?
    Christmas comes but once a Year. (With Chettle, Dekker and Webster). 1602.
    Lady June, pt. 1. 1602. (With the above and Wentworth Smith).
Pageants for 1632 and 1633. (*See* Lord Mayor's Pageants, pt. 1; ed. Fairholt. Percy Soc. 3. 1843).
Pageants for 1631; 1635; 1637; 1638; 1639. (*See* vols. 4 and 5 of Pearson's ed. Heywood's Dram. Works).
An Apology for Actors. 1612; ed. w. introd. Collier. Sh. Soc. Pub. 1841. (Answered in A Refutation, by T. G. 1615).
Funeral Elegy on the Death of Prince Henry. 1613.

Marriage Triumphe; or, The Nuptials of the Prince Palatine and the Princess Elizabeth. 1613; ed. Collier. Percy Soc., v. 6. 1842.
England's Elizabeth; her Life and Troubles during her Minority from the Cradle to the Crown. 1631. Harl. Misc. 10. 1808.
✤Dramatic Works, w. notes and memoir. 6 v. London. Pearson. 1874. 63/.
Best Plays; ed. A. W. Verity, w. introd. by Symonds. (Mermaid Series). Lond. Scott. 1889. ea. 2/6.
Dramatic Works, ed. w. life. Collier. Sh. Soc. Pub. 1850—'51. (Fair Maid of the West, 2 pts. Royal King and Loyal Subject. If you know not me, you know nobody. Golden Age. Silver Age).
Fair Maid of the Exchange; ed. Barron Field. Sh. Soc. Pub. 1837.
Four Prentices of London, 2 pts.; ed. Barron Field. Sh. Soc. Pub. 1842.
Late Lancashire Witches. Tr. by Tieck in Sh.'s Vorschule, 1. Leipzig. 1823.
† Dict. Nat. Biog. (Ward).
Edin. Rev. Apr., 1841.
Fleay. Biog. Chron. Eng. Drama.
Gosse. Jacobean Poets.
Henslowe. Diary.
Herford. Studies in Literary Relations of England and Germany in Sixteenth Cent.
Lamb. Specimens of Early Dram. Poetry.
Marmion, Shackerley. Cupid and Psyche. (Repr. Singer, 1820). (Commend. Verses).
On the Time-Poets.
Retro. Rev. 11: 126—54. 1825.
Symonds. Shakspere's Predecessors.

HOLIDAY, (Dr.) BARTEN. —1661.

Marriages of the Arts. 1618. (Univ.)
† Gosse. Jacobean Poets.
Nichols. Progresses of King James. 3: 713.

JONES, INIGO. 1573—1652.

Masques. (Scenic and Mechanical).

    Blackness. (With Jonson). 1605.
    Alba. 1605.
    Ajax Flagellifer. 1605.
    Vertumnus. 1605.
    Hymen. (With Jonson). 1606.
    Hue and Cry after Cupid. (With Jonson). 1608.
    Queens. (With Jonson). 1609.
    Tethys' Festival. (With Daniel). 1610.
    Middle Temple and Lincoln's Inn Masque. (With Chapman). 1613.
    Time Vindicated. (With Jonson). 1623.
    Pan's Anniversary. (With Jonson). 1623?
    ?Neptune's Triumph. (With Jonson). 1624.
    Love's Triumph through Callipolis. (With Jonson). 1630.
    Chloridia. (With Jonson). 1630.
    Albion's Triumph. (With Townsend). 1632.
    Tempe Restored. (With Townsend). 1632.
    Triumph of Peace. (With Shirley). 1634.

Coelum Britannicum. (With Carew). 1634.
Love's Mistress. (With Heywood). 1634.
Temple of Love. (With Davenant). 1635.
Florimène. (French). 1635.
Britannia Triumphans. (With Davenant). 1638.
Luminalia. 1638.
Salmacida Spolia. (With Davenant). 1640.
† Blomfield, Reginald T. Series of papers in Portfolio for 1889, pp. 88, 113, 126.
Cunningham, Peter. Life of Inigo Jones. (With facsimile of drawings). Sh. Soc. Pub. 1848.
Fleay. Biog. Chron. Eng. Drama.
Gifford. Memoir of Ben Jonson, revised by Cunningham. 1875.
Jonson. Conversations with Drummond. Tale of a Tub.
Loftie, (Rev.) W. I. Inigo Jones and Wren. N. Y. Macmillan. 1893. $4.50.
Nichols. Progresses of James I.
Symonds. Ben Jonson. (Eng. Worthies). Lond. Longmans. 1888. 1/6.
Walpole. Anecdotes of Painting in Eng. Lond. Wornum. 1849.

JONSON, BEN. 1573?—1637.

Hot Anger soon Cold. (With Chettle and Porter. Not extant). 1598.
Case is Altered. 1598?
*Every Man in his Humour. 1598.
Every Man out of his Humour. 1599.
Page of Plymouth. (With Dekker. Not extant). 1599.
Robert II., King of Scots. (With Chettle, Dekker and other gentlemen. Not extant). 1599.
Cynthia's Revels. 1600.
Poetaster. 1601.
Tale of a Tub. 1601?
("Additions" to Jeruoymo). 1601.
Richard Crookback. (Not extant). 1602.
Sejanus. 1603.
*Eastward Ho. 1604.
*Volpone; or, The Fox. 1605.
*Epicoene; or, The Silent Woman. 1609.
*Alchemist. 1610.
Catiline. 1611.
Bartholomew Fair. 1614.
Sad Shepherd. 1615?
Devil is an Ass. 1616.
Staple of News. 1625.
New Inn. 1629.
Magnetic Lady. 1632.

Masques.

Satyr. 1603.
Entertainment to King James in London in passing to his Coronation. 1604.
Penates. 1604.
Blackness. (With Inigo Jones). 1605.
Hymen. (With Inigo Jones). 1606.
Entertainment at Theobalds of the Kings of Great Britain and Denmark. (Partly in Latin). 1606.

Entertainment at Theobalds to the King and Queen. 1607.
Beauty. 1608.
Hue and Cry after Cupid. (With Inigo Jones). 1608.
Queens. (With Inigo Jones). 1609.
Speeches at Prince Henry's Barriers. 1610.
Oberon the Fairy Prince. 1611.
Love freed from Ignorance and Folly. 1611.
Challenge at Tilt at a Marriage. 1613.
Irish Masque. 1613.
Mercury Vindicated from the Alchemists. 1615.
Golden Age Restored. 1616.
Christmas. 1616.
Lovers made Men. 1617.
For the Honor of Wales. 1618.
News from the New World discovered in the Moon. 1621.
Metamorphosed Gipsies. 1621.
Masque of Augurs. 1622.
Time Vindicated. (With Inigo Jones). 1623.
Pan's Anniversary. (With Inigo Jones). 1623?
Fortunate Isles. 1624.
Neptune's Triumph. (With Inigo Jones?) 1624?
Masque of Owls. 1624.
Love's Triumph through Callipolis. (With Inigo Jones). 1630.
Chloridia. (With Inigo Jones). 1630.
Love's Welcome. (At Walbeck). 1633.
Love's Welcome. (At Balsover). 1634.

✸Dram. Works. First Folio; (ed. by author). v. 1, 1616; v. 2, 1631. Repr. 1640 (2 v.); 1641 (2 v.); 1692 (1 v.); 1715 or '16 (6 v.); 1756 (7 v., w. life and notes by Whalley). 1811. (Coleman's ed. Pub. by Stockdale in 4 v. with Plays by Beaumont and Fletcher). 1816. (Gifford's ed. in 9 v.) 1838. (Barry Cornwall's ed.) 1861. (Routledge repr. of Barry Cornwall's ed.) 1865. (New ed. of Gifford by Cunningham). 1870. (Repr. in 3 v.)
Works; w. notes and memoir, ed. Gifford, re-ed. Cunningham. 9 v. Lond. Bickers. 1875. 105/. 3 v. Lond. Chatto. 1876. 18/.
Works; ed. Gifford. Lond. Routledge. 1879. 10/6.
Best Plays; ed. Nicholson and Herford. 3 v. (Mermaid Series). Lond. Unwin. 1890—'94. Ea. 3/6. N. Y. Scribner. 1890—'94. Ea. $1.
Alchemist, Fox, Silent Woman, Sad Shepherd? (Morley's Universal Libr.) Lond. Routledge. 1885. 1/.
Every Man in his Humour; ed. w. notes by Wheatley. Lond. Longmans. 1877. 2/6.
Masques; ed. Morley. (Carisbrooke Libr. 9). Lond. Routledge. 1890. 2/6.
Poems; ed. Wm. Sharp. (Canterbury Poets). Lond. Scott. 1886. 1/.
Timber; ed. Schelling; w. introd. and notes. Bost. Ginn. 1892. 90c.
Conversations with Drummond of Hawthornden. Ed. Laing. Sh. Soc. Pub. 1842. (Abstract in Drummond's Works, 1711. Abstract in Gifford's Jonson. In Masson's Life of Drummond).

† Anglia. 10: 361.
Austin. Poets Laureate. (60 pp.)
Baudissin, W. G. Ben Jonson und seine Schule. Leipzig. 1816.
Brit. Rev. 1870. 52: 394—428. (Ben Jonson's Quarrel with Shakespeare).
Buff, A. The Quarto ed. of Ben Jonson's "Every Man in his Humour." (Engl. Studien, 1: 181—86).

Coleridge. Lectures upon Shakespeare and some of the Old Dramatists. Lit. Remains. v. 2.
Dekker. Satiro-Mastix. (In answer to Jonson's Poetaster).
Disraeli. Amenities of Lit. Curiosities of Lit. Quarrels of Authors.
Dryden. Essay of Dram. Poetry.
Dunham. Lit. and Sci. Men. v. 2.
Elze. Sh. Jahrbuch. 3: 150; 4: 112.
Fleay. Biog. Chron. Eng. Drama. (See also Sh. Soc. Pub. 1. 1883—'84).
Friesen. Eine Studie. Sh. Jahrbuch, 10, 1875.
Fuller. Worthies of England.
Gilchrist, O. Examination of the charges maintained by Messrs. Malone, Chalmers, and others, of Ben Jonson's enmity, etc., towards Shakespeare. 1808.
Gosse. Jacobean Poets.
Hazlitt. Lectures on the Eng. Comic Writers. Lectures on the Dram. Lit. of the Age of Eliz.
Henslowe. Diary.
Hermann, E. Shakspeare's Tempest and Jonson's Volpone. 117 pp. (In his Shakes. Studien, 2).
Holthausen, F. Die Quelle von Ben Jonson's Volpone. (Anglia, 12: 519—525).
Jeaffreson in Athenæum. March 6, 1886.
Ljungren, Carl Aug. Poetical Gender of Substantives in Ben Jonson. Diss. Lond. 1892.
Masson. (Prof.) D. Life and Writings of Drummond of Hawthornden. Lond. Macmillan. 1873. 10/6.
Retro. Rev. 1: 1—16.
Return fr. Parnassus. (See Index).
Saegelken, H. Ben Jonson's Römer-dramen. Bremen. 1880. Diss. Jena. (Notice by Max Koch. Englische Studien, 8: 120—30).
Schmidt, A. The plays and poems of Shakespeare ... w. an essay relative to ... Sh. and Jonson. 1. 1790.
Shakespeare and Jonson. Dramatic, versus Wit-Combats. 1864.
Soergel. Die englischen Maskenspiele.
Swinburne. Study of Ben Jonson. Lond. Chatto. 1889. 7/. (Nineteenth Cent., Apr. and May, 1888). Study of Shakespeare. p. 118—124, 143.
Symonds, J. A. Ben Jonson. (Eng. Worthies). Lond. Longmans. 1888. 1/6.
Uellner, (Dr.) Critical examination of the poetic genius of Ben Jonson. Dusseldorf. 1857.
Ward. Eng. Dram. Lit.
Whipple. Lit. of the Age of Eliz.
Wilke, W. Anwendung der rhyme-test u. double-ending-test auf Ben Jonson's dramen. (Anglia, 10: 512—521).

KILLIGREW, HENRY, (D. D.) 1613—1700.

Conspiracy. 1638. (Published in 1653 under title of Pallantus and Eudora).
† Fleay. Chronicle of the Eng. Drama.
Pepys. Diary.

KIRKE, JOHN. Fl. 1625.

*Seven Champions of Christendom. 1638.

LOVELACE, RICHARD. 1618—'58.

Scholar. (Univ.) 1636? (Not extant. Prol. and epil. in Lucasta. 1649).
Soldier. (Not acted and not extant).

Non-Dram. Works.

    Lucasta. (Lyrics). 1649; ed. w. memoir, W. C. Hazlitt. Lond. Smith. 1864.
    Posthume Poems. 1659.

MACHIN, LEWIS. Fl. 1608.

*Dumb Knight. 1608. (With Markham).
† Dict. Nat. Biog. (*Under* Henry Machin).

MARKHAM, GERVASE. 1568?—1637.

*Dumb Knight. 1608. (With Lewis Machin).
Herod and Antipater. Pr. 1622; played much earlier. (With Wm. Sampson).
Sacred Poems. (Lamentations of St. John, 1600; Marie Magdalene's Lamentations, 1601); ed. Grosart w. memoir. 1871.

MARMION, SHACKERLEY. 1603—'39.

*Holland's Leaguer. 1632.
*Fine Companion. 1633.
*Antiquary. 1640.
‡Dramatic Works, ed. Maidment and Logan. Edin. 1876.
Cupid and Psyche. (Poem). 1637. Repr. Singer. 1820.
† Heywood, Thomas. Pleasant Dialogues and Dramas. 1637. (Commend. Verses).
Jonsonus Virbius. 1638. (A Funeral Sacrifice to the Sacred Memory of his thrice-honoured Father, Ben Jonson).

MASON, JOHN. Fl. 1606.

Turk. 1609.
† Fleay. Biog. Chron. Eng. Drama.

MASSINGER, PHILIP. 1583—1640.

*Duke of Milan. 1618? (Revived at Drury Lane, 1816).
*Unnatural Combat. 1619?
*Bondman. Licensed 1623. (Revived 1661; 1719; 1799).
Renegado. Licensed 1624.
Parliament of Love. Licensed 1624.
*New Way to Pay Old Debts. 1625? (Thirteen revivals. 1748—1827).
Roman Actor. Licensed 1626. (Revived 1722; 1796; 1822).
?Maid of Honour. (Revived 1785).
Great Duke of Florence. Licensed 1627.
*Picture. Licensed 1629. (Revived 1783).
Emperor of the East. Licensed 1631.
Believe as You List. (Refused license 1631).
*City Madam. Licensed 1632. (Revived 1783).
*Guardian. Licensed 1633.
Bashful Lover. Licensed 1636. (Revived 1798).

In Collaboration.
  *Second Maiden's Tragedy. Licensed 1611. (With Tourneur?)
  Honest Man's Fortune. 1613. (With Fletcher, Field, Daborne.)
  *Thierry and Theodoret. 1613? (With Fletcher, Field, Wilkins?)
  Bloody Brother. 1613? (With Fletcher, Field, Wilkins?)
  Knight of Malta.' 1616? (With Fletcher).
  Queen of Corinth. 1617? (With Fletcher).
  *Fatal Dowry. Before 1619? (With Field). (Cf. Rowe's Fair Penitent).
  ?Virgin Martyr. Licensed 1620. (With Dekker).
  Custom of the Country. Date? (With Fletcher).
  Double Marriage. 1620? (With Fletcher).
  *False One. 1620? (With Fletcher).
  Little French Lawyer. 1620? (With Fletcher).
  Sea Voyage. Licensed 1622.' (With Fletcher).
  Beggar's Bush. 1622? (With Fletcher).
  Prophetess. Licensed 1622. (With Fletcher).
  Spanish Curate. Licensed 1622. (With Fletcher).
  Fair Maid of the Inn. Licensed 1626. (With Fletcher).
  ?A Very Woman; or, The Prince of Tarant. Licensed 1634. (With Fletcher).
  Lovers' Progress. Licensed 1634. (With Fletcher).
     [For alleged lost plays by Massinger see Dict. Nat. Biog.]

*Dram. Works; ed. Coxeter. 4 v. 1759; re-issued w. introd. by Davies. 1761.
Dram. Works; ed. J. Monck Mason. 4 v. 1779.
Plays; ed. Wm. Gifford. 4 v. 1805; 1813. (Edin. Rev. 1808; 12: 99).
Expurgated Plays; ed. Harness. 3 v. 1830—'31.
Massinger and Ford. Dram. Works, w. introd. Hartley Coleridge. 1 v. 1840.
  Lond. Routledge. 1865. 10/6.
Plays; ed. Cunningham fr. text of Gifford (1813). (w. add. of Believe as You
  List). Lond. Chatto. 1867; 1872. 6/. (Lit. Liv. Age. 100: 266).
Selected Plays; ed. A. Symons. 2 v. (Mermaid Series). Lond. Vizetelly.
  1889. ea. 2/6.
A New Way to Pay Old Debts; ed. Deighton, w. introd. and notes. (Eng.
  Classics). Lond. Bell. 1894. 2/6.
Believe as You List; ed. T. C. Croker. Percy Soc. 1848.
Lafond, E. Contemporains de Sh. (Fr. trans.) Paris. 1864.
† Balser, J. E. Acad. 37: 430.
Boyle, R. Beaumont, Fletcher and Massinger. Engl. Studien, 5: 74; 7: 66;
  8: 39; 9: 299; 10: 383.
Choate. Wells of English.
Coleridge. Literary Remains.
Fleay. Biog. Chron. Eng. Dram. (Under Fletcher).
Gardiner, S. R. The Political Element in Massinger. Sh. Soc. Trans.
  1875—'76. (Contemp. Rev. Aug., 1876; 28: 495, art. John Fletcher).
Gaspary, Alfred. Allgemeine Aussprüche in den Dramen Philip Massinger.
  Marburg, 1890.
Hazlitt. Dram. Lit. of Age of Eliz.
Lamb. Specimens of Dram. Poets.
Lowell. Massinger and Ford. Harper's, 85: 942. Also Old Eng. Dramatists.
Macaulay, G. C. Francis Beaumont. A Crit. Study. Lond. Paul. 1883. 5/.
  On the Time-Poets.
Phelan, Jas. On Philip Massinger. Halle diss. 1878. Anglia, 2: 1, 44, 504.
Stephen, L. Cornh. Mag. 36: 440. (Same in Ecl. Mo. 89: 688, and Lit. Liv.
  Age, 135: 228). Hours in a Library, 2: 141—76.

Swinburne. Fortn. Rev. 52:1.
Ward. Eng. Dram. Lit.
Whipple. Essays and Reviews. Lit. of the Age of Eliz.

MAY, THOMAS. 1595—1650.

*Old Couple. 1620?
*Heir. Acted 1620.
Cleopatra. Acted 1626.
Julia Agrippina. Acted 1628.
Antigone. Pr. 1631.
Julius Cæsar. (Latin). MS.
[For Poems, Translations and Prose Works, see Dict. Nat. Biog.]
† Dunham. Lives of Lit. and Sci. Men, 2.
Gosse. Jacobean Poets.

MAYNE, JASPER. 1604—'72.

City Watch. Acted 1639. (Revised by Bromfield, 1755, as The Schemers, and by Planché, 1828, as the Merchant's Wedding).
Amorous War. Pr. 1648.
[For Poems, Translations and Prose Works, see Dict. Nat. Biog.]
✠ Two Plays. By J. M. of Ch. Ch. in Oxon. 1658.
† Pepys. Diary. Sept. 28, 1668.
Walker, John. Sufferings of the Clergy. Lond. 1714.

MEAD, ROBERT. 1616—'53.

Combat of Love and Friendship. (Univ.) circ. 1636.
† Cowley, Abraham. Poetical Blossoms. 1633. (Commend. Verses by Mead).
Jonsonus Virbius. 1638.

MIDDLETON, THOMAS. 1570?—1627.

Old Law. 1599? (With Rowley and Massinger?)
*Blurt, Master Constable; or, The Spaniard's Nightwalk. 1600.
Cæsar's Fall. 1602. (With Dekker, Drayton, Monday, Webster. Not extant).
Two Harpies. 1602. (With Dekker, Drayton, Monday, Webster. Not extant).
Chester Tragedy; or, Randolph, Earl of Chester. 1602. (Not extant).
*Mayor of Quinborough. 1602?
*?Honest Whore, pt. 1. 1604. (With Dekker).
Michaelmas Term. 1604?
Phœnix. 1606?
*Trick to catch the Old One. 1606.
*A Mad World, My Masters. 1606?
*?Puritan; or, The Widow of Watling Street. 1606.
Family of Love. 1607?
Five Gallants. (Five Witty Gallants). 1607.
*Roaring Girl. 1608—'11? (With Dekker).
Chaste Maid in Cheapside. 1611—'13?
No Wit, No Help, like a Woman's. 1613?
*Women Beware Women. 1613?
Fair Quarrel. 1616? (With Wm. Rowley).
*Changeling. 1621. (With Wm. Rowley).

*More Dissemblers besides Women. 1622?
*Spanish Gipsy. 1623? (With Wm. Rowley?)
Anything for a Quiet Life. 1623?
Game at Chess. 1624.
?Widow. Pr. 1652. (With Jonson and Fletcher?)
?Witch. Pr. 1778.

Pageants.

Entertainment to King James. 1604. (With Dekker).
Triumphs of Truth. (Lord Mayor). 1613.
Lordship's Entertainment at the Opening of the New River. 1613.
Mask of Cupid. (Merchant Taylors. Not extant). 1614.
Civitatis Amor. (Whitehall). 1616.
Triumphs of Honor. (Lord Mayor). 1617.
Inner Temple Masque; or, Masque of Heroes. 1618.
Triumphs of Love. (Lord Mayor). 1619.
World Tost at Tennis. "Courtly Masque." 1620.
Sun in Aries. 1621.
Invention (for the Lord Mayor, at an entertainment in his house). 1622.
Triumphs of Honor and Virtue. (Lord Mayor). 1622.
Triumphs of Integrity. (Lord Mayor). 1623.
Triumphs of Health and Prosperity. (Lord Mayor). 1626.
Honorable Entertainments composed for the Service of this Noble City. (Ten minor masques). Pr. 1621. (*See* Athen. Oct. 2, 1886).

[For misc. works in verse and prose ascribed to Middleton see Dict. Nat. Biog. (Herford)].

✣Works; ed. Dyce. 5 v. Lond. Lumley. 1840.
Works; ed. Bullen. 8 v. Lond. Nimmo. 1885—'86. ea. 7/6. (Ath., 1886, 1:625. Atlantic, 56:853. Sat. Rev., 61:305).
Selected Works; ed. Ellis, w. introd. by Swinburne. 2 v. (Mermaid Series). Lond. Vizetelly. 1887—'90. ea. 2/6.
† Arnheim. Herrig's Archiv. 78:1; 129:369.
Choate. Wells of English.
Gosse. Jacobean Poets.
Hazlitt. Dram. Lit. of the Age of Eliz.
Henslowe. Diary.
Holthausen, F. Zu Middleton's No Wit, No Help, like a Woman's. (Anglia, 12:526—527).
Hornby, T. Game of Chess. Sh. Soc. Trans. 2. 1845.
Jonson. Conversations with Drummond. Staple of News, 3:1.
Pearson, Jas. L. Repr. of an unknown Pageant, Triumphs of Honor and Virtue, w. introd. Sh. Soc. Trans. 2. 1845.
Pepys. Diary. Feb. 23, 1661. (The Changeling).
Retro. Rev. 1823. 8:125.
Spalding. On the Witch-Scenes in Macbeth. Sh. Soc. Trans. 1877—'79.
Swinburne. Nineteenth Cent. Jan., 1886. 19:138. (*Same.* Ecl. Mo. 106:335).
Webster. Duchess of Malfi. 1623. (Commend. Verses by Middleton).

MILTON, JOHN. 1608—'74.

Arcades, Masque, presented before the Countess Dowager of Derby. 1633?
*Comus. Masque, presented at Ludlow Castle. 1634.
*Samson Agonistes. 1671.

✱Works in Verse and Prose; ed. w. life, J. Mitford. 8 v. Lond. 1867.
Poetical Works; ed. w. life and notes, D. Masson. 3 v. Lond. Macmillan. 1874. Globe ed. Lond. Macmillan. 1877. 3/6.
Poetical Works; ed. w. life, introd. bibliog., etc., Jno. Bradshaw. 2 v. Lond. Bell. 1893. ea. 2/6. N. Y. Macmillan. 1893. ea. 75c.
Arcades and Comus; ed. w. introd. and notes, A. W. Verity. Lond. Camb. Press. 1891. 3/. N. Y. Macmillan. 1891. 90c.
Comus; ed. w. introd. and notes, Bell. (Eng. Classics). Lond. Macmillan. 1890. 1/6. N. Y. Macmillan. 1890. 40c.
Illustrations to Comus, by Wm. Blake. (Reprod. of the 8 orig. drawings). Lond. Quaritch. 1890. 42/.
Comus, adapted to the stage. Altered by J. Dalton. Lond. 1738. (Bell's Br. th., 1; Br. dr., 2; Dibdin's Lond. th., 10; Mod. Br. dr., 2).
Comus. Altered by G. Colman. As performed in Covent Garden. Lond. 1772. (Bell's Br. th., 9; Br. dr., 12; Inchbald's Farces, 7; Lond. stage, 2; Mod. Br. dr., 5).
Samson Agonistes; ed. Jerram. Lond. Rivington. 1890. 2/. ed. Percival. (Eng. Classics). Lond. Macmillan. 1890. 1/6. N. Y. Macmillan. 1890. 40c. ed. J. Churton Collins. Oxf. Clar. Press. 1/. N. Y. Macmillan. 25c. ed. A. W. Verity, w. introd. and notes. Camb. Press. 1892. 2/6. N. Y. Macmillan. 1892. 70c.
Samson. Adapted as oratorio by N. Hamilton. Oxford. 1749.
Samson. Set to music by Handel. Lond. 1762.
Handel's Oratorio, Samson. Words chiefly fr. Milton. Compiled by T. Morell. Lond. 1840.
† Arnold. Essays in Criticism.
Bagehot. Lit. Studies.
Birrill. Obiter Dicta.
Bridges, Rob. Milton's Prosody. Clar. Press. 1893. 8/6. N. Y. Macmillan. 1893. $3.00.
Brooke, Stopford A. Milton. Lond. Macmillan. 1879. 1/6.
Cleveland, C. D. Concordance to Milton's Poetical Works. Lond. Low. 1867. 6/.
Coleridge. Seven Lectures on Sh. and Milton.
De Quincey. Works. (1883). 6: 311—25; 10: 79—98.
Dowden. Transcripts and Studies. Lond. 1888.
Elze. Ein Gegenbild zu Sh. Sh. Jahrbuch, 12. 1877.
Garnett, Richard. Life of John Milton. (Bibliog. by Anderson). Lond. Scott. 1890. 2/6.
Lowell. Among My Books.
Macaulay, Th. B. Crit. and Hist. Essays. 2 v. Lond. 1854. 1: 1—28.
Masson, D. Essays. Cambridge. 1856. Life of John Milton. Cambridge. 1859—'80. 8 v. (New ed. 1881).
Pattison, Mark. Milton. (Eng. Men of Letters). Lond. 1879.
Rossetti, Wm. Michael. Lives of Famous Poets. Lond. 1878.
Scherer. Essays on Eng. Lit.

MONTAGUE, WALTER. 1603?—'77.

Shepherd's Paradise. 1633.
† Clarendon. Hist. of the Rebellion.
Dict. Nat. Biog.
Prynne. Histrio-mastix.
Suckling. Session of the Poets.

NABBES, THOMAS. Fl. 1635.

*Covent Garden. 1633.
*Tottenham Court. 1633.
*Hannibal and Scipio. 1635.
*Bride. 1638.
*?Unfortunate Mother. 1639.

Pageants.
   Microcosmus. Pr. 1637.
   Spring's Glory. Pr. 1638.
   Presentation on the Prince's Birthday. Pr. 1638.
✠Spring's Glory, a Maske. Together with sundry Poems, Epigrams, Elegies, and Epithalamiums. 1639.
   Bullen, A. H. Collection of Old Eng. Plays. New Series. 1887. (Vols. 1 and 2. Nabbes' Coll. Works, w. introd. by Bullen).
† Bridges. Censura Literaria and Restituta.
   Fleay. Biog. Chron. Eng. Drama.

NEVILE, ROBERT. —1694.

Poor Scholar. 1673.
† Notes and Queries. 1st ser. 11 : 367, 436; 3rd ser. 1 : 80.

NICCOLS, RICHARD. 1584—1616.

Twins' Tragedy. 1612. (Not extant, unless identical with "Twins," pub. as by Wm. Rider. 1655. (See Fleay. Biog. Chron. Eng. Drama).

Non Dram. Works.
   Epicedium. A Funeral Oration upon the Death of Elizabeth. Wr. by Infelice Academico Ignoto. 1603.
   Cuckow: 1607. Sackville's Mirror for Magistrates, re-ed. w. continuations by Niccols in 1619. (See Haslewood's ed. 1815).
   Three Sisters' Tears, shed at the Funerals of Prince Henry. 1613.
   Epigrams. 1614. (Harl. Misc. 10 : 1).
   Monodia. 1615. (Harl. Misc. 10 : 11).
   London's Artillery. 1616.
   Sir Thomas Overbury's Vision. 1616. (Harl. Misc. 7 : 178. Hunterian Club. Glasgow, 1853).

PHILLIPS, (Philips) AMBROSE. 1671—1749.

*Distrest Mother. (Tr. of Racine's Andromaque).
† Spectator, 290.

QUARLES, FRANCIS. 1592—1644.

Virgin Widow. 1649.
Emblems: Divine and Moral.
[For complete list of works see Lowndes' Bibliographer's Manual].
† Gosse. Jacobean Poets.

RANDOLPH, THOMAS. 1605—'35.

Aristippus; or, The Jovial Philosopher. Pr. 1630.
Conceited Pedlar. Pr. 1630.

Jealous Lovers. Acted 1632.
*?Amyntas. Pr. 1638.
*Muses' Looking-glass. Pr. 1638.
?Plutophthalmia Plutogamia.
Cornelianum Dolium. Pr. 1638.
Prodigal Scholar. S. R. 1660.
✠Poet. and Dram. Works; ed. w. memoir and notes, W. C. Hazlitt. Lond. Reeves and Turner. 1875. 15/.
† Choate. Wells of English.
Gosse. Jacobean Poets.
Masson. Life of Milton. 1: 218.
Retro. Rev. 6: 61.
Shirley. Faithful Servant. (Verses by Randolph prefixed).
Ward. Eng. Dram. Lit. 1: XLIV.—XLVI.

RAWLINS, THOMAS. —1670?

*Rebellion. Pr. 1639.

RICHARDS, NATHANIEL. Fl. 1640.

Messalina. Pr. 1640.
✠Sacred and Satirical Poems. 1630. 1641.

ROWLEY, SAMUEL. Fl. 1605.

*Henry VIII.; or, When you see me you know me. Pr. 1605.
Spanish Soldier. Pr. 1634. (See Fleay. Biog. Chron. Eng. Drama. under Dekker).
Lost Plays.
  Judas. 1601. (With Bourne).
  Joshua. 1602.
  Hymen's Holiday; or, Cupid's Vagaries. Acted 1612. (Perhaps by Wm. Rowley. See Fleay. Biog. Chron. Eng. Drama).
  Richard III.; or, The English Profit. 1623. (See Fleay. Biog. Chron. Eng. Drama).
  Hard Shift for Husbands; or, Bilbo's Best Blade. 1623.
✠Henry VIII.; or, When you see me you know me; ed. w. introd. and notes, by K. Elze. Dessau and Lond. 1874.
† Henslowe. Diary.
Ward. Eng. Dram. Lit.

ROWLEY, WILLIAM. Fl. 1610.

Travels of Three English Brothers. 1607? (With Day and Wilkins).
*Match at Midnight. 1607?
A Shoemaker's a Gentleman. 1609?
Hymen's Holiday; or, Cupid's Vagaries. (Not extant. See Samuel Rowley).
Fortune by Land and Sea. 1609? (With Heywood, ed. Barron Field. Sh. Soc. Pub. 1845).
Old Law; or, A New Way to Please You. 1615? (With Middleton and perhaps Massinger).
Fair Quarrel. 1616? (With Middleton).
Cure for a Cuckold. 1618? (With Webster? Cf. Fleay. Biog. Chron. Eng. Drama. 2: 98—99; and Gosse. Seventeenth Cent. Studies, John Webster, 66—67).

*Changeling. 1621. (With Middleton).
All's Lost by Lust. 1622.
*Maid of the Mill. 1623. (With Fletcher).
Witch of Edmonton. 1623? (With Dekker and Ford).
*Spanish Gipsy. 1623? (With Middleton? See Fleay. Biog. Chron. Eng. Drama).
*New Wonder; or, A Woman never Vext. Pr. 1632.
*Birth of Merlin; or, The Child has lost a Father. Pr. 1662. (Ascribed on title-page to Shakespeare and Rowley).
† Bodenstedt. Shakespeare's Zeitgenossen. 1.
Bullen, *in pref. to his* Day's Dram. Works. Chiswick Press. 1881. £3, 5/.
Gosse. Jacobean Poets.
Hazlitt. Dram. Lit. of the Age of Eliz.
Lamb. Specimens Eng. Dram. Poets.

RUTTER, JOSEPH. Fl. 1635.

*Shepherd's Holiday. Pr. 1635.
Cid. 2 pts. (Tr. fr. Corneille). Pr. 1638.
† Jonson. Shepherd's Holiday. Commend. Verses. Underwoods, 22.
Jonsonus Virbius.

SAMPSON, WILLIAM. Fl. 1625.

Herod and Antipater. Pr. 1622.
Widow's Prize. 1625? (Not extant).
Vow Breaker; or, The Fair Maid of Clifton. Pr. 1636.

?SAVILLE, J. Fl. 1603.

King James's Entertainment at Theobalds and his Welcome to Lond. 1603. (Arber Reprints). Lond. and N. Y. Macmillan. (But *see* Fleay. Biog. Chron. Eng. Drama, 2: 175).

SHARPE, LEWIS. Fl. 1640.

Noble Stranger. Pr. 1640.

SHARPHAM, EDWARD. Fl. 1606.

Fleire. 1606?
Cupid's Whirligig. 1607? (Founded on Boccaccio's Decameron, 7: 6).

SHIRLEY, JAMES. 1596—1666. (Dates usually of license).

School of Compliment. 1625.
Maid's Revenge. 1626.
Wedding. 1626?
*Brothers. 1626. (*See* Fleay. Biog. Chron. Eng. Drama).
Witty Fair One. 1628.
Faithful Servant. 1629.
*Traitor. 1631.
Duke. 1631.
Love's Cruelty. 1631.
Changes; or, Love in a Maze. 1632.

Hyde Park. 1632.
Contention for Honor and Riches. S. R. 1632.
*Ball. 1632. (With Chapman).
Arcadia. Acted 1632?
Beauties. 1633.
Nightwalker. 1633. (Wr. by Fletcher; re-modelled by Shirley).
Young Admiral. 1633.
*Gamester. 1633.
Triumphs of Peace. Presented at Whitehall. 1633. (With Inigo Jones).
Example. 1634.
Opportunity. 1634.
Coronation. 1635. (With Fletcher? See Fleay. Biog. Chron. Eng. Drama. 2: 241).
Chabot. 1635. (With Chapman).
Lady of Pleasure. 1635.
Duke's Mistress. 1635.
*Saint Patrick for Ireland. Acted (at Dublin) 1636—7.
Constant Maid. Acted 1637?
Royal Master. Acted 1637.
Politician. Acted 1637—'39? (See Fleay. Biog. Chron. Eng. Drama).
Gentleman of Venice. 1639.
?General. Acted 1636—'38? (Pr. Halliwell, 1853).
Triumph of Beauty. 1640?
Rosania. 1640.
Imposture. 1640.
Politic Father. 1641.
Cardinal. 1641.
Sisters. 1642.
Court Secret. Wr. 1642.
Cupid and Death. Acted 1653.
Contention of Ajax and Achilles. Pr. 1659.
✠Dram. Works; w. notes by W. Gifford, and added notes and some account of Shirley and his writings, by Dyce. 6 v. Lond. 1833. £6. (Quart. Rev. 49: 1, 1833; and 16: 103, 1834).
Selections; ed. w. introd. and notes by Gosse. Lond. Vizetelly. 1888. 2/6. (Mermaid Ser.)
Poems. Campbell. Brit. Poets. 5: 1—63.
† Blackwoods, 4: 66. (The Traitor).
Dunham. Lives of Lit. and Sci. Men.
Fleay. Annals of the Careers of James and Henry Shirley. (Anglia, 8: 405—414. 1885).
Ford. Love's Sacrifice. (Prefatory lines by Shirley).
Heywood. Queen's Mask. (Coridon the Clown=Shirley).
Hogarth. Memoirs of the Opera. 1: 55. (Triumphs of Peace).
Kingsley, Chas. Plays and Puritans. Lond. Macmillan. 1889. 5/.
Swinburne. Fortn. Rev. 53: 461.
Ward. Eng. Dram. Lit.

SHIRLEY, HENRY. Fl. before 1638.

*Martyred Soldier. Pr. 1638.
† Fleay. Annals of the Careers of James and Henry Shirley. (Anglia, 8: 405—414, 1885).

?SMITH, WILLIAM. Fl. 1615.
Possibly identical with Wentworth Smith.

Hector of Germany. 1613? (Pr. 1615).
Freeman's Honour. 1614? (Not extant).
Fair Foul One. Licensed 1623. (Not extant).
Saint George for England. (MS. destroyed by Warburton's cook).

SQUIRE, JOHN. Fl. 1620.

Triumphs of Peace. (Lord Mayor). 1620. Repr. Nichols: Progresses of King James, 3: 619.

STEPHENS, JOHN. Fl. 1613.

Cynthia's Revenge. Pr. 1613. (See Fleay. Biog. Chron. Eng. Drama).

STRODE, WILLIAM. 1599—1644.

Floating Island. Acted by Christ Church students before Charles I. at Oxford, 1636.

SUCKLING, (Sir) JOHN. 1609—'41?

Aglaura. Acted 1637?
*Goblins. Acted 1638?
Brennoralt; or, Discontented Colonel. Wr. 1639?
Sad One. (Unfinished). Wr. 1640?
✣Works. 2 v. Lond. 1770.
Poems, Plays and other Remains, ed. W. C. Hazlitt. 2 v. Lond. Reeves and Turner. 1892. 8/.
Selected Works; w. memoir, A Suckling. Lond. 1836.
† Anderson. Brit. Poets, 3.
Hazlitt. Eng. Comic Writers.
Retro. Rev. 9: 19. 1824.
Wotton. Word Portraits.

SWINHOE, GILBERT. Fl. 1650.

Unhappy Fair Irene. Pr. 1658. (Founded on Painter: Palace of Pleasure. Nov. 40).

TAILOR, ROBERT. Fl. 1614.

*Hog hath lost his Pearl. Pr. 1614.
† Fleay. Biog. Chron. Eng. Drama, 2: 256—7.

TAYLOR, JOHN. 1580—1654.

Triumphs of Fame and Honor. (Lord Mayor). 1634.
Ovatio Caroli. 1641.
✣Works. 1630. (Folio ed.) Repr. Spenser Soc. Manchester. 1869.
Works not in 1630 Folio. Repr. Spenser Soc. 1870—'78.
Early Prose and Poet. Works. Morison. Glasgow. 1888. 5/.

TOMKINS, JOHN. Fl. 1615.

*Albumazar. Acted 1615.

TOURNEUR (Turner) CYRIL. Fl. 1610.

Atheist's Tragedy. 1603? Pr. 1611.
*Revenger's Tragedy. Pr. 1607.
Non-Dram. Works.
 Transformed Metamorphosis. Pr. 1600.
 Funeral Poem on the Death of Sir Francis Vere. Pr. 1609.
 Grief on the Death of Prince Henry. Wr. 1612. Pr. 1613.
✠Plays and Poems; ed. w. crit. introd. and notes, J. Churton Collins. 2 v. Lond. Chatto. 1878. 18/.
 Tragedies;, ed. w. introd. and notes, Symonds. Lond. Vizetelly. 1888. (Mermaid Series).
† Choate. Wells of English.
 Gosse. Jacobean Poets. Seventeenth Cent. Studies: John Webster, p. 59.
 Hazlitt. Age of Eliz. Lecture 3.
 Henley. Views and Reviews.
 Jahrbuch. (Sh.) 23: 132.
 Lamb. Specimens of the Eng. Drama. Poets.
 Retro. Rev. 1823. 7: 331—52.
 Swinburne. Nineteenth Cent. 1887. 21: 415—27. (*Same*, Ecl. Mo. 108: 599).

TOWNSEND, AURELIAN. Fl. 1630.

Albion's Triumph. Masque. 1631. (With Inigo Jones).
Tempe Restored. Masque. 1631. (With Inigo Jones).

WEBSTER, JOHN. 1591—?

Cæsar's Fall. 1602. (With Drayton, Middleton, Monday and "the rest." Not extant).
Two Harpies. 1602. (With Drayton, Dekker, Middleton, Monday. Not extant).
Lady Jane. 2 pts. 1602. (With Chettle, Dekker, Heywood, Smith. Pub. 1607 as The Famous Hist. of Sir Thomas Wyatt).
Christmas comes but once a Year. 1602. (With Chettle, Dekker, Heywood. Not extant).
Westward Ho. 1603? (With Dekker).
Northward Ho. 1605. (With Dekker).
?White Devil; or, Vittoria Corombona. 1607?
*Appius and Virginia. 1609?
Devil's Law Case. 1610?
*Duchess of Malfi. 1612?
?Late Murther of the Son upon the Mother. Licensed 1624 as a "new tragedy." (With Ford).
Monuments of Honour. (Lord Mayor). 1624.
?Cure for a Cuckold. Pr. 1661. (Cf. Fleay: Biog. Chron. Eng. Drama, and Gosse: Seventeenth Cent. Studies).
✠Works; ed. w. memoir and notes, Dyce. 4 v. Lond. 1830.
 Dram. Works; ed. Hazlitt. 4 v. Lond. Smith. 1857. 20/.
 White Devil, and Duchess of Malfi; ed. w. introd. and notes, Symonds. Lond. Vizetelly. 1888. 2/6. (Mermaid Ser.)

† Acad. 42 : 339.
Blackwood's. 2 : 656. (Duchess of Malfi). 3 : 556, (White Devil).
Bodenstedt. Sh.'s Zeitgenossen, 1.
Gosse. Seventeenth Cent. Studies.
Hazlitt. Dram. Lit. of the Age of Eliz.
Lamb. Specimens of Eng. Dram. Poetry.
Lowell. Old Eng. Dramatists.
Meiners, M. Metrische Untersuchungen den Dramatiker J. Webster. Halle diss. 1893.
Retro. Rev. 1823. 7 : 87.
Swinburne. Nineteenth Cent. June, 1886. 19 : 861. Same, Ecl. Mo. 107 : 227. Same, Littell's Liv. Age. 170 : 67.
Symonds. Italian By-ways. (Vittoria Accoramboni). Lond. Smith and Elder. 1883. 10/6.

WHITE, ROBERT. Fl. 1617.

Cupid's Banishment. Masque. 1617.
† Nichols. Progresses of James I. 3 : 283.

WILKINS, GEORGE. Fl. 1607.

*Miseries of inforced Marriage. 1607.
*Travels of the Three English Brothers. 1607. (With Day and W. Rowley).
† Fleay : Biog. Chron. Eng. Drama.
Jahrbuch. (Sh.) 3 : 169 ; 23 : 132 ; 27 : 143, 155.

WILSON, ARTHUR. 1595—1652.

*Inconstant Lady. (Also known as Better Late than Never). Pr. 1814.

RESTORATION DRAMA.

DRAMATISTS.

Behn, Mrs.
Betterton.
Boyle. (Orrery).
Cavendish, Margaret.
Cavendish, Wm.
Chamberlayne.
Cokayne.
CONGREVE.
Crowne.
D'AVENANT.
Digby.
DRYDEN.
ETHEREGE.
FARQUHAR.
Hopkins.
Howard, Edw.
Howard, (Sir) Robt.
Killigrew, Th.
Killigrew, Th., the Younger.
Killigrew, (Sir) Wm.
Lacy.
Lee.
Lower.
Mountford.
OTWAY.
Pix, (Mrs.)
Sedley.
Settle.
Shadwell.
Stapylton.
Tate.
Tatham.
Tuke.
VANBRUGH.
Villiers.
Wilson.
WYCHERLEY.

BEHN, (Mrs.) APHRA. 1640—'89.

Forc'd Marriage. 1671.
Amorous Prince. 1671.
Dutch Lover. 1673.
Abdelazar. 1676.
Rover. Part 1. 1677.
Debauchee. 1677.
Town Fop. 1677.
Sir Patient Fancy. 1678. (From Molière's Malade Imaginaire).
Rover. Part 2. 1681.
Roundheads. 1682.
City Heiress. 1682.
False Count. 1682.
Young King. 1683.
Lucky Chance. 1687.
Emperor of the Moon. 1687.
Widow Ranter. Pub. 1690.
Younger Brother. Pub. 1696.
✻Plays, Histories and Novels, with Life and Memoir. Lond. Pearson. 1871. 6v. 52/6.
† Bayle. Dictionary. 3 : 140 ; 10 : 126.
Dunham. Lives of Lit. and Sci. Men. 3.
Fitzgerald. Hist. of the Eng. Stage. 1 : 188–190.
Forsyth. Novels and Novelists.
Jeafferson. Novels and Novelists. 1. 20 pp.
Kavanagh. Eng. Women of Letters.
Periodicals.
   Mrs. Behn and her Novels. Dub. Univ. 47 : 536. *Same.* Littell's Liv. Age. 49 : 800.
   Dram. Writings. Retros. Rev. 17 : 1.
   England's First Lady Novelist. St. James. 7 : 351.
   Works. Amer. Bibliopolist. 4 : 303.
   Temple Bar. 71 : 388. *Same.* Ecl. Mag. 103 : 400.
Robertson. Eng. Poetesses.
Williams. Literary Women.

BETTERTON, THOMAS. 1635 (?)—1710.

Roman Virgin ; or, The Unjust Judge. 1670. (1679). (Alteration of Webster's Appius and Virginia).
Prophetess ; or, The History of Diocletian. 1690. (Founded on The Prophetess of Beaumont and Fletcher).
✻King Henry IV., with the Humours of Sir John Falstaff. 1700. (Sh.'s Henry IV. with omissions).
Amorous Widow ; or, The Wanton Wife. 1706. (Adaptation of Georges Daudin).
✻Bondman ; or, Love and Liberty. 1719. (Altered from Massinger).
Woman made a Justice.
✻Revenge ; or, A Match in Newgate. 1680. (Alteration of Marston's Malcontent). Assigned by Langbaine to Mrs. Behn.
† Anonymous. The Life of Mr. Thomas Betterton. 1710.
Austin and Ralph. Poets-laureate.
Baker. Eng. Actors. 1 : 50. Betterton and his Associates.

Cibber, Colley. Apology. 1740.
Dibdin. Hist. of the Stage.
Doran. Annals of the Stage. 1.
Fitzgerald. New Hist. of the Eng. Stage. 1.
Galt. Lives of Players. 1.
Life and Times of Betterton; by the editor of "Life of Quin." Lond. Reader. 1888. 7/6.
Russell, W. Rep. Actors.
Tatler. 1, 2, and 4.

BOYLE, ROGER. Baron Broghill and first Earl of Orrery. 1621—'79.

*Henry V. 1664.
*Mustapha, the Son of Solyman the Magnificent. 1665.
Black Prince. 1667.
Guzman. 1669.
Tryphon. 1672.
Mr. Anthony. 1690.
Herod the Great. (1694).
Altemira. (1702).
⁂The Complete Dram. Works of the Earl of Orrery. (Without Mr. Anthony). 1743.
†?Clarendon. Hist. of the Rebellion.
Evelyn. Diary.
Morrice, T. Life of the Earl of Orrery. 106 p. (*In* Boyle, R. *Earl of Orrery.* Collection of State Letters. v. 1. Dublin. 1743).
Pepys. Diary.
?Ware. Writers of Ireland.
?Whitelocke. Memorials.

CAVENDISH, MARGARET. Duchess of Newcastle. 1624 (?)—'74.

Love's Adventures.
Second Part of Love's Adventures.
Several Wits.
Youth's Glory and Death's Banquet.
Second Part of Youth's Glory and Death's Banquet.
Lady Contemplation. Part I.
Lady Contemplation. Part II.
Wit's Cabal. Part I.
Wit's Cabal. Part II.
Unnatural Tragedy.
Public Wooing.
Matrimonial Trouble. Part I.
Matrimonial Trouble. Part II.
Nature's Three Daughters, Beauty, Love and Wit. Part I.
Nature's Three Daughters. Part II.
Religions.
Comical Hash.
Bell in Campo. Part I.
Bell in Campo. Part II.
Apocryphal Ladies.
Female Academy.
 [The above plays were printed by the Duchess in folio, 1662].
Convent of Pleasure.

Sociable Companions; or, The Female Wits.
Presence.
Bridals.
Blazing World.
[The above plays were printed by the Duchess in folio, 1668].
✠Plays. Lond. 1762—8. 2 v.
Select Poems. 1813.
True Relation of the Birth, Breeding and Life of Margaret Cavendish, Duchess of Newcastle, written by Herself. 1814.
† Badard. Memories of British Ladies. 1775.
Blackwood's. (Notice of Poems and Plays. '5 p.) 4: 300. 1818. Blackwood's. (On the "World's Olio." 4 p.) 5: 30. 1819.
Connoisseur. 2: 265. ed. 1774.
Jeafferson. Novels and Novelists. 1.
Letters and Poems in Honour of the incomparable Princess Margaret, Duchess of Newcastle, Written by several Persons of Honour and Learning. In the Savoy. 1676.
Life; w. a Selection from her Poems, Opinions, Orations and Letters. Ed. Edward Jenkins. Macmillan. 1872. 4/6.
Pepys. Diary. 30 March, 1667. 12 April, 1667.
Retro. Rev. 1. 1853.
Walpole. Royal and Noble Authors.

CAVENDISH, WILLIAM. Duke of Newcastle. 1592—1676.

Country Captain. 1649.
Variety. 1649.
Humorous Lovers. 1677.
Triumphant Widow; or, The Medley of Humours. 1677.
† Cavendish, William and Mary. Joint Lives; ed. M. A. Lower. Library of Old Authors. Lond. Smith. 1872. Ed. C. H. Firth. 1886.
Life of the Duke of Newcastle, by the Duchess. Lond. 1667. Repr. of first ed. M. A. Lower. Library of Old Authors. 1872. 5/. Another ed., w. notes and illus. papers, by C. H. Firth. Lond. Nimmo. 1886. 21/.

CHAMBERLAYNE, WILLIAM. 1620—'89.

Love's Victory. Pub. 1658. (Acted in 1678 under title of Wits led by the Nose; or, A Poet's Revenge).
† Retro. Rev. 1, pt. 2: 258. 1820. (Rev. of Love's Victory).

COKAYNE, (COKAIN) (Sir) ASTON. 1608—'84.

*Obstinate Lady. 1657.
*Trappolin supposed a Prince. 1658.
Mask at Brethie. 1658.
*Ovid's Tragedy. 1669.
✠Small Poems of Divers Sorts. Lond. 1658. (Contains "Obstinate Lady," "Trappolin," etc. Some copies are entitled,"A Chaine of Golden Poems").
Poems; w. Obstinate Lady, Trappolin, and Tragedy of Ovid, 1662.
Plays. 1669.
Dram. Works. Lond. Sotheran. 1872. 10/6.
† British Bibliographer. 2: 450—63.

CONGREVE, WILLIAM. 1672—1728.

*Old Bachelor. 1693.
*Double-Dealer. 1693.
*Love for Love. 1695.
*Mourning Bride. 1697.
*Way of the World. 1700.
 Judgment of Paris. Masque.
 Semele. Opera.
✻Dram. Works. Dublin. 1731.
 Dram. Works; w. biog. and crit. notices by Leigh Hunt. Lond. Routledge. 1865. 10/6.
 Plays; ed. Jos. Knight. Lawrence and Bullen. *In prep.*
 Best Plays. (Mermaid Series). Lond. Vizetelly. 1887. 2/6.
 Letters; written by and between Dryden, Wycherley, Congreve, and Dennis. Lond. 1696. Another ed. Select works of J. Dennis, v. 2. Lond. 1718. *See also references under IV., Stage Polemics.*
† Cibber. Lives of the Poets.
 Gosse, E. Life of Congreve. Lond. Scott. 1888. 1/. (Great Writers). Bibliog. by Anderson.
 Hazlitt, W. View of the Eng. Stage. Lond. 1818. "Love for Love," p. 226—29. Eng. Comic Writers.
 Johnson. Lives of the Poets.
 L'Estrange, A. G. Hist. of Eng. Humour. 2 v. Lond. 1878. Congreve, I: 355—58.
 Macaulay. Comic Dramatists of the Restoration. (Crit. and Hist. Essays).
 Swinburne. Miscellanies.
 Thackeray. Eng. Humourists.
 Thompson, Jas. Poem to the Memorie of Congreve. Ed. Cunningham. Percy Soc., 9. 1844.

CROWNE, JOHN. —1703?

*Juliana; or, The Princess of Poland. 1671.
*Charles the Eighth. 1672.
*Calisto; or, The Chaste Nymph. Court Masque. 1675.
*Country Wit. 1675.
*Destruction of Jerusalem. Two parts. 1677.
*Ambitious Statesman; or, The Loyal Favorite. 1679.
 Misery of Civil War. 1680. (Founded on the Second Part of Henry VI.)
 Henry the Sixth, First part. 1681.
*Thyestes. 1681. (Founded on Seneca).
*City Politiques. 1683?
*Sir Courtly Nice; or, It Cannot Be. 1685. (Taken from the Spanish).
*Darius, King of Persia. 1688.
*English Frier; or, The Town Sharks. 1690.
*Regulus. 1694.
*Married Beau; or, The Curious Impertinent. 1694. (Taken from Don Quixote).
*Caligula. 1698.
✻Dram. Works; w. pref., memoir and notes. Edinb. 1873—'74. 4 v. Sotheran. 42/.
† Dunham. Lit. and Sci. Men.

Fitzgerald. New Hist. of the Eng. Stage. (Anecdote). 1: 173.
Rochester. Poems. 1685. Timon, a Satyr.
Rochester and Buckingham. Tryal of the Poets for the Bayes.

D'AVENANT, (Sir) WILLIAM. 1606—'68.

*Albovine, King of the Lombards. 1629.
*Cruel Brother. 1630.
*Just Italian. 1630.
*Temple of Love. A Masque. 1634.
*Prince d'Amour. 1635.
*Platonick Lovers. 1636.
*Wits. 1636.
*Britannia Triumphans. A Masque. 1637.
*Salmacida Spolia. 1639.
*Unfortunate Lovers. 1643.
*Love and Honour. 1649.
*Entertainment at Rutland House, by Declamations and Musick; after the manner of the Ancients. 1657.
*Siege of Rhodes. Made a Representation by the Art of Prospective in Scenes and the story sung in recitative Musick. 1656.
Cruelty of the Spaniards in Peru. 1658.
History of Sir Francis Drake. 1659.
[Two plays above subsequently incorporated in "The Playhouse to be Let, first printed in folio collection, 1673].
*Law against Lovers. 1662. (Alteration of Measure for Measure).
*Rivals. 1668. (Alteration of The Two Noble Kinsmen).
*Tempest; or, The Enchanted Island. (With Dryden). 1670. (Alteration of The Tempest).
*Macbeth. 1667? (Alteration of Macbeth).
*Man's the Master. 1669.
Also
    *News from Plymouth.
    *Fair Favorite.
    *Distresses. (Spanish Lovers).
    *Siege.
✠Plays. Folio Ed. 1673.
Collected Dramas; w. memoir. 5 v. ed. Laing and Maidment. Edinb. Sotheran. 1872—'74.
† Austin and Ralph. Lives of the Poets-laureate.
Clarendon. Hist. of the Rebellion.
Delius. Sh.'s Macbeth u. Davenant's Macbeth. Jahrbuch, (Sh.) 20, 1885.
Disraeli. Quarrels of Authors.
Dunham. Lives of Lit. and Sci. Men. 3.
Elze, Karl. "Sir William Davenant." (Sh. Jahrb. 4. 1869).
Fischer, H. Gibt es einen von Dryden und Davenant bearbeiteten Julius Cæsar? (Anglia, 8: 415—18).
Gosse. Shakspere to Pope.
Hogarth. Dramas of Davenant. Memor. of the Opera. 1: 72.
Malone. Hist. Account of the Eng. Stage.
Morgan, A. Shakespeare's Literary Executor. Mag. Am. Hist. 16: 516.
Pepys' Diary.
Robinson, E. Retrosp. Rev. n. s. 2. 1854.
Whitelocke. Memorials.
            For Davenant's "Gondibert" and its reviews, see Peabody Cat.

DIGBY, GEORGE, Second Earl of Bristol. 1612—'77.
* Elvira; or, The Worst not always True. A Comedy Written by a Person of Quality. Lond. 1667.
*?Adventures of Five Hours. 1663. (With Sir Samuel Tuke).
† Cunningham. Lives of Eminent and Illustrious Englishmen. 1837. 3: 29—32.
Clarendon. Hist. of the Rebellion.
Lodge. Portraits. 1850. 6: 23—39.

DRYDEN, JOHN. 1631—1700.

Wild Gallant. 1663.
Rival Ladies. 1663.
Indian Queen. (With Sir Robert Howard). 1664.
*Indian Emperor. 1665.
Secret Love; or, The Maiden Queen. 1667.
Sir Martin Mar-all. 1667. (Founded on the Duke of Newcastle's translation of Molière's L'Etourdi).
*Tempest. (With D'Avenant). 1667. (Altered from Shakespeare).
Evening's Love; or, The Mock Astrologer. 1668.
Tyrannic Love; or, The Royal Martyr. 1669.
Conquest of Grenada. 2 pts. 1670. 1672.
Marriage à la Mode. 1672.
Assignation; or, Love in a Nunnery. 1672.
Amboyna: or, The Cruelties of the Dutch to the English Merchants. 1673.
*State of Innocence. An Opera. Not Acted. 1674. (Founded upon Milton's Paradise Lost, pub. 1669).
*Aurengzebe; or, The Great Mogul. 1675.
*All for Love. 1677—'78.
Kind Keeper; or, Mr. Limberham. 1678.
*Œdipus. (Acts I. and III. The rest by Lee). 1679.
Troilus and Cressida. 1679. (Adapted from Shakespeare).
*Spanish Friar; or, The Double Discovery. 1681.
Duke of Guise. (With Lee). 1682.
Albion and Albanius. An Opera. 1685.
*Don Sebastian. 1690.
*Amphitryon. 1690.
King Arthur. 1691. (Sequel to Albion and Albanius).
Cleomenes. (Finished by Southerne). 1692.
Love Triumphant. 1694.
*Rehearsal. 1671. (Satiric drama ridiculing the heroic tragedies of the day and especially, under the name of Bayes, Dryden. Written ostensibly by the Duke of Buckingham, with possible help from Butler, Sprat and others).
Essay on Dram. Poesy. 1668. (Neander=Dryden).
Essay on Heroic Plays. 1670.
Essay on Dram. Poetry of the Last Age. 1672.
(See also references under IV., Stage Polemics).
✱Works; ed. Sir W. Scott; re-ed. G. Saintsbury. 18 v. Lond. Paterson. 1889. Ea. 10/6.
Works; ed. Peter Cunningham. Lond. 1854.
Aurengzebe; ed. K. Deighton, with biog. introd. and notes. Lond. Constable. 1892. 6/.
Essays; Selected and ed. C. D. Yonge. Lond. Macmillan. 1881. 2/6.

Letters; written by and between Dryden, Wycherley, Congreve and Dennis. Lond. 1696. Another ed. Select Works of J. Dennis, 2. Lond. 1718.
† Beljame, Alex. Le Public and les Hommes de Lettres on Angleterre. 1881.
Bobertag, F. Dryden's Theorie des Dramas. (Eng. Studien, 4: 373—404).
    Dryden's Trauerspiel Antonius u. Kleopatra. Deutsch von Fr. Ohlsen. Altona. 1886. Engl. Studien, 10: 125.
Clough, A. Prose Remains. p. 325.
Coleridge, H. Essays, 2: 28.
Delius. Dryden u. Sh. Jahrbuch, 4. 1869.
De Quincey. Literary Criticism. p. 401—5. Dryden's Hexastich. Same. Note book of an Eng. Opium-eater, p. 281—5.
Gosse. Eighteenth Cent. Lit. ch. 12.
Hazlitt. Eng. Poets.
Holzausen, P. Dryden's Heroisches Drama. (Eng. Studien, 13: 414—45; 15: 13—52; 16: 201—229).
Johnson. Lives of the Poets.
Lowell. Among my Books.
Macaulay. Crit. and Misc. Essays, 1.
Malone. Life of Dryden. (In Dryden's Misc. Prose Works. 1).
Masson. Dryden and the Lit. of the Restoration. (In his Three Devils, etc.)
Ohlsen, Fr. Dryden as a Dramatist and Critic. Progr. d. Realgym., etc. Zu Altona. 1883. (Notice by F. Bobertag. Eng. Studien, 7: 379).
Perry. Eng. Lit. of the Eighteenth Cent.
Rossetti. Famous Poets.
Saintsbury, G. Dryden. Lond. Macmillan. N. Y. Harper. 1881. 75c. (Eng. Men of Letters).
Scott, Sir W. Life of Dryden. (In Dryden's Compl. Works. 1808).
Swinburne. Miscellanies.
Taine. Eng. Lit.

ETHEREGE, (Sir) GEORGE. 1636?—'94?

Comical Revenge; or, Love in a Tub. 1664.
*She Would if she Could. 1667.
*Man of Mode; or, Sir Fopling Flutter. 1676.
✠ Works; ed., w. introd. and notes, A. W. Verity. Lond. Nimmo. 1888. 16/.
Works. Lond. 1704.
Lady of Pleasure; A Satire; Madam Nelly's Complaint; A Satire. (Villiers, G. Duke of Buckingham. Works, 1).
(MS. The Letterbook of Sir George Etheredge, Brit. Museum).
† Athen. 1888. 2: 409.
Bell, R. Comedies of Etherege. (Fortn. Rev. 3: 298. 1866).
Dunham. Lit. and Sci. Men. 3: 175.
Gosse. Seventeenth Cent. Studies. Same. Cornhill, 43: 284. Littell's Liv. Age. 149: 259.
Hazlitt. Eng. Comic Writers.

FARQUHAR, GEORGE. 1678—1707.

Love and a Bottle. 1699.
*Constant Couple; or, A Trip to the Jubilee. 1699.
*Sir Harry Wildair. 1701.
*Inconstant; or, The Way to Win him. 1702.

*Twin Rivals. 1702.
Stage Coach. Farce. (With Motteux). 1704.
*Recruiting Officer. 1706.
*Beaux' Stratagem. 1707.
⁂Dram. Works; w. biog. and crit. notices by L. Hunt. Lond. Routledge. 1865. 10/6. ·(With Wycherley).
Dram. Works; ed. Alec. C. Ewald, w. life and notes. 2 v. Lond. Unwin. 1892. 21/.
† Baker, G. P. Harper's Mo. Mag. 3: 54.
Chetwood. Hist. of the Stage. 1749.
Dunham. Lives of Lit. and Sci. Men. 3.
Egerton. Memoirs of Mrs. Oldfield. 1731.
Fitzgerald. Hist. of the Stage.
Galt. Lives of Players.
Gosse. Gossip in a Library.
Guiney, Louise Imogen. A Little Eng. Gallery. "George Farquhar." N. Y. $1.00. Harper. 1894.
Hazlitt. Eng. Comic Writers.
Huntington, H. A. Athen. 49: 399.
Life of Wilkes. Pub. by Curll. 1733.
Macaulay. Comic Dramatists of the Restoration. (Crit. and Hist. Essays).
O'Bryan, Daniel. Memoirs of Wilkes. 1732.
Thackeray. Eng. Humourists.
Ware. Writers of Ireland.

HOPKINS, CHARLES. 1664—1700.

Pyrrhus, King of Epirus. 1695. (Prologue by Congreve).
*Boadicea, Queen of Britain. 1697.
Friendship Improved; or, The Female Warrior. 1697.
† Jacob, Giles. Poetical Register, or Lives and Characters of the English Dramatic Poets. 1723. 1: 318.
Scott, Sir W. Dryden's Life and Works. 1821. 18: 163.

HOWARD, EDWARD. 1624?—?
(Brother of Sir Robert Howard).

Usurper. 1668.
Six Days' Adventure; or, The New Utopia. 1671.
Women's Conquest. 1671.
Man of Newmarket. 1678.
British Princes; An Heroic Poem. Lond. 1669.
Poems and Essays, with a paraphrase on Cicero's Laelius in heroic verse. Lond. 1674.
† Gent. Mag. 1850. 2: 369.
Pepys. Diary. April 12, 1667.

HOWARD, (Sir) ROBERT. 1626—98.

Blind Lady. (Pub. with his Poems, 1660).
Four New Plays. 1665.
   Surprisal. Comedy.
  *Committee. Comedy.
   Vestal Queen. Tragedy.
   Indian Queen. Tragedy. (With Dryden).

Great Favorite; or, The Duke of Lerma. Tragedy. 1668.
✠Howard's Plays. (Excepting The Blind Lady). Fol. ed. 1692. 1722.
Indian Queen; by Howard and Dryden. (*In* Dryden's Works. 1, 1808). (*See also references under IV., Stage Polemics*).
† Cibber. Lives of the Poets.
Dryden. Essay of Dram. Poesy. (Crites=Howard).
Evelyn. Diary.
Hogarth. Memoirs of Opera.
Pepys. Diary.
Shadwell. The Sullen Lovers. 1668. (Howard ridiculed under the character of Sir Positive At-All).
Suckling. Session of the Poets. (Contemptuous reference to Howard).

KILLIGREW, THOMAS. 1612—'83.

Contents of Folio Edition, 1664.
　Princess; or, Love at First Sight.
　*Parson's Wedding.
　Pilgrim.
　First Part of Cicilia and Clorinda; or, Love in Arms.
　Second Part of Cicilia and Clorinda.
　Thomaso; or, The Wanderer.
　The Second Part of Thomaso.
　Claracilla.
　Prisoners.
　First Part of Bellamira her Dream; or, The Love of Shadows.
　Second Part of Bellamira.

KILLIGREW, THOMAS. (The Younger). 1657—1719.

Chit Chat. 1719.
† Carew. Poem on "The Marriage of T. K. and C. C."
Clarendon. History of the Rebellion.
Fleay. Chronicle of the Eng. Drama.
Genest. Account of the Eng. Stage.
Halliwell. Ancient Documents concerning the Office of Master of the Revels.
Quarles. "Sighes at the contemporary Deaths of Mistress Cicely Killigrew" and her sister, the Countess of Cleveland.

KILLIGREW, (Sir) WILLIAM. 1606—'95.

Three Plays, pub. 1665.
　Selindra.
　Pandora.
　Ormasdes.
Four New Plays. 1666.
　The Same, with the addition of
　Siege of Urbin.
　Love and Friendship, being another title for Ormasdes.
† Dict. Nat. Biog.

LACY, JOHN.   —1681.

*Old Troop; or, Monsieur Raggou. 1664? 1672.
*Sawny the Scot. 1667. 1698.
*Dumb Lady. 1669. 1772.
*Sir Hercules Buffoon; or, The Poetical Squire. 1684.
✠Dramatic Works; with Pref., Memoirs and Notes. Lond. Sotheran. 1875. 10/6.
† Aubrey. Letters by Eminent Persons. 1813.
  Doran. Annals of the Stage.
  Dub. Univ. 45 : 278. Mem. of Lacy Family.
  Pepys. Diary.
  NOTE. *Not to be confused with Lacy, Th. Hailes, (1809–'73) ed. Lacy's Acting Edition of Plays. 1848—1873. 99 v. 1,485 plays. Retired in spring of 1873, when his business was transferred to Samuel French of New York. Also proprietor of John Cumberland's British Theatre, (399 dramas in 48 v.) and of Cumberland's Minor Theatre, (152 plays in 16 v.) Left £8,000 to Gen. Theatre Fund. Made such plays as Pickwickians, Martin Chuzzlewit, Clarissa Harlowe; and translations from the French.*

LEE, NATHANIEL. 1658?—'92.

*Nero. 1675.
 Gloriana; or, The Court of Augustus Cæsar. 1676.
 Sophonisba; or, Hannibal's Overthrow. 1676.
*Rival Queens; or, The Death of Alexander the Great. 1677.
 Mithridates, King of Pontus. 1678.
*Œdipus. 1679. (With Dryden).
 Cæsar Borgia. 1680.
*Theodosius; or, The Force of Love. 1680.
*Lucius Junius Brutus, the Father of his Country. 1681.
 Princess of Cleve. Comedy. 1681.
 Duke of Guise. 1682. (With Dryden).
 Constantine the Great. 1684.
✠Tragedies Collected. 1713. 2 v.
 Works. Lond. 1722. 3 v.
 Dramatick Works. Lond. 1734—'35. 3 v.
† Addison. The Spectator. 39.
  Beljame's Le Public et les Hommes de Lettres. 1660—1744.
  Cibber. Lives of the Poets.
  Dunham. Lives of Lit. and Sci. Men. 3.
  Mosen. Engl. Studien, 2 : 416.
  Retro. Rev. 3 : 240-68. 1821.
  Wotton, M. E. Theatre. 2 : 76. 1886.

LOWER, (Sir) WILLIAM. 1600?—'62.

Phœnix in her Flames. 1639.
Polyeuctes; or, The Martyr. 1655. (From Corneille).
Horatius. 1656. (From Corneille).
Three Dorothies. 1657. (MS.) (From Scarron).
Don Japhet of Armenia. 1657. (MS.) (From Scarron).
Amorous Fantasme. 1659. (From Quinault).
Noble Ingratitude. 1661.
Enchanted Lovers. 1661. Pastoral.
† Dict. Nat. Biog.

MOUNTFORD, WILLIAM. 1664?—'92.

Injur'd Lovers; or, The Ambitious Father. 1688.
Life and Death of Dr. Faustus. 1697. (Taken from Marlowe).
Successful Strangers. 1690. (Founded on a novel by Scarron).
King Edward the Third. 1691.
Greenwich Park. 1691.
Zelmane. Pr. 1720.
✠Six Plays written by Mr. Mountford, ed. Bancroft. Lond. 1720.
† Cibber. Lives of the Poets.
Doran. Their Majesties' Servants.
Galt. Lives of the Players.

OTWAY, THOMAS. 1651—'85.

Alcibiades. 1675.
Don Carlos. 1676.
Titus and Berenice. 1677. (Taken from Racine).
*Cheats of Scapin. 1677. (Taken from Molière).
Friendship in Fashion. 1678.
History and Fall of Caius Marius. 1680.
*Orphan; or, The Unhappy Marriage. 1680.
Soldier's Fortune. 1681.
*Venice Preserved; or, A Plot Discovered. 1682.
Atheist; or, The Second Part of the Soldier's Fortune. 1684.
✠Works; w. a sketch of his life, enlarged from that written by Dr. Johnson. Lond. 1812. 2 v.
Works; w. crit. and explan. and a life of the author by T. Thornton. Lond. 1813. 3 v.
Selections; ed. R. Noel, with introd. and notes. Lond. Scott. 1888. 2/6. (Mermaid Ser.)
Letters. See Wilmot, J. Second Earl of Rochester, and others. Familiar Letters.
† Barante, A. G. P. B. de. (In his Mélanges Historiques, 3).
Dunham. Lives of Lit. and Sci. Men.
Gosse. Seventeenth Cent. Studies.
Johnson, Samuel. Life of Otway. (In Chalmers' Eng. Poets, 8).
Mosen, R. Ueber T. Otway's Leben u. Werke. (Engl. Studien, 1: 425—56).
Periodicals.
    Cornh. 36: 679. Templ. Bar. 57: 95. Same. Appleton, 22: 392. Spec. 62: 645.
Ward. Eng. Dram. Lit.
Wotton. Word Portraits, 231.

PIX, (Mrs.) MARY. Reign of Wm. III.

Spanish Wives. 1696.
Ibrahim the Thirteenth. 1696.
Innocent Mistress. 1697.
Deceiver Deceived. 1698.
Queen Catherine. 1698.
False Friend. 1699.
Beau Defeated. n. d.

Czar of Muscovy. 1701.
Double Distress. 1701.
Conquest of Spain. 1705.
Adventures in Madrid. n. d.
(Ridiculed, with Mrs. Manley and Mrs. Cockburn, in comedy of The Female Wits).

SEDLEY, (Sir) CHARLES. 1639?—1728?

Mulberry Garden. 1668. (Partly founded on Molière's L'Ecole des Maris).
*Anthony and Cleopatra. 1677. (Reprinted in 1702 as Beauty the Conqueror or, The Death of Mark Antony).
Bellamira; or, The Mistress. 1687. (Founded on the Eunuchus of Terence).
Grumbler. 1702. (Translation from the French).
Tyrant King of Crete. 1702. (Alteration of Henry Killigrew's The Conspiracy, pr. 1638, or of its revised edition, Pallantus and Eudora, pr. 1653).
✠Works. 2 v. Lond. 1722.
† Dryden. Essay of Dram. Poesy. (Lisideius=Sedley).
Dunham. Lives of Lit. and Sci. Men. 3.
Lond. Mag. 6: 265. Memoirs of Sedley.
Pepys. Diary.

SETTLE, ELKANAH. 1648—1724.

Cambyses, King of Persia. 1671.
Empress of Morocco. 1673.
Love and Revenge. 1675.
Conquest of China by the Tartars. 1676.
Ibrahim, the Illustrious Bassa. 1677.
Pastor Fido; or, The Faithful Shepherd. 1677.
Fatal Love; or, The Forced Inconstancy. 1680.
Female Prelate, being the History of the Life and Death of Pope Joan. 1680.
Heir of Morocco. 1682.
Distressed Innocence; or, The Princess of Persia. 1691.
New Athenian Comedy. 1693.
Ambitious Slave; or, A Generous Revenge. 1694.
Philaster; or, Love lies a Bleeding. 1695.
World in the Moon. 1697.
Virgin Prophetess; or, The Fate of Troy. An Opera. 1701.
Siege of Troy. 1707.
City Ramble; or, The Playhouse Wedding. 1711.
Lady's Triumph. 1718.
Triumphs for the Inauguration of the Lord Mayor.
Drolls for Bartholomew Fair.
† Dryden. Absalom and Achitophel. Second Part. (Doeg=Settle).
Dunton, J. Life and Errors. 1705. Re-pr. in 1818, w. life by J. B. Nichols; also in Nichols's Lit. Anecd.
Morley, Henry. Memories of Bartholomew Fair. Lond. Chatto. 1880. 7/6.

SHADWELL, THOMAS. 1640—'92.

Sullen Lovers; or, The Impertinents. 1668. (Founded on Les Fâcheux of Molière).
*Miser. 1671. (Founded on Molière's L'Avare).
Humourists. 1671.

Psyche. (Opera). 1674.
Epsom Wells. 1675.
Virtuoso. 1676.
Libertine. 1676. (Founded on Molière's Le Festin de Pierre).
The History of Timon of Athens, the Man-Hater. 1678. (Taken from Shakespeare).
True Widow. 1679.
Woman-Captain. 1680.
Lancashire Witches, and Tegue O'Divelly, the Irish Priest. 1681.
Squire of Alsatia. 1688.
Bury-Fair. 1689.
Amorous Bigot, with the Second Part of Tegue O'Divelly. 1690.
Volunteers; or the Stock-Jobbers. 1692.
Scourers. 1693.

[For Controversy with Dryden, see Shadwell: The Medal of John Bayes, and Dryden; Second Part of Absolom and Achitophel, Mac Flecknoe].

✠Dramatic Works. 4 v. Lond. 1720.
Selections; ed. w. introd. and notes. G. Saintsbury. Lond. Vizetelly. 1880. 2/6.
† Austin. Poets-laureate.
Dunham. Lives of Lit. and Sci. Men. 3.
Retro. Rev. 2:55. 1828.

STAPYLTON, (Sir) ROBERT.   —1669.

Slighted Maid. 1663.
Stepmother. 1664.
*Hero and Leander. 1669.

TATE, NAHUM. 1652—1715.

Brutus of Alba. 1678.
Loyal General. 1680.
King Lear. (Altered from Shakespeare). 1681.
Richard II. 1681.
Ingratitude of a Commonwealth: or, The Fall of Coriolanus. 1682.
Cuckolds' Haven. 1685.
*Duke and No Duke. (Altered from Cokayne's Trappolin). 1685.
Island Princess. 1687.
Injured Love. 1707.
Dido and Æneas.
† Austin. Poets-laureate.
Baker. Biographia Dramatica.

TATHAM, JOHN. (City Poet to Chas. I.)

*Love Crowns the End. 1640.
*Distracted State. 1651.
*Scots Figaries. 1652.
*Rump. 1660.
Pageants for 1657, 1658, 1659, 1660, 1661, 1662, 1663, 1664.
✠Dram. Works. Lond. Sotheran. 1879. 10/6.

TUKE, (Sir) SAMUEL.   —1673.

*Adventures of Five Hours. 1662. (Adapted from Calderon).

VANBURGH, (Sir) JOHN. Circ. 1666—1726.

*Relapse; or, Virtue in Danger. 1697. (Sequel to Cibber's Love's Last Shift).
*Provoked Wife. 1697.
False Friend. 1702.
*Confederacy. 1705.
*Mistake. 1705.
Country House. 1705.
A Journey to London. (4 acts). (Fifth Act added by Colley Cibber, who produced the play as *The Provoked Husband. 1728).
✠Dram. Works; w. biog. and crit. notices by L. Hunt. Lond. Routledge. 1865. 10/6. (With Wycherley, Dram. Works).
Plays; ed. W. C. Ward. 2 v. Lond. Lawrence and Bullen. 1893. 25/.
Selections; ed. w. introd. and notes, W. C. Ward. Lond. Vizetelly. 1890. 2/6. (Mermaid Ser.)
Relapse; an adaptation of, by R. W. Buchanan. Theatre, 24: 256.
Letters. Athen. 1890. 2: 289, 321.
(See also references under IV., Stage Polemics).
† Birrell, Augustine. Essays about Men, Women and Books.
Cunningham, A. Sir J. Vanbrugh. (In his Lives of British Painters. v. 4).
Dunham. Lives of Lit. and Sci. Men.
Fitzgerald. Hist. of the Eng. Stage. I.: 337. II.: 328—29.
Hazlitt. Eng. Comic Writers.
Macaulay. Comic Dramatists of the Restoration.
Thackeray. Eng. Humourists.
Ward. Eng. Dram. Lit.

VILLIERS, GEORGE, Duke of Buckingham. 1627—'88.

*Rehearsal. 1672. (Arber Reprint).
✠Works. 2 v. 3d ed. Lond. 1715.
† Brown, T. Some Memoirs on G. Cate, Duke of Buckingham. (Villiers, G., etc. Works, v. 1).
Disraeli. Curiosities of Lit.
Döhler, E. Der Angriff George Villiers auf die heroischen Dramen, u. Dichter Englands in 17 Jahrh. (Anglia, 10: 38—75).
Lodge, E. Portraits.
Menzies, S. Royal Favorites.
Thomson, K. B. and J. C. Wits and Beaux of Society, v. 1.

WILSON, JOHN. —1666.

*Cheats. 1662.
*Projectors. 1664.
*Andronicus Comnenius. 1664.
*Belphegor; or, The Marriage of the Devil. 1691.
✠Dram. Works; ed. w. memoir, Maidment and Logan. Lond. Sotheran. 1874. 10/6.

WYCHERLEY, WILLIAM. 1640—1715.

Love in a Wood; or, St. James Park. 1672.
Gentleman Dancing Master. 1672.
*Country Wife. 1673.

*Plain Dealer. 1674.
✠Dram. Works; w. biog. and crit. notices by L. Hunt. Lond. Routledge. 1865. 10/6.
Selected Plays; ed. W. C. Ward, w. introd. and notes. Lond. Vizetelly. 1888. 2/6. (Mermaid Ser.)
Country Girls. Lacy's (French's) Acting Ed. of Plays. No. 1515.
Letters; written by and between Dryden, Wycherley, Congreve and Dennis. Lond. 1696. Another Ed. Select Works of J. Dennis, 2. Lond. 1718.
Letters on Several Occasions. Pub. by John Dennis. Lond. 1696.
Pope, A. Correspondence, ed. W. J. Courthope. 4 v. Lond. Murray. 1880. 10/6. (See also references under IV., Stage Polemics).
† Clarke, C. C. Gent. Mag. n. s., 7: 823.
Dunham. Lit. and Sci. Men.
Fitzgerald. New Hist. of the Eng. Stage. 1: 183—4.
Granville, G. Genuine Works. 2. (Char. of Wycherley).
Hazlitt. Eng. Comic Writers.
Klette, J. W. Wycherley's Leben u. dram. Werke Mit besonderer berücksichtigung von Wycherley als plagiator Molières. Münster. 1883. Coppenrath. 74 p.
Macaulay. Hist. aud Crit. Essays, 4: 369. Ediu. Rev. 72: 490.
Molloy, J. F. Tinsley, 32: 235.
Mosen, R. Engl. Studien, 8: 131—33.
Sandman. Molière u. Garrick. Herrig's Archiv. 77: 47.
Spence. Anecdotes.
Thackeray. Eng. Humourists.
Ward. Eng. Dram. Lit.

English Drama.—A Working Basis.

EIGHTEENTH CENTURY.

THE REFORMED DRAMA.

THE NEW COMEDY.

PLAYWRIGHTS, ADAPTERS AND TRIFLERS.

Eighteenth Century.

The Reformed Drama.

ADDISON.   STEELE.

The New Comedy.

GOLDSMITH.   SHERIDAN.

Playwrights, Adapters and Triflers. (*Names Only*).

Arbuthnot, John.
Bickerstaff, Isaac.
Boaden, James.
Brevel, John Durant.
Brooke, Henry.
Bullock, Christopher.
Carey, Geo. Saville. (Son of Henry Carey).
Carey, Henry.
Centlivre, (Mrs.) Susanna.
Chetwood, William Rufus.
Cibber, Colley.
Cibber, Theophilus. (Son of Colley Cibber).
Cockburn, (Mrs.) Catherine Trotter.
Colman, George. (The Elder).
Colman, George. (The Younger).
Cowley, (Mrs.) Hannah.
Cumberland, Richard.
Dennis, John.
Dibdin, Chas. (The Elder).
Dibdin, Chas. (The Younger).
Dibdin, Th. (Son of Charles Dibdin, the Elder).
Dodsley, Robert.
D'Urfey, Thomas. ("Tom Durfey.")
Fielding, Henry.
Foote, Samuel.
Francklin, (Dr.) Thomas.
Garrick, David.
Gay, John.
Gentleman, Francis.
Gildon, Charles.
Granville, George.
Harvard, William.
Hill, Aaron.
Holcroft, Thomas.
Home, John.
Hoole, John.
Hughes, John.
Inchbald, (Mrs.) Elizabeth.
Johnson, Chas.
Johnson, Samuel.
Kelly, Hugh.
Lillo, George.
Manley, (Mrs.) Mary de la Rivière.
Mason, William.
Miller, James.
More, (Mrs.) Hannah.
Motteux, Peter Anthony.
Murphy, Arthur.
Oldmixon, John.
Rowe, Nicholas. [*Better than his company*].
Smith, Edmund.
Smollet, Tobias.
Southern, Thomas.
Theobald, Lewis.
Thomson, James.
Townley, James.
Whincop, Thomas.
Whitehead, William.

THE REFORMED DRAMA.

DRAMATISTS.

ADDISON, JOSEPH. 1672—1719.

Fair Rosamond. 1707. (Opera).
*Cato. 1713.
*Drummer. 1713.
✠Addison's Works. W. notes of Bishop Hurd. A short memoir, and a portrait of Addison after G. Kneller. Ed. H. G. Bohn. 6 v. ea., $1.00. Half calf, $2.25 each. v. 1. Plays; Poems; Poemata.
 Works; ed. G. W. Greene, w. notes, etc., Lond. and N. Y. Routledge. 1887. 6 v. 21/.
 Addison's Cato, in Lacy's Acting Edition of Plays. No. 1484.
† Aiken, L. Life of Addison. 2 v. Lond. Longmans. 1843.
 Courthope, W. J. Addison. N. Y. Harper. 1884. 75 cts. (Eng. Men of Letters).
 Ficke. A Critical Exam. of Addison's Cato. Ramscheid. 1885. Eng.? Studien, 9: 367. Anglia, 8: 45—48.
 Johnson, S. Addison. (*In his* Six Chief Lives of the Poets, 1879, p. 273—326).
 Macaulay, T. B. Essays, 5, Life and Writings of Addison. *Same.* Edinb. Rev. 78: 193—260 and Ecl. Mo. 3: 261.
 Phillips, (Sir) R. Addisoniana. 2 v. Lond. 1803.
 Taine. Eng. Lit. 1874. 3: 150—197.
 Thackeray, W. M. Congreve and Addison. (*In his* Eng. Humourists. 1879. p. 156—191).
 Tickell, T. Life of Addison. (*In* Addison, Jos., Works, 1856. 1: 3—12).

STEELE, (Sir) RICHARD. 1671—1729.

*Funeral; or, Grief à-la-Mode. 1702.
 Lying Lover. 1703.
*Tender Husband. 1705.
*Conscious Lovers. 1722.
✠Complete Plays; ed. G. A. Aitken. (Mermaid Ser.) Lond. Unwin. 1894. 3/6. N. Y. Scribner. 1894. $1.25.
 Selected Plays, ed. Geo. R. Carpenter. Bost. Ginn. (Athen. Press Series).
† Aitken, G. A. Life of Richard Steele, w. bibliog. 2 v. Bost. Houghton, Mifflin. 1889. $8.00. Lond. Isbister. 1889. 32/.
 Dennis, J. Sir R. Steele. (*In his* Studies in Eng. Lit. Lond. 1876. p. 148—191. Lond. Stanford. 1876. 7/6).
 Disraeli, I. Sir R. Steele. (*In his* Calamities and Quarrels of Authors. 1859. p. 168—172).
 Dobson, A. R. Lond. Longmans. 1886. 1/. N. Y. Appleton. 75 cts.
 Forster, J. Hist. and Biog. Essays. 2. Lond. Murray. 1860. 12/. Paper on Sir R. Steele. Lond. Quar. Rev. April, 1855.
 Hartmann, H. Steele als Dramatiker. Kneiphöfische Mittelschule. Könisberg. 1880.

Hazlitt, W. Eng. Comic Writers. Lect. 8
McCarthy, J. H. Hours with Eminent Irishmen. p. 109—16.
Macaulay, T. B. Crit. and Hist. Essays.
Minto, W. Enc. Brit. 9th ed. Steele.
Montgomery, H. R. Memoirs of the Life and Writings of Sir R. Steele. 2 v. Edinb. Simpkin. 1865. 24/.
Thackeray. Eng. Humourists.

THE NEW COMEDY.

DRAMATISTS.

GOLDSMITH, OLIVER. 1728—'74.

*Good Natur'd Man. 1768. (Produced at Covent Garden).
*She Stoops to Conquer. 1773. (Produced at Covent Garden).
✷Works. 5 v. Lond. Bohn. ea. $1. (Plays. In separate vol. 50c.)
 Plays; ed. H. Littledale. (Blackie's School Classics). Lond. Blackie. 1884. 2/ and 3/.
 Plays; ed. Austin Dobson. Lond. Dent. 1892. 2/6. N. Y. Macmillan. $1.00.
 Good Natured Man. Lacy's (French's) Acting Ed. of Plays. No. 1629.
† Black, W. Goldsmith. Lond. Macmillan. 1878 and 87. 1/ and 1/6. N. Y. Harper. 75c. and 15c.
 Davies, T. Memoirs of the Life of D. Garrick. 2: 142—164. 2 v. Lond. 1780.
 De Quincey, T. Works. Masson's ed. 1890. 4: 288—322.
 Dobson, H. A. Goldsmith. Lond. Scott. 1889. 1/ and 2/6. (Great Writers). *Bibliog. by Anderson.*
 Forster, J. Life and Adventures of Goldsmith. Lond. 1848 and '54. Life and Times. Lond. Ward. 1890. 2/.
 Hazlitt. Eng. Comic Writers. Lect. 8.
 Hunt, L. Classic Tales. Lond. 1806. 1: 41—80. (Writings and Genius of Goldsmith).
 Hutton, L. Lit. Landmarks of London. p. 118—126. Lond. Unwin. 1885. 3/6 and 2/6.
 Irving, W. Life of Goldsmith. N. Y. Putnam. 1882. $1.75.
 Macaulay, T. B. Enc. Brit., 8th and 9th eds. Goldsmith. *Same.* Misc. Works.
 Prior, (Sir) James. Life of Goldsmith. 2 v. Lond. Murray. 1836. 30/. 1849. 21/.
 Rossetti. Lives of Famous Poets.
 Thackeray. Eng. Humourists.

SHERIDAN, RICHARD BRINSLEY. 1751—1816.

*Rivals. 1775.
 St. Patrick's Day. 1775.
*Duenna. 1775.
*Trip to Scarborough. 1777.
*School for Scandal. 1777.

*Critic. 1779.
*Pizarro. 1799.
(Sheridan's first three plays were produced at Covent Garden, and the others at Drury Lane, in which he became share-holder, 1776).

✠Dram. Works; w. biog. and crit. sketch by Leigh Hunt. Lond. Moxon. 1848. 4/6.
Works; (dramas, poems, translations, speeches, and unfinished sketches), ed. F. Stainforth. Lond. Chatto. 1874. 7/6.
Dram. Works, Complete. With Life by G. G. S., and Portrait. Bohn. $1.00. (Plays in separate volume. 50c.)
Dram. Works; w. introd. by R. Grant White. N. Y. 1883. Dodd, Mead & Co. $15.00.
Dram. Works; w. memoir by J. P. Browne, and extracts from life by T. Moore. Phil. Lippincott. 1876. $3.50. Lond. Ward. 1891. 3/6.
Dram. Works. Lond. Gibbings. 1891. 7/6. Bost. Houghton. $1.50. (Standard Brit. Classics).
Plays; ed. by Dircks. Lond. Scott. 1891. 2/. Camelot Ser. 1/.
Plays; w. introd. by H. Morley. Lond. Routledge. 1892. 2 eds. 5/ and 2/.
Rivals; w. introd. and notes by B. Matthews; ill. by E. A. Abbey and C. S. Reinhart. Lond. Chatto. 1885. 12/6. Boston. Osgood. 1884. $3.00.
School for Scandal, ill. by F. M. Gregory. N. Y. Dodd. 1892. $3.50. Lond. Stevens. 16/.
Lacy's (French's) Acting Ed. of Plays. Trip to Scarborough. No. 1540. St. Patrick's Day. No. 1702.
† Bardsley, S. A. Critical remarks on Pizarro, a tragedy taken from the German Drama of Kotzebue and adapted to the Eng. Stage by Sheridan. Lond. 1800.
Brougham. Statesmen of the time of George III., v. 1.
Byron, (Lord). Monody on the death of Sheridan. Lond. 1816. Works, 1818, v. 5; p. 171—79.
Crawfurd, O. J. F. ed. Eng. Comic Dramatists. Lond. Paul. 1884. 6/. N. Y. Appleton. $1.25.
Engl. Studien, 4: 361—64 and 7: 169—171.
Fitzgerald, Percy. Lives of the Sheridans. 2 v. Lond. Bentley. 1887. 30/.
Hazlitt. Eng. Comic Writers. Lect. 8.
Klapperich, J. Zur Sprache des Lustspiel Dichters R. B. Sheridan. Ostern. 1892. Lpz. G. Fock. 1 m. (J. G. C. Schuler. Engl. Studien, 17: 280—284).
Lefanu, A. Memoirs of the Life and Writings of Mrs. Frances Sheridan, with remarks for a late life of R. B. Sheridan. Lond. 1824.
McCarthy, J. H. Hours with Eminent Irishmen. p. 117—25. N. Y. Ford's Nat. Lib. 1886. $1.00.
Mangin, E. Letter to T. Moore on the subject of Sheridan's School for Scandal. Bath. 1826.
Matthews, Brander. Princ. Rev. n. s. 13: 292—303. Sheridan and his Biographers. A review of lives of S. by Watkins, Moore, Smyth, Mrs. Oliphant and Rae. Also of the sketches by Leigh Hunt, "The Octogenarian," Grace and Philip Wharton, and G. S. Sigmund.
Moore, T. Memoirs of the Life of R. B. Sheridan. 2 v. Lond. Middleton. 1825. $3.00. (Blackwood's, v. 19 and 20. Westminster Rev., 4: 371—407. Quarterly Rev., 33: 561—93).
Minto, W. R. B. Sheridan. Ency. Brit. 9th ed.
Molloy, J. F. Famous Plays; their Histories and Authors. p. 175—218, Rivals, and School for Scandal.

Oliphant, *Mrs.* Marg. O. (Wilson). R. B. Sheridan. N. Y. Harper. 1883. 75c. (Eng. Men of Letters). Macmillan. 1883 and 1889. 2/6 and 1/6.
Pearson, Chas. H. Reviews and Crit. Essays.
Rae, W. F. R. B. Sheridan. Lond. Isbister. 1873. 18/. (*In his* Wilkes, Sheridan, Fox). N. Y. Appleton. 1874. $2.00. Holt. 1896. $7.00.
Sanders, Lloyd C. Life of R. B. Sheridan. Lond. Scott. 1890. 2/6 and 1/. N. Y. Scribners. 1890. (Great Writers). *Bibliog. by Anderson.*
Sheridan and his Times; by an Octogenarian who stood by his knee in youth and sat at his table in manhood. 2 v. Lond. Hope. 1859. 21/.
Sheridaniana; or Anecdotes of the Life of R. B. Sheridan; his Table-talk, and Bon-mots. Lond. 1826.
Watkins, J. Memoirs of the Public and Private Life of R. B. Sheridan, with a particular account of his family and connexions. Lond. 1817.
Whipple, Essays and Reviews. 1873. 2: 250—302. *Same.* No. Amer. Rev. 66: 72.

NINETEENTH CENTURY.

GEORGIAN DRAMA.
VICTORIAN DRAMA.

GEORGIAN DRAMA.

DRAMATISTS.

Baillie, Joanna.
Beddoes.
BYRON.
COLERIDGE.
Keats.

Lamb.
Marston, John Westland.
Mitford, Mary Russell.
SHELLEY.
Wordsworth.

BAILLIE, JOANNA. 1762—1851.

Plays on the Passions.
1798.
    Basil. Tragedy on Love.
    Trial. Comedy on Love.
    De Monfort. Tragedy on Hatred. (Staged by Kemble and Mrs. Siddons and, later, by Kean).
1802.
    Election. Comedy on Hatred. (Produced with music at Eng. Opera House).
    Ethwald. Tragedy on Ambition. (Two Parts).
    Second Marriage. Comedy on Ambition.
1812.
    Orra. Tragedy on Fear.
    Dream. Tragedy on Fear.
    Siege. Comedy on Fear.
    Beacon. Musical Drama on Hope.

1836.
    Romiero. Tragedy on Jealousy.
    Alienated Manor. Comedy on Jealousy.
    Henriquez. Tragedy on Remorse. (Produced at Drury Lane).

Miscellaneous Plays.
1804.
    Rayner. Tragedy.
    Country Inn. Comedy.
    Constantine Paleologus; or, The Last of the Cæsars. (Produced at Edinb. and at Drury Lane).
1810.
    Family Legend. Tragedy. (Produced in Edinb. and at Drury Lane).
1826.
    Martyr. Drama.
1836.
    Separation. Tragedy. (Produced at Covent Garden).
    Stripling. Tragedy.
    Phantom. Musical Drama.
    Enthusiasm. Comedy.
    Witchcraft. Tragedy.
    Homicide. Tragedy.
    Bride. Drama.
    Match. Comedy.
✠Dram. and Poet. Works, (w. life). Lond. Longmans. 1853. 21/. Lond. Bohn. 1860. 10/6.
† Adams, W. H. D. Celebrated Englishwomen of Victorian Era.
Chorley. Authors of England.
Mitford, Mary R. Recollections of a Literary Life.
Robertson, E. S. Eng. Poetesses.
Wotton, M. E. Word Portraits.

BEDDOES, THOMAS LOVELL. 1803—'49.

Bride's Tragedy. 1822.
Death's Jest Book; or, The Fool's Tragedy. 1850. (Writing begun in 1825).
Dramatic Fragments.
    Love's Arrow Poisoned.
    Second Brother.
    Torrismond.
    Last Man.
✠Death's Jest Book; ed. Kelsall. Lond. Pickering. 1849. 5/.
Poems; ed. Kelsall, w. memoir. Lond. Pickering. 1850. 7/6.
Works; ed. Kelsall. 2 v. Lond. Pickering. 1851. 12/.
Poetical Works; ed. Gosse, w. memoir. Lond. Dent. 1890. 10/6.
Letters; ed. Gosse, w. brief notes. Lond. Mathews and Lane. 1894. 5/.
† Kelsall, T. F. T. L. Beddoes. Fortn. Rev. n. s. 12: 67.

BYRON, GEORGE GORDON. (Lord). 1788—1824.

Manfred. Dramatic Poem. 1817.
Marino Faliero. 1820. (Produced at Drury Lane).
Sardanapalus. 1821.
Two Foscari. 1821.
Cain. Mystery. 1821.

Werner. 1822.
Heaven and Earth. Mystery. 1823.
Deformed Transformed. 1824.
✠Complete Poetical Works; ed. W. B. Scott. 3 v. Lond. Routledge. 1885. 10/6. N. Y. Lovell. 1885. $3.75.
Poetical Works. N. Y. Worthington Co. 1886. $3.00.
Poetical Works. N. Y. Routledge. 1890. $1.50.
† Anton, H. S. Byron's Manfred. (A lecture). Naumberg. 1875.
Arnold. Essays in Criticism. 2d Ser., p. 163—204.
Boyle, G. English and American Poets and Dramatists of the Victorian Age, w. biog. notices. Frankfurt. A. Gestewitz. 1886. 3.60 m. (F. Dow. Engl. Studien, 11 : 316—17).
Dimond, W. The Bride of Abydos; Romantic Drama in three acts, from Byron's poem. Arranged by T. H. Lacy. Lond. 1866. (Lacy's Acting Ed. of Plays, 70).
Elze, K. Lord Byron; Biography w. critical essay on his place in literature. Lond. Murray. 1872. 16/.
Gerard, W. Byron Re-studied in his Dramas. Essay. Lond. F. V. White. 1886. 5/.
Hazlitt. Spirit of the Age.
Hodgkins. Nineteenth Century Authors. *Bibliography*.
Howell, O. Abel: written, but with great humility, in reply to Byron's Cain. Lond. 1843.
Journal of the Conversations of Lord Byron with the Countess of Blessington. New ed. Rev. and annotated. Lond. Bentley. 1894.
Kölbing, E. Byron's Siege of Corinth. Mit einleitung u. anmerkungen. Berlin. E. Felber. 1893. 3 m. (L. Boescholdt. Engl. Studien, 18: 236—38).
Mazzini, J. Life and Writings. 6 v. Lond. Smith and Elder. 1870. ea. 9/. 6: 61—97, Byron and Goethe.
Milner, H. M. Mazeppa; or, The Wild Horse of Tartary. Romantic Drama in 3 acts. Dram. from Byron's Poem. Lond. 1828. Cumberland's Minor Theatre. Lacy's Acting Ed. 96.
Moore, T. Life and Letters. Lond. Murray. 1873. 7/6.
Morley, J. Critical Miscellanies. Lond. 1886. 1: 203—251.
Noel, R. Byron. Lond. Scott. 1890. *Bibliog. by Anderson*. (Great Writers).
Stöhsel, K. Lord Byron's Trauerspiel "Werner" u. seine Quelle. Eine rettung. Erlangen. Junge. 1891. 1.80 m. (E. Kölbing. Engl. Studien, 17: 141—47).
Swinburne. Essays and Studies.
Swinburne. Miscellanies. p. 63—156, Wordsworth and Byron.
Trelawny, E. J. Recollections of the Last Days of Shelley and Byron. Lond. Moxon. 1858. Bost. Ticknor and Fields. 1858.
Westenholz, F. Uber Byron's historische Dramen. Ein beitrag zu ihrer ästhetischen Würdigung. Stuttgart. F. Frommann's. (E. Hauff). 1890. 1.20 m.

COLERIDGE, SAMUEL TAYLOR. 1772—1834.

Fall of Robespierre. 1794. (First Act by Coleridge. Second and Third by Southey).
Remorse. 1813. (Produced at Drury Lane).
Zapolya. 1817.
Osorio. 1873. (Written 1797).

114   *English Drama.—A Working Basis.*

Dramatic Translations.

 Schiller's Piccolomini. 1800.
 Schiller's Death of Wallenstein. 1800.
✠Poetical and Dramatic Works. 4 v. Lond. Macmillan. 1880. 31/6.
 Poetical Works. 2 v. N. Y. Scribner. 1885. $4.00.
 Poetical Works. Pocket Lib. N. Y. Routledge. 40c.
 Poetical Works; ed. W. M. Rosetti. Lond. 1880. 3/6. (Moxon's Pop. Poets).
 Schiller, F. Works. 2, The Piccolomini. Death of Wallenstein. Tr. by Coleridge. Lond. Bohn. N. Y. Macmillan.
 Letters; ed. Ern. Hartley Coleridge. (Grandson). Lond. Heinemann.
† Brooke, S. A. Theol. in the Eng. Poets.
 Caine, T. Hall. Cobwebs of Criticism. Lond. Stock. 1884. 5/. p. 54—87.
 Coleridge. Lond. Scott. 1887. 1/. *Bibliog. by Anderson.* (Great Writers).
 Campbell, J. Dykes. Life of Sam. Taylor Coleridge. Lond. Macmillan. 1894. 10/6. N. Y. Macmillan. 1894. $3.00.
 Carlyle, T. Life of J. Sterling. Lond. Chapman and Hall. 1851. 10/6. p. 69—80.
 Chancellor, E. Beresford. Literary Types.
 Courthope, W. J. Liberal Movement in Eng. Lit., p. 159—194, Poetry, Music and Painting; Coleridge and Keats.
 De Quincey, T. Works; ed. Masson. 2.
 Dowden. Studies in Literature. p. 44—48, The Transcendental Movement in Literature.
 Hodgkins, L. M. Nineteenth Cent. Authors. *Bibliography.*
 Pater. Appreciations.
 Rossetti, W. M. Lives of Famous Poets. p. 237—255.
 Sarrazin. Le Renaissance de la Poesie Anglaise.
 Shairp, J. C. Studies in Poetry and Philosophy. p. 116—226.
 Southey, R. Life and Correspondence. 6 v. Lond. Longmans. 1849—50. 63/. Lond. Bohn. 1862. 27/.
 Swinburne. Essays and Studies. p. 250—275.

KEATS, JOHN. 1795—1821.

 Otho the Great. 1819. (With Charles Armitage Brown).
 King Stephen. 1819. (Unfinished).
✠Poetical Works and Other Writings; ed. H. B. Forman. 4 v. Lond. Reeves and Turner. 1890. 52/6. N. Y. Scribner and Welford. 1884. $3.20.
 Poetical Works; ed. W. T. Arnold. 2 v. N. Y. Dodd. $3.00.
 Poetical Works; ed. Lord Houghton. Bost. Roberts. 1887. $1.50.
 Poetical Works; ed. W. M. Rossetti. Lond. Ward and Lock. 1888. 5/.
 Letters to Fanny Brawne; ed. H. B. Forman. Lond. Reeves. 1890. 6/.
 Letters; ed. S. Colvin. Macmillan. 1888. 6/.
† Caine, T. Hall. Cobwebs of Criticism. p. 158—190.
 Colvin, S. Keats. Lond. Macmillan. 1890. 1/. (Eng. Men of Letters).
 Courthope, W. J. Liberal Movement in Eng. Lit. p. 159—194, Coleridge and Keats.
 Hodgkins, L. M. Nineteenth Cent. Authors. *Bibliography.*
 Lowell. Among my Books. 2nd Series, p. 303—327.

Masson. Wordsworth, Shelley, Keats. Lond. Macmillan. 1874 and '81. 5/. p. 143—191.
Rossetti, W. M. Keats. Lond. Scott. 1887. *Bibliog. by Anderson.* (Great Writers). Lives of Famous Poets. p. 349—61.

LAMB, CHARLES. 1775—1834.

John Woodvil. 1802.
Mr. H——. 1806.
(Pawnbroker's Daughter).
✠Works; ed. C. Kent. N. Y. Routledge. 1890. $1.50.
Poems, Plays, and Misc. Essays. Notes by A. Ainger. N. Y. Armstrong. 1885. $1.50. *Same ed.* Lond. Macmillan. 1884. 5/.
Plays; (and Dram. Essays) ed. w. Introd. Rud. Dircks. Lond. Scott. 1893. 1/6.
Letters, arranged by A. Ainger. 2 v. Lond. Macmillan. 1888. 10/.
† Ainger, A. C. Lamb. Lond. Macmillan. 1888. 1/6.
Chancellor, E. Beresford. Lit. Types. Edin. Rev. Apr., 1803.
Fitzgerald, P. Life, Letters and Writings. New ed. 6 v. Lond. Stark. 1886. 21/.
Hodgkins, L. M. Nineteenth Cent. Authors. *Bibliography.*
Martin, B. E. In the Footprints of C. Lamb. *p. 147—193, Bibliog. by E. D. North.* N. Y. Scribner. 1890. $2.50.

MARSTON, JOHN WESTLAND. 1819—'90.

Patrician's Daughter. 1841.
Borough Politics. 1846.
Heart and the World. 1847.
Strathmore. 1849.
Philip of France. 1850.
Anne Blake. 1852.
Life's Ransom. 1857.
Hard Struggle. 1858.
Wife's Portrait. 1862.
Pure Gold. 1863.
Donna Diana. 1863.
Favorite of Fortune. 1866.
Hero of Romance. 1867.
Life for Life. 1869.
Broken Spells. 1873.
Put to the Test.
Under Fire. 1885.
Not Published.
  Montezuma.
  At Bay.
  Charlotte Corday.
✠Dram. and Poet. Works. 2 v. Lond. Chatto. 1876. 18/.
  For Anne Blake, Hard Struggle, Life's Ransom and Patrician's Daughter, *see* Spencer, W. V., Bost. Theatre, v. 8, 21, 14 and 5.
† Athenæum. 1890. Jan. p. 57.
Horne. New Spirit of the Age. Rob. Browning and J. W. Marston.
Miles. Poets and Poetry of the Century.
Powell. Living Authors of England.

MITFORD, MARY RUSSELL. 1787—1856.

Julian. 1823. (Produced by Macready at Covent Garden).
Foscari. 1826. (Produced at Covent Garden).
Rienzi. 1828. (Produced at Drury Lane).
*Charles I. 1834. (Produced at Victoria Theatre).
✠Dram. Works. 2 v. Lond. Hurst and B. 1854. 21/. (Autobiog. introduction).
    See also Cumberland's Brit. Theatre: Rienzi, v. 32; Julian, v. 38; Foscari, v. 24.
Dramatic Scenes, Sonnets, and other Poems. Lond. 1827.
Recollections of my Literary Life. Lond. Bentley. 1888. 6/.
† Adams, W. H. D. Celebrated Englishwomen of the Victorian Era.
Browning, Eliz. B. Letters to R. H. Horne.
Chorley. Authors of England.
L'Estrange, A. Friendships of,— as told in Letters to her. 2 v. Lond. Hurst. 1882. 21/. Life as told in her letters. 1st ser. 3 v. Lond. Bentley. 1870. 31/6. 2nd ser. ed. H. Chorley. 2 v. Lond. Bentley. 1872. 21/.
Martineau, H. Biog. Sketches.
Robertson. English Poetesses.
Wotton. Word Portraits.

SHELLEY, PERCY BYSSHE. 1792—1822.

Prometheus Unbound. 1820.
Cenci. 1820.
Œdipus Tyrannus. 1820.
Hellas. 1822.
Dram. Fragments.
    Charles the First.
    Of an Unfinished Drama.
Dram. Translations.
    Cyclops of Euripides.
    From Calderon's Magico Prodigioso.
    From Goethe's Faust.
✠Complete Poetical Works; ed. G. E. Woodberry. 4 v. Bost. Houghton. 1892. $7.00.
Works; ed. H. B. Forman. 8 v. Lond. Reeves and Turner. 1880. ea. 12/6.
Works; ed. R. H. Shepherd. 5 v. Lond. Chatto. 1888. Ea. 3/6. Phila. Lippincott. 1888. $6.25.
Poetical Works; ed. W. M. Rossetti. Lond. Stark. 1885. 21/ or 36/. Bost. Estes. 1886. $10.50.
Riverside Ed. 2 v. Bost. Houghton. $3.00.
Scudder, Vida D. Prometheus Unbound. Bost. Heath. 1893. 65c.
† Dowden. Life of Shelley. 2 v. Lond. Paul. 1887. 36/.
Ellis, Fred S. Lexical Concordance to the Poetical Works of Shelley. Lond. Quaritch, 1892. 31/6.
Forman, H. B. The Shelley Library; *An Essay in Bibliography*. Lond. Reeves and Turner. 1886. 3/6.
Hodgkins, L. M. Nineteenth Cent. Authors. *Bibliography*.
Hutton, R. H. Essays, Theological and Literary. Lond. 1877. 2: 118—152, Shelley's Poetical Mysticism.
Masson, D. Wordsworth, Shelley and Keats. Lond. Macmillan. 1881. 5/.
Rabbé, Felix. Shelley, the Man and the Poet. Lond. Ward and Downey. 1888. 21/.

Rossetti, W. M. Memoir of Shelley. Shelley Soc. Pub. 4:2. Shelley's Prometheus Unbound. A Study of its Meaning and Personages. Lond. 1886. (Privately printed).
Sarrazin, O. Le Renaissance de la Poesie Anglaise.
Salt, H. S. Shelley Primer. Shelley Soc. Pub. Lond. 1887.
Sharp, W. Shelley. Lond. Scott. 1887. 1/. *Bibliog. by Anderson.* (Great Writers).
Shelley, Mrs. Memorials of Shelley. Lond. King. 1876. 5/.
Shelley Soc. Pub. Lond. Reeves and Turner. 1886—'90.
Symonds, J. A. Shelley. Lond. Macmillan. N. Y. Harper. 75c. (Eng. Men of Letters).
Todhunter, J. Study of Shelley. Lond. Paul. 1880. 7/.
Trelawny, E. J. Recollections of the Last Days of Shelley and Byron. Lond. Moxon. 1858. 9/. Bost. Ticknor and F. 1858.

WORDSWORTH, WILLIAM. 1770—1850.

Borderers. 1842. (Written 1795—'96).
✠Poetical Works; ed. W. Knight. 8 v. N. Y. Macmillan. 1889. $25.00.
Poetical Works; introd. J. Morley. N. Y. Macmillan. 1889. $1.75.
† Pater. Appreciations.
Poole, W. F. Bibliog. of Review and Magazine Articles. (Trans. of the Wordsworth Soc. 1883, 5: 90—100).
Shairp, J. C. Studies in Poetry and Philosophy. Edinb. Edmonston and Douglas. 1872. New ed. Hamilton. 1878. 6/. p. 1—103.

NOTE.—Scott's " Dramatic Pieces " merit no more than a passing reference.

VICTORIAN DRAMA.

DRAMATISTS.

Arnold, (Sir) Edwin.
Arnold, Matthew.
Austin, Alfred.
Bailey, P. J.
Bridges, Robert.
Browning, Mrs.
BROWNING, ROBERT.
Buchanan.
Bulwer-Lytton.
Butler.
Clough.
Cross, Mrs. ("Geo. Eliot.")
Davidson.
Dobell.
"Field."
Gilbert.
Gosse.
Henley and Stevenson.
Horne.
Jones.
Kingsley.
Knowles.
Landor, Robert.
LANDOR, WALTER SAVAGE.
Moore.
Nichol.
Pinero.
Shaw.
Skrine.
Smith, Alex.
SWINBURNE.
Talfourd.
Taylor, (Sir) Henry.
Tennyson.
Webster, Mrs.

ARNOLD, (Sir) EDWIN. 1832—

Adzuma; or, The Japanese Wife. Lond. Longmans. 1893. 6/6. N. Y. Scribner. 1893. $1.50.
✠Poetical Works. 8 v. Lond. Trübner. 1880. 48/. Lond. Longmans. 1891. N. Y. Funk. 1891.

ARNOLD, MATTHEW. 1822—'88.

Strayed Reveller. 1848.
Empedocles on Etna. 1852.
*Merope. 1858.
✠Complete Poetical Works. 3 v. Lond. Macmillan. 1882. Ea. 7/6.
Letters. 2 v. Lond. and N. Y. Macmillan. 1895.
† Bost. Pub. Lib. Bulletin. 6: 84—87. 1884. Bibliog. of Arnold's Writings with Critical References.
Forman. Our Living Poets.
Hodgkins, L. M. Nineteenth Cent. Authors. *Bibliography.*
Hutton, R. H. Literary Essays. Mod. Guides of Eng. Thought.
Smart, Thos. B. Bibliog. of Matthew Arnold. (Incl. 235 separ. wks., pubns. or edns. attrib. to him; *also* list of over 300 critiques and reviews).
Stedman. Victorian Poets.
Swinburne. Essays and Studies.

AUSTIN, ALFRED.

Savonarola. 1881. Lond. Macmillan. 7/6.
Prince Lucifer. 1887. Lond. and N. Y. Macmillan. 6/ and $2.00.

BAILEY, PHILIP JAMES. 1816—

Festus. 1839. (Expanded from 10,000 lines to 40,000, 1889).
✠Festus; a Poem. 10th ed. Lond. Longmans. 1877. 12/6.
Festus; Anniversary ed. Lond. and N. Y. Routledge. 1889. 3/6 and $1.50.
† Blackwood's Mag. 1854. 5: 75. Firmilian: A Tragedy. (Aytoun. Satiric review fatal to "The Spasmodic School.")
Firmilian; A Spasmodic Tragedy, by T. Percy Jones. Blackwood. 1854. 5/.
Horne, R. H. New Spirit of the Age. Henry Taylor and the author of "Festus."
Stedman. Victorian Poets.
Whipple. Essays and Reviews.

BRIDGES, ROB. SEYMOUR. 1844—

Nero. 1890.
Palicio. (In Eliz. manner). 1890.
Return of Ulysses. 1890.
Christian Captives. 1890.
Achilles in Cyros. 1892.
Humours of the Court. 1893.
Feast of Bacchus. 1894.
✠Plays. Lond. Bell. 1885—'94, ea. 2/6.
Poetical Works. 3 v. Lond. Bell. 1886—'94. 18/.

BROWNING, ELIZABETH BARRETT. 1809—'61.

Seraphim. 1838.
Drama of Exile. 1840.

Dramatic Translation.

    Prometheus Bound. 1833. (Amended version, 1850).
✠ Poetical Works. 6 v. Lond. Smith and Elder. 1890. Ea. 5/.
Poetical Works. 5 v. N. Y. Dodd. 1884. $6.25.
Poems. N. Y. Routledge. 1887. 40c.
Horne's Letters of E. B. Browning; ed. R. H. Stoddard. 2 v. N. Y. J. Miller. 1877. $2.50.
Letters; ed. S. R. T. Mayer. Lond. Bentley. 1876. 21/.
† Bayne, P. Two Great Englishwomen. E. B. Browning and C. Brontë. Lond. Clarke. 1880. 7/6.
Browning Soc. Papers. Nos. 1 and 2.
Colvin. Landor. (q. v.)
Forster. Life of Landor. (q. v.)
Hodgkins, L. M. Nineteenth Cent. Authors. *Bibliography.*
Ingram, J. H. Eliz. B. Browning. (Eminent Women Ser.) Lond. Allen. 1889. 3/6. Bost. Roberts. $1.00.
Jameson, Mrs. Memoirs.
Mitford. Recollections of a Literary Life.
Orr, Mrs. S. Life and Letters of R. Browning. 2 v. Bost. Houghton. 1891. $3.00.
Robertson. Eng. Poetesses.
Shairp, W. Rob. Browning. Lond. Scott. 1890. 1/. (Great Writers).
Stedman. Victorian Poets.

BROWNING, ROBERT. 1812—'89.

Paracelsus. 1835.
Strafford. 1837. (Produced by Macready and Miss Faucit at Covent Garden Theatre).
Pippa Passes. 1841.
King Victor and King Charles. 1842.
Return of the Druses. 1843.
Blot in the 'Scutcheon. 1843. (Produced at Drury Lane).
Colombe's Birthday. 1844.
Luria. 1845.
Soul's Tragedy. 1845.

Dramatic Translations.

    Balaustion's Adventure; including a Transcript from Euripides. ("Alcestis.") 1871.
    Aristophanes' Apology, including a Transcript from Euripides, being the Last Adventure of Balaustion. ("Herakles.") 1875.
    Agamemnon of Æschylus. 1877.
✠ Poetical Works. 17 v. Lond. Smith, Elder & Co. 1889. Ea. 5/. N. Y. Macmillan. Ea. $1.50. New ed. 9 vols. 1895. $20.00; or $2.25 ea.
Poetical and Dramatic Works. Riverside Ed. 6 v. Boston. Houghton. 1889. $10.00, or $1.75 ea. (Also, complete in one vol. $3.00).
Complete Works. New ed., w. prefaces and notes by Augustine Birrell. 2 v. N. Y. Macmillan. $3.50.

Blot in the 'Scutcheon, Colombe's Birthday, and A Soul's Tragedy; ed. W. J. Rolfe and H. E. Hersey. N. Y. Harper. 1887. 56c.
Strafford; a Tragedy. Notes and Preface by E. H. Hickey. Introd. by S. R. Gardiner. Lond. Bell. 1884. 2/6.
† Alexander, W. J. Introd. to the Poetry of R. Browning. Bost. Ginn. 1889. $1.10.
Bagehot, Walter. Literary Studies.
Berdoe, (Dr.) Edw. The Browning Cyclopædia. Lond. Sonnenschein. 1891. N. Y. Macmillan. 1891. $3.50. Browning's Message to his Time. Lond. Sonnenschein. 1891. 2/6. N. Y. Macmillan. 90c. Browning Studies, being Select Papers by Members of the Browning Society. N. Y. Macmillan. 1895.
Browning Soc. Papers. Lond. Trübner. 1881—'91. 59 nos.
Birrell. Obiter Dicta. 1st Ser. Lond. Stock. 1888. 6/.
Cooke, G. W. Guide book to the Poetic and Dramatic Works of R. Browning. Bost. Houghton. 1891. $2.00.
Corson, H. Introd. to the Study of Browning's Poetry. Bost. Heath. 1886. $1.50.
Courtney, W. L. Studies New and Old. R. Browning, Writer of Plays, p. 100—123. Lond. Chapman. 1888. 6/.
Dowden. Studies in Literature, p. 191—239, Tennyson and Browning. Transcripts and Studies.
Everett, C. C. The Tragic Motive in Browning's Dramas. And. Rev. Feb., 1889.
Forman. Our Living Poets.
Fotheringham, J. Studies in the Poetry of Robert Browning. Lond. Paul. 1888. 6/.
Furnivall, F. J. Bibliog. of R. Browning, fr. 1833—'81. Lond. Browning Soc. Papers. 1881—'84. Pts. 1 and 2.
Gosse, Edmund. Robert Browning Personalia. Bost. Houghton. 75c.
Hodgkins, L. M. Nineteenth Cent. Authors. *Bibliography.*
Hutton. Literary Essays.
Jones, H. Browning as a Philos. and Relig. Teacher. N. Y. Macmillan. 1891. $2.25.
Lowell, J. R. Browning's Plays and Poems. No. Amer. Rev. 66: 357.
Macready, W. C. Macready's Reminiscences and Sel. from his Diaries and Letters. 2 v. Lond. Macmillan. 1876. 7/6.
McNicoll, T. Essays on Eng. Lit. Browning and Landor. Lond. 1861.
Molineaux, Marie Ada. Phrase Book from the Works of Robert Browning. Boston. Houghton. 1896. $3.00.
Nettleship, J. T. Essays on Robert Browning's Poetry. Lond. Mathews. (1868) 1890. 7/6.
Noel, Roden. Essays on Poetry and Poets. Lond. Paul. 1887. 12/.
Orr, Mrs. S. Handbook to the Works of Browning. Lond. Bell. 2nd ed. 1886. 6/. N. Y. Scribner and Welford. 1888. $2.25.
Poet Lore, 1889. A Browning Reference List. 1: 490—531.
Quarterly Review, April, 1890.
Sarrazin. Le Renaissance de la Poesie Anglaise.
Scudder, V. D. Life of the Spirit in the Mod. Eng. Poets. (Ch. on Browning as a Humorist).
Shairp, W. Rob. Browning. *Bibliog. by Anderson.* (Great Writers) Lond. Scott. 1890.
Stedman. Victorian Poets.

Symons, A. Introd. to the Study of Browning. Lond. and N. Y. Cassell. 1886. 2/6. Is Browning Dramatic? Browning Soc. Papers, Pt. 7, p. 1—12.

BUCHANAN, ROBERT. 1841—

Piper of Hamelin; a Fantastic Opera in two Acts. Lond. Heinemann. 1893. 2/6.
✠Poetical Works. Lond. Chatto. 1885—'93. (1888. 6/.)
† Noble, Jas. Ashcroft. Sonnet in England, and other Essays. "Robert Buchanan." Lond. Mathews and Lane. 1893. 5/.

BULWER, EDWARD GEORGE EARLE LYTTON, (1st Baron Lytton). 1805—'73.

Duchess de la Vallière. 1836.
Lady of Lyons. 1838.
Richelieu; or, The Conspiracy. 1839.
Sea Captain; or, The Birthright. 1839.
Money, 1840. (Produced at the Haymarket).
Not So Bad As We Seem.
✠Dram. Works. Lond. Routledge. 1890. 3/6. (Red Line Poets).
Dram. Works. Handy Vol. Ed. N. Y. Stokes. 1889. $1.00.
Lady of Lyons and other Plays. Lond. Scott. 1890. 1/. (Canterbury Poets).
Complete Poems and Dramas. 4 v. N. Y. Routledge. 1883. $5.00.
Lacy's (French's) Acting Edition of Plays.
    Lady of Lyons. No. 1732.
    Richelieu. No. 1752.
    Money. No. 1772.
† Bayne. Essays in Biography.
Cooper, T. Lord Lytton; a Biography. 1873.
Horne, R. H. New Spirit of the Age. Sir E. Lytton Bulwer.
Life, Letters and Remains; ed. by his son. 2 v. Lond. Paul. 1883. 32/. N. Y. Harper. 1884. $2.75.
Stedman. Victorian Poets.
Westm. Rev. 27: 247. 1837. Bulwer's Tragedies.

BUTLER, ARTHUR GRAY.

Harold; a Drama in four Acts. (Wr. 1877). Lond. Froude. 1892. 5/.

CLOUGH, ARTHUR HUGH. 1819—'61.

Dipsychus. 1869. (Wr. 1850).
✠Poems and Prose Remains, with a sel. from his Letters and a Memoir; ed. by his wife. 2 v. Lond. Macmillan. 1862, '69 and '88. Ea. 7/6.
Poems, with Memoir by F. T. Palgrave. Lond. Macmillan. 1862.
† Dowden. Contemp. Rev. 12: 513.
Hutton. Literary Essays.
Norton, C. E. Atl. Mon. 9: 462.
Perry, T. S. Atl. Mon. 36: 409.
Symons, J. A. Fortn. Rev. n. s. 1868.
Waddington, S. A Monogram. 1883,

CROSS, MARIAN EVANS. (George Eliot). 1819—'80.

Spanish Gypsy. 1868.
Works of George Eliot. (Cab. Ed. 20 v.) Edinb. and Lond. 1878. Blackwood. £5.
Poems. (Compl.) N. Y. Crowell. 1887. $2.50.
Complete Poems of Geo. Eliot, with introd. notice by M. Browne. Illust. Ed. Bost. Estes. 1889. $6.00.
Life and Works. 24 v. Edinb. Blackwood. 1888. Ea. 5/.
Spanish Gypsy. 5th ed. Edinb. Blackwood. 1875. 7/6. Bost. Houghton. 1881. $1.50.
† Bray, A. E. Autobiography. Lond. Chapman. 1884. 10/6.
Browning, O. Geo. Eliot. Lond. Scott. (Great Writers). *Bibliog. by Anderson.*
Cooke, G. W. Geo. Eliot; a Critical Study of her Life, Writings and Philosophy. Lond. Low. 1883. 10/6. Bost. Osgood. 1883. $2.00.
Dowden. Studies in Literature. p. 240—272.
Geo. Eliot's Life as related in her Letters and Journals. Ed. J. W. Cross. Edinb. Blackwood. 1885. 15/. In 1 v., 1887. 7/6. N. Y. Harper. 3 v. $3.75.
Forman. Our Living Poets.
Hodgkins, L. M. Nineteenth Cent. Authors. *Bibliography.*
Hutton. Essays Theol. and Lit., v. 2. Essays on some Mod. Guides of Eng. Thought.
Monthly Ref. Lists, Providence Pub. Lib. 1881. Geo. Eliot. 1 : 5.
Robertson. Eng. Poetesses. p. 327—334.

DAVIDSON, JOHN.

Unhistorical Pastoral.
Romantic Farce.
Bruce; a Chronicle Play.
Smith; a Tragic Farce.
Scaramouch in Naxos; a Pantomime.
✠Plays. Lond. Mathews and Lane. 1894. 7/6.
Poetical Works. Lond. Mathews and Lane. 1892—'94.

DOBELL, SYDNEY THOMPSON. 1824—'74.

Roman. Lond. Bentley. 1850. 5/.
Balder. Lond. Smith and Elder. 1854. 7/6.
England in Time of War; Poem. Lond. Smith and Elder. 1856. 5/.
✠Poetical Works. 2 v. Lond. Smith and Elder. 1875. 21/.
Life and Letters. 2 v. Lond. Smith and Elder. 1878. 28/.
Thoughts in Art, Philosophy, etc. Lond. Smith and Elder. 1876. 7/6.
Select Edition of Poems; ed. by Sharp. Lond. Scott. 1887. 1/. (Cant. Poets).
† Buchanan, R. Look around Literature. Lond. 1887. (Sidney Dobell and "The Spasmodic School.")

"FIELD, MICHAEL." (Two women).

Callirrhoe. 1884.
Fair Rosamond. 1884.
Father's Tragedy. 1885.

William Rufus. 1885.
Loyalty or Love? 1885.
Brutus Ultor. 1886.
Canute the Great. 1887.
Cup of Water. 1887.
Tragic Mary. 1890.
Stephania. 1892.
Question of Memory. 1893. (Produced at the Independent Theatre. Lond. Oct. 27, 1893).
✠Poetical and Dramatic Works. Clifton, Baker. 1887—'92.
Brutus Ultor, 1/. Callirrhoe; Fair Rosamond, 6/. Canute the Great; Cup of Water, 7/6. Father's Tragedy; William Rufus; Loyalty or Love? 7/6. Tragic Mary, 6/. Stephania, 6/. (All Lond. Mathews and Lane).

GILBERT, W. S. 1836—

Original Plays, 2 Series. Lond. Chatto. 1875—'79. Ea. 2/6.
Series I.
    Wicked World.
    Pygmalion.
    Charity.
    Princess.
    Palace of Truth.
    Trial by Jury.
Series II.
    Broken Hearts.
    Engaged.
    Sweethearts.
    Gretchen.
    Dan'l Druce.
    Tom Cobb.
    H. M. S. Pinafore.
    Sorcerer.
    Pirates of Penzance.

GOSSE, (Prof.) EDM. W.

King Eric; a Tragedy; w. introd. by Theod. Watts. Lond. Heinemann. 1893. 5/.

HENLEY and STEVENSON. W. E. and R. L. 1850—'95.

Deacon Brodie.
Beau Austin.
Admiral Guinea.
✠Three Plays. Lond. Nutt. 1892. 7/6. N. Y. Scribner. 1892. $2.00.
† Monkhouse, Allan. Books and Plays. "Stevenson and Henley's Plays." Lond. Mathews and Lane. 1894. 5/.

HORNE, RICHARD HENGIST. 1803—'84.

Cosmo di Medici. 1837.
Death of Marlowe. 1837.
Gregory VII.; a Tragedy. 1840.
Judas Iscariot. 1848.

Prometheus, the Fire Bringer. 1864.
South-Sea Sisters; a Lyric Masque. 1866.
Laura Dibalzo. 1880.
King Nihil's Round Table; or, The Regicide's Symposium. 1881.
Bible Tragedies. 1881.
    Judas Iscariot. (Reprinted).
    John the Baptist; or, The Valour of the Soul.
    Rahman, the Apocryphal Book of Job's Wife.
✠Cosmo di Medici, and Other Poems. Lond. Rivers. 1875. 7/.
Laura Dibalzo. Lond. Newman. 1880. 4/.
Bible Tragedies. Lond. Newman. 1881. 7/6.
Marlowe. Bullen's Ed. Marlowe's Works. v. 3. (Death of Marlowe). Lond. Smith and Elder. 1844. 24/. N. Y. Harper. 1844.
† Browning, Mrs. Letters to R. H. Horne.
Forman. Our Living Poets.
Horne. New Spirit of the Age.
Stedman. Victorian Poets.

JONES, HENRY ARTHUR.

Saints and Sinners. Lond. Macmillan. 1891. 3/6.
Crusaders. Lond. Macmillan. 1893. 2/6.
Judah. Lond. Macmillan. 1894. 2/6.
Michael and his Lost Angel. Lond. Macmillan. 1896. 2/6.
Renascence of the Eng. Drama; Essays, Lectures, and Fragments Rel. to the Mod. Eng. Stage. N. Y. Macmillan. 1895. $1.75.

KINGSLEY, CHARLES. 1819—'75.

Saint's Tragedy. 1848. (Fraser, 37: 328. N. Brit. Rev. 15: 442).
✠Works. 17 v. Lond. Macmillan. 1890. ea. 3/6.
Poems. Lond. Macmillan. 1889. 3/6.
Letters, and Memories of his Life: ed. by his wife. Lond. Macmillan. 1890. 6/.
† Müller, F. M. Biogr. Essays.
Stephen. Hours in a Lib. Ser. 3.

KNOWLES, JAMES SHERIDAN. 1784—1862.

Caius Gracchus. 1815.
Virginius. 1820.
William Tell. 1825.
Alfred the Great; or, The Patriot King. 1831.
Hunchback. 1832.
Wife; a Tale of Mantua. 1833.
Beggar of Bethnal Green. 1834.
Daughter. 1837.
Love Chase. 1837.
Woman's Wit. 1838.
Maid of Mariendorpt. 1838.
Love. 1839.
John of Procida; or, The Bridals of Messina. 1840.
Old Maids. 1841.

Rose of Arragon. 1842.
Secretary. 1843.

[Knowles' plays were written for the stage, and were successfully produced at Drury Lane, Covent Garden, and other leading theatres].

✠Dram. Works. Lond. and N. Y. Routledge. 1890. 2/6.
Hunchback and Love Chase. N. Y. Cassell. 1887. 10c.
† Doran. Their Majesties' Servants.
Hazlitt. Spirit of the Age.
Horne. New Spirit of the Age. Knowles and Macready.
Knowles, R. B. Life. Lond. 1872.
Macready. Reminiscences. Lond. Macmillan. 1876. 7/6.

LANDOR, ROBERT EYRES. 1781—1869.

Count Arezzi. 1823.
Earl of Brecon. 1841.
Faith's Fraud. 1841.
Ferryman. 1841.
Fawn of Sertorius. 1846.
Fountain of Arethusa. 1848.

LANDOR, WALTER SAVAGE. 1775—1864.

Count Julian. 1810—'11.
Andrea of Hungary. 1839.
Giovanna of Naples. 1839.
Fra Rupert. 1841.
Siege of Ancona. (Written soon after Fra Rupert).

Dramatic Fragments.

> Don Pedro. Circ. 1820.
> Ines de Castro. Circ. 1820.
> Ippolito di Este. Containing two scenes from *Ferranti and Gisilio*, burned by the author in 1811).

See also

> Scenes.
> Hellenics.
> Imaginary Conversations.

✠Works, ed. w. life. J. Forster. 8 v. Lond. Chapman. 1876. Ea. 14/.
Gebir; Count Julian. N. Y. Cassell. 1887. 10c.
† Chancellor, E. Beresford. Literary Types.
Colvin, S. Landor. (Eng. Men of Letters). N. Y. Harper. 1881. 75c.
De Vere. Essays. 2 v. Lond. Macmillan. 1888. 12/. Landor's Poetry, 2: 143.
Evans, Edw. J. Walter Savage Landor: a Critical Study. N. Y. Putnam. 1892. $1.25.
Horne. New Spirit of the Age.
Lowell. Latest Lit. Essays. Bost. Houghton. 1892. $1.00.
Martineau. H. Biog. Sketches.
Stedman. Victorian Poets.
Swinburne. Miscellanies.

MOORE, GEO.

Strike at Arlingford. A Play in Three Acts. Lond. Scott. 1893. 5/.

NICHOL, (Prof.) JOHN.

Hannibal; a Drama. Lond. Macmillan. 1872. 7/6.

PINERO, ARTHUR W.

Plays. Lond. Heinemann. 1891—'95, *in prog.* Each 1/6.
Cabinet Minister.
Dandy Dick.
Hobby Horse.
Lady Bountiful.
Magistrate.
Profligate.
Lords and Commons.
Schoolmistress.
Squire.
Sweet Lavender.
Times.
Weaker Sex.
Amazons.
Benefit of the Doubt.
Notorious Mrs. Ebbsmith.
Second Mrs. Tanqueray.

SHAW, GEO. BERNARD.

Widowers' Houses; a Comedy. (Indep. Theatre Series). Lond. Henry. 1893. 2/6.

SKRINE, JOHN HUNTLEY.

Columba; a Drama. Lond. Blackwood. 1892. 6/.

SMITH, ALEXANDER. 1829 (or '30) ?—'67.

Life Drama. 1852. Lond. Macmillan. 1855. 2/6.
† Wilson, J. G. Poets and Poetry of Scotland. 2.

SWINBURNE, ALGERNON CHARLES. 1843—

Atalanta in Calydon. 1864.
Chastelard. 1865.
Bothwell. 1874.
Erectheus. 1876.
Maria Stuart. 1881.
Marino Faliero. 1885.
Locrine. 1887.
Sisters. 1892.
✠Poetical Works. 16 v. Lond. Chatto. 1889.
† Courtney. Studies New and Old. Lond. Chapman. 1888. 6/.
Lowell. My Study Windows.
Shepherd, R. H. Bibliog. of Swinburne. Lond. Redway. 1887. 6/.
Stedman. Victorian Poets.

TALFOURD, (Sir) THOMAS NOON.
(Called Sergeant Talfourd and Ion Talfourd). 1795—1854.

— Ion. 1835. (Produced by Macready at Covent Garden Theatre).
Athenian Captive. 1838.
Glencoe; or, The Fate of the Macdonalds. 1840.
✠Tragedies. Lond. and N. Y. Routledge. 1889. 1/ and 40c.
Dram. Works. Lond. Moxon. 1852. 6/.
† Horne. New Spirit of the Age.
Tuckerman, H. T. Characteristics of Lit. 2 v. Phila. 1849—'51. Talfourd as a Dramatist.
Whipple. Essays and Reviews. 1 : 181.

TAYLOR, (Sir) HENRY. 1800—

Isaac Comnenus. 1827.
Philip Van Artevelde. 1834. (Produced by Macready at the Princess Theatre in 1847).
Edwin the Fair. 1842.
Virgin Widow. (A Sicilian Summer). 1850.
St. Clement's Eve. 1862.
✠Complete Works. 5 v. Lond. Paul. 1878. 30/.
Philip van Artevelde; The Virgin Widow. Lond. Paul. 1879—'80. Ea. 3/6.
Philip van Artevelde. Phila. Lippincott. 1876. $1.25.
Autobiog. 2 v. Lond. Blackwood. 1885. 32/. N. Y. Harper. 1885. $3.00.
Correspondence; ed. Dowden. Lond. Blackwood. 1888. 16/. N. Y. Longmans. 1888. $2.50.
† De Vere. Essays, 1.
Forman. Our Living Poets.
Horne. New Spirit of the Age. Henry Taylor and the author of " Festus."

TENNYSON, (Lord) ALFRED. 1809—'92.

Queen Mary. 1875. (Produced by Irving at the Lyceum).
Harold. 1877.
Falcon. 1879. (Produced at St. James's Theatre).
Cup. 1881. (Produced by Irving at the Lyceum).
Promise of May. 1882. (Produced at the Globe Theatre).
Becket. 1884. (Produced by Irving at the Lyceum).
Foresters. 1892. (Produced at Daly's Theatre in New York).
✠Complete Works. 8 v. Lond. Macmillan. 1888. Ea. 5/.
Dram. Works. 4 v. Lond. Macmillan. 1887. Ea. 10/6.
† Brooke, (Rev.) Stopford A. Tennyson, his Art and Relations to Modern Life. Lond. Isbister. 1894. 7/6.
Dowden. Studies in Lit.
Hodgkins, L. M. Nineteenth Cent. Authors. *Bibliography.*
Hutton. Literary Essays.
Luce, Morton. New Studies in Tennyson. Clifton. Baker. 1893. 1/.
Records of Tennyson, Ruskin and Browning. Lond. Macmillan. 1892. 10/6.

Ritchie, A. T. Lord Tennyson and his Friends. Lond. Unwin. 1893. 12/6.
Robertson, J. M. Essays towards a Critical Method. Lond. Unwin. 1889. 7/6.
Sarrazin. Le Renaissance de la Poesie Anglaise.
Stedman. Victorian Poets.
Vandyke, H. Poetry of Tennyson. Lond. Mathews. 1893. 5/6.
Waugh. Tennyson, a Study. Lond. Heinemann. 1893. 6/.

WEBSTER, (Mrs.) AUGUSTA. —1895.

Translations.
    Prometheus Bound: Æschylus. 1866.
    Medea: Euripides. 1868.
Original.
    Dramatic Studies. 1866.
    Auspicious Day. 1872.
    Disguises. 1879.
    In a Day. 1882.
    Sentence. 1887.
† Athenæum.
    1888, 2: 313. 1894, 2: 355. 1895, 2: 346.
Forman. Our Living Poets.
Robertson. Eng. Poetesses.

WILDE, OSCAR. 1856—

Dramatic Works. Lond. Mathews and Lane. 1893. 7/6.
Lady Windermere's Fan.
Woman of No Importance.
Duchess of Padua.

NOTE.—For the more prominent playwrights of the modern period, as Boucicault, Taylor, Wills, Albery, Robertson, Sims, Pettitt and Grundy, *see* Archer's Eng. Dramatists of Today. Lond. 1882. Archer's About the Theatre. Lond. 1886. Buchanan's A Look round Literature, "The Modern Stage," Lond., 1887, and "Dramatic Notes, a Chron. of the Lond. Stage," 1879—1882. Lond. 1883. *See* for tendencies of modern drama as exemplified in Ibsen, Sardou, Daudet and English playwrights, Walkley's Playhouse Impressions. Lond. 1892. (Sharp's Vistas, Chicago, Stone and Kimball, 1895, is an English expression of the method of Maeterlinck). For list of French's Acting Editions of Modern Plays, send to Samuel French, 89, Strand, London.

BOOKS OF GENERAL REFERENCE.

I.

BIBLIOGRAPHICAL.

ADAMS, W. DAVENPORT.
   Dictionary of the Drama. Lond. Chatto. 1883. 12/6.

ALLIBONE, S. A.
   Dictionary of English Literature. 3 v. Phil. Lippincott. 1888. $22.50.
   Supplement by J. F. Kirk. 2 v. Phil. Lippincott. 1891. $15.

ANDERSON, J. P. (Brit. Museum).
   Bibliographies in Great Writers Series.
     (Dramatists); Browning, Byron, Coleridge, Congreve, George Eliot, Goldsmith, Keats, Milton, Shelley, Sheridan. Lond. Scott. *In prog.* ea. 1/6.

ARBER, (Prof.) E.
   Transcript of Registers of Stationers' Company. 5 v. and Index. (1554—1640). Lond. Arber. 1875—'77.

BARKER, J.
   List of Plays to 1814. Lond. Barker. 1814.

BREWER, E. C.
   Authors and their Works, with Dates. Lond. Chatto. 1884. 2/.

BRITISH MUSEUM.
   Catalogue of Books in English Language printed up to 1640. 3 v. 1884. 30/-

CHAPMAN, J. K.
   Complete List of Theatrical Entertainments, Dramas, Masques, etc., from the time of Henry VIII. to the present day.

COLLIER, J. PAYNE.
   Bibliographical and Critical Account of the Rarest Books in the English Language. 4 v. N. Y. Scribner. 1866. $12. 2 v. Lond. Lilly. 1865. 40/.
   Extracts from the Registers of the Stationers' Company, 1557—1570, 1570—1587, w. notes and illustrations. Sh. Soc. Pub. 1848, 1849.

FOSTER, F. W.
  Title list of Catalogues of English Plays, Notes and Queries, 5th ser. 12: 203, 204, 261, 262, 381, 382. (Additions to the list are suggested by J. Brander Matthews, 6th ser. 1: 154).

HALLIWELL-PHILLIPS, J. O.
  Dictionary of Old English Plays. (To end of 17th Cent.) Lond. Smith. 1860. 12/.

HAZLITT, W. C.
  Handbook to the Popular, Poetical and Dramatic Literature of Great Britain to the Restoration. Lond. Smith. 1867—'68 31/6.
  Bibliographical Collections and Notes. Lond. Quaritch. 1876, '82, '86. Ser. 1, 24/; 2, 36/; 3, 24/.
  Manual for the Collector and Amateur of Old English Plays. Lond. Pickering and Chatto. 1892. 21/.

HENSLOWE, PHILIP.
  Diary. 1591—1609; ed. Collier. Sh. Soc. Pub. 1845.

HODGKINS, LOUISE M.
  Guide to the Study of Nineteenth Century Authors. (Dramatists; Arnold, M., Browning, Eliz., Browning, R., Coleridge, Geo. Eliot, Keats, Lamb, Shelley, Tennyson, Wordsworth). Boston. Heath. 1890. $1.

INGLIS, R.
  Dramatic Writers of Scotland. Glasgow. Muckellar. 1868.

KIRKMAN, FRANCIS.
  Exact Catalogue of all the English Stage Plays. (App. to John Dancer's tr. of Corneille's Nicomede, 1671).

KÖRTING, (Dr.) GUSTAV.
  Grundriss der Geschichte der Englischen Literatur. Münster, 1887. 4/.

LOWE, R. W.
  Bibliographical Account of English Theatrical Literature. Lond. Nimmo. 1888. 18/. N. Y. Bouton. 1887. $5.

LOWNDES, W. T.
  The Bibliographer's Manual. 10 pts. (Pt. XI.: Publications of Learned Societies and Private Presses, 5/.) Lond. Bohn. 1864. ea. 3/6.

MEARS, W.
  "A compleat cat. of all the plays that were ever yet printed in the Eng. language. Containing the dates and number of plays written by every part. author; an acc. of what plays were acted with applause, and of those wh. were never acted; and also the authors now living. In two separate alphabets. Cont. to the present year, 1726."

MORLEY, HENRY.
  English Writers. Cited in full under II. *(See the bibliog. appendices, especially to v. 11)*.

NICHOLS, J. GOUGH.
  Bibliographical List of Lord Mayor's Pageants. Lond. 1831.

PASCOE, C. E.
  Dramatic List, 1879.
RYLAND, FRED.
  Chronological Outlines of English Literature. Lond. and N. Y. Macmillan. 1890. $1.40.
SONNENSCHEIN, W. S.
  Best Books. Lond. Sonnenschein. 1891. 21/. N. Y. Putnam. 1891. $5.
  First Supplement; Readers' Guide to Contemporary Literature. N. Y. Putnam. 1895. $7.50.
WATT, (Dr.) R.
  Bibliotheca Britannica. 4 v. Edin. 1819—'24. £5.
WHINCOP, TH.
  Scanderbeg. (List of English Dramatic poets affixed). Lond. 1747.

II.

DRAMATIC HISTORY AND CRITICISM.

ADAMS, W. H. D.
  Celebrated Englishwomen of the Victorian Era. 2 v. Lond. White. 1884. 12/.
AIKEN, LUCY.
  Memoirs of the Court of Queen Elizabeth. 2 v. Lond. 1819. New ed. Lond. Ward. 1875. 3/6 and 2/. 2 v. in 1. N. Y. Putnam. 1868. $2.
ANDERSON, ROBERT.
  Works of the British Poets, w. memoirs and criticisms. 13 v. Lond. 1795.
ANGLIA.
  Ed. Wülker, Trautmann, Flügel, Schirmir. Halle. *In prog.* ea. v. 20/.
(ANON.)
  On the Time-Poets. (In Choice Drollery, Songs and Sonnets, 1656; repr. Halliwell, Sh. Soc. Trans. v. 3, 1847.
(ANON.)
  Shakspere and Johnson. Dramatic, versus Wit-Combats. Lond. 1864.
ARBER, (Prof.) E.
  An English Garner. Ingatherings from our History and Literature. 3 v. Lond. 1877—'80.
ARCHIV FUR DAS STUDIUM DER NEUREN SPRACHEN.
  Ed. L. Herrig. Brunswick. *In prog.* 1846— ea. v. 6/.
ARISTOTLE.
  The Poetic of Aristotle, tr. by T. Buckley. Lond. Bohn. 5/. (Bound w. his Treatise on Rhetoric).
  Poetics; text and trans. by E. R. Wharton. Lond. Parker. 1883. 2/6.

ARNOLD, MATTHEW.
  Essays in Criticism. 2nd. ser. Lond. and N. Y. Macmillan. 1888. 7/6.

ARREAT, L.
  La Morale dans le Drame, l'Epopée et le Roman. Paris. 1884. Alcan. 2 fr. 50c.

AUBIGNAC, FRANCOIS HEDELIN, ABBE d'.
  Practique du Théatre. 2 v. Amsterdam. 1715.

AUSTIN, W. S. and RALPH J.
  Poets-laureate. Lond. 1853.

BAGEHOT, WALTER.
  Literary Studies; ed. R. H. Hutton. 2 v. Lond. Longmans. 1879. 28/.

BAKER, DAVID ERSKINE.
  Biographia Dramatica. (Comp. by Baker to 1764, by Isaac Reed on to 1782, and by Stephen Jones on to 1811). 3 v. in 4. Lond. 1812.

BAYNE, PETER.
  Essays in Biography and Criticism. Boston. 1871.

B., G. S.
  A Study of the Prologue and Epilogue in English Literature fr. Shakespeare to Dryden. Lond. Paul. 1884.

BELJAME, ALEX.
  Histoire du Public et des Hommes de Lettres au Dixhuitième Siècle. 1660–1744. Paris. 1881.

BIRRELL, AUGUSTINE.
  Obiter Dicta. Ser. 1. Obiter Dicta. Ser. 2. Res Judicatæ. Essays about Men, Women and Books. Lond. Stock. 1892. ea. 5/. N. Y. Scribner. 1892. ea. $1.

BLACKWOOD'S MAGAZINE.
  Greek and Romantic Drama. 59:54.

BOAS, F. S.
  Shakspere and his Predecessors. (Univ. Extens. Manuals). Lond. Murray. 1896. 6/. N. Y. Scribner. 1896. $1.50.

BODENSTEDT, F. M.
  Shakespeare's Zeitgenossen und ihre Werke. (Ford, Greene, Lily, Marlowe, Webster). 3 v. Berlin. 1858—'60.

BOHTZ, AUG. W.
  Idee des Tragischen. Göttingen. 1836.

BOSSUET, J. B.
  Maximes et Réflexions sur la Comédie. Paris. 1881. (Œuvres complètes 10 v. Paris. 1877. Contant-Laguerre).

BOYLE, G.
  English and American Poets and Dramatists of the Victorian Age, w. biog. notices. Frankfurt. Gestewitz. 1886. mk. 3.60.

(ENCYCLOPAEDIA) BRITANNICA.
 Ninth Edition.

BRYDGES, (Sir) SAMUEL EGERTON.
 Archaica. Reprint of Prose Tracts. (Braithwait, Breton, Greene, Harvey, Nash, Southwell). 2 v. Lond. 1815.
 Censura Literaria and Restituta. Titles, abstracts and opinions of old English books. 10 v. in 9. Lond. Longmans. 1805—9.

BULLEN, ALEX. H.
 Editions of Eliz. and Jacob. Dramatists, w. introd. and notes. Beaumont and Fletcher. (In prep.) Dekker, 4 v. 1887. Marlowe, 3 v. 1888. Marston. 3 v. 1887. Middleton, 8 v. 1885—'86. Peele, 2 v. 1888. Old English Plays, 4 v. 1882. New Ser., 3 v. 1887. Lond. Nimmo. ea. v. 7/6. Day, 1881. Chiswick Press. £3, 5/.

BUTCHER, S. H.
 Aristotle's Theory of Poetry and Fine Art. (With crit. text and trans. of the Poetics). Lond. and N. Y. Macmillan. 1894. $3.25.

CAMPBELL, T., (and others).
 Lives of British Dramatists. 2 v. Phil. 1846.

CHALMERS, A.
 Works (w. memoirs) of the English Poets fr. Chaucer to Cowper. 21 v. Lond. 1810.

CHANCELLOR, E. BERESFORD.
 Literary Types. N. Y. Macmillan. 1895. $1.50.

CHOATE, J. B.
 Wells of English. Bost. Roberts Brothers. 1892. $1.50.

CHORLEY, H. F.
 Authors of England. Lond. 1861.

CIBBER, T.
 Lives of the Poets of Great Britain and Ireland. 5 v. Lond. 1753.

COLBY, J. ROSE.
 Some Ethical Aspects of Later Elizabethan Tragedy. Ann Arbor. 1886.

COLERIDGE, HARTLEY.
 Essays and Marginalia. (Sh. and his contemporaries, 1: 353—66). Lond. 1851.

COLERIDGE, S. T.
 Lectures on Shakespeare and other Dramatists; ed. T. Ashe. Lond. Bohn. 1888. 3/6. Bost. Little, Brown. $1.40. N. Y. Scribner. $1.40.
 Miscellanies. Lond. Bohn. 1888. 3/6.

COLLIER, J. P.
 History of English Dramatic Poetry to the time of Shakespeare, and Annals of the Stage to the Restoration. 3 v. Lond. Bell. 1879. 70/.

COLLINS, JOHN CHURTON.
 Essays and Studies. "The Predecessors of Shakspere." Lond. and N. Y. Macmillan. 1895. 9/.

CORNEILLE, PIERRE.
  Œuvres. 12 v. (Vol. 1). Paris. 1862—'68.
COURTHOPE, W. J.
  Liberal Movement in English Literature. (Byron, Coleridge, Keats, Scott, Shelley, Wordsworth). Lond. Murray. 1886. 6/.
CRAWFURD, OSWALD J. F. (Ed.)
  English Comic Dramatists. (Selections w. brief Criticisms). Lond. Paul. 1884. 6/. N. Y. Appleton. 1884. $1.25.
CREIGHTON, M.
  Age of Elizabeth. Lond. and N. Y. Longmans. 1876. 2/6. N. Y. Scribner. 1876. $1.
CUNLIFFE, (Dr.) JOHN W.
  The Influence of Seneca on Elizabethan Tragedy. Lond. Macmillan. 1893. 4/.
DICTIONARY OF NATIONAL BIOGRAPHY.
  Ed. L. Stephen and S. Lee. Lond. Smith and Elder. 1885— ea. v. 15/. N. Y. Macmillan. 1885— ea. v. $3.75.
DIDEROT, DENIS.
  De la Poësie Dramatique. (*In his* Œuvres de Théâtre). Paris. 1763.
DISRAELI, ISAAC.
  Curiosities of Literature. 3 v. 1791—1823.
  Calamities and Quarrels of Authors. 1812—'14.
  Amenities of Literature. 1841.
  Miscellanies of Literature. 1841. Lond. Routledge. 1881—'84. ea. v. 3/6.
DONNE, W. B.
  Essays on the Drama. Lond. Tinsley. 1862. 5/.
DOWDEN, (Prof.) EDWARD.
  Studies in Literature. Lond. Paul. 1878. 12/.
  Transcripts and Studies. Lond. Paul. 1887. 12/.
DRYDEN, J.
  Essay of Dramatic Poesy; ed. Thos. Arnold, w. notes. Oxford, Clarendon Press. 1890. 3/6.
DU MERIL, E.
  Historie de la Comédie. Paris, 1864.
DUNHAM, S. A.
  Lives of British Dramatists. 2 v. Lond. Longmans. 1847. 7/.
  Lives of the most eminent Literary and Scientific Men of Great Britain and Ireland. 3 v. Lond. 1836—'38.
DYCE, ALEX.
  Editions of Eliz. and Jacob. Dramatists, w. introd. and notes. Beaumont and Fletcher, 11 v. Lond. Moxom. 1843—'46. £8. Greene and Peele. (1828, 31). 1886. Lond. Routledge. 7/6. Marlowe. (1850). 1884. Lond. Routledge. 7/6. Middleton. 5 v. 1840. Lond. Lumley. 42/. Shirley. (Ed. w. Gifford). 6 v. 1833. Lond. £6. Webster. (1840). 1885. Lond. Routledge. 7/6.

ELZE, KARL.
: Notes on Eliz. Dramatists w. conjectural emendations of the text. Halle.
  1880. 5/.

ENGLISCHE STUDIEN.
: Ed. E. Kölbing. (In prog.) 1877— ca. v. 15/.

EVERETT, C. C.
: Poetry, Comedy and Duty. Bost. Houghton. 1888. $1.50.

FAIRHOLT, F. W.
: Lord Mayors' Pageants. Percy Soc. 1843.

FARQUHAR, G.
: Works. (v. 1, p. 81—107, Discourse upon Comedy). Lond. 1742.

FITZGERALD, PERCY.
: Principles of Comedy and Dram. Effect. Lond. Tinsley. 1870. 12/.

FLEAY, F. G.
: Biographical Chronicle of the English Drama. Lond. Reeves and Turner. 1891. 30/.

FORMAN, H. B.
: Our Living Poets. Lond. Tinsley. 1871. 12/.

FREYTAG, G.
: Die Technik des Dramas. Leipzig. 1881. Hirzel. mk. 5. Trans. E. J. MacEwan. Chicago. Griggs. 1894. $1.50.

FULLER, S. M.
: Papers on Literature and Art. (Pt. 2: 100—151, The Modern Drama). N. Y. 1848.

GERVINUS, GEORG GOTTFRIED.
: Shakespeare Commentaries. Trans. F. E. Bunnett. Lond. Smith and Elder. 1877. 14/. N. Y. Scribner. 1877. $5.25.

GILFILLAN, GEORGE.
: Specimens with Memoirs of the less known British Poets. Edin. and Lond. 1860.

GIRARDIN, SAINT-MARC.
: Cours de Littérature Dramatique, ou, De l'Usage des Passions dans le Drame. Paris. Charpentier. 1876. 17 fr. 50c.
: Lectures on Dram. Lit. (The same, trans. R. G. Barnwell). N. Y. 1849.

GOETHE, J. W.
: Theater und dramatische Poesie. Werke. Weimar. 1887—'95.

GOSSE, EDMUND W.
: From Shakespeare to Pope. Camb. Press. 1885. 6/. N. Y. Dodd. 1885. $1.75.
: The Jacobean Poets. Lond. Murray. 1894. 3/6. N. Y. Scribner. 1894. $1.
: Seventeenth Cent. Studies. Lond. Paul. 1883. 10/6.
: History of English Literature in the Eighteenth Cent. Lond. and N. Y. Macmillan. 1889. 7/6 and $1.75.
: Gossip in a Library. Lond. Heinemann. 1892. 7/6. N. Y. U. S. Book Co. $2.50.

GREEN, J. R.
    Short History of the English People. Lond. and N. Y. Macmillan. 1889.
        12/ and $2.25. N. Y. Harper. 1888. $1.20. N. Y. Macmillan. 1890.
        4 v. ea. 75c.
GRIFFITHS, L. M.
    Evenings with Shakspere. Bristol and Lond. Simpkin. 1889. 15/.
GUIZOT, F. P. G.
    Shakespeare and his Times. (p. 124—57, Dram. Construction). N. Y. Harper.
        1855.
HALLAM, HENRY.
    Introduction to the Literature of Europe, in the Fifteenth, Sixteenth, and
        Seventeenth Centuries. 4 v. Lond. Murray. 1871. 16/.
HAMILTON, W.
    Poets Laureate of England. Lond. Stock. 1879. 7/6.
HASLEWOOD, J. (ed.)
    Ancient Critical Essays upon English Poets and Poesy. (Puttenham, Webbe,
        James. I., Campion, Daniel, Boulton; Letters of Harvey and Spenser).
        2 v. Lond. 1811—'15.
HAZLITT, WILLIAM.
    Lectures on Dramatic Literature of the Age of Elizabeth. Lond. Bohn. 1889.
        3/6. N. Y. Scribner. $1.40. Macmillan. $1.00.
    Lectures on the English Poets and Comic Writers. Lond. Bohn. 1869. 3/6.
        N. Y. Macmillan. $1.00.
    Spirit of the Age. Lond. Bohn. 1858. N. Y. Macmillan. $1.00.
HEGEL.
    Werke. 18 v. Berlin. 1833—'48. (Vol. 10).
HENLEY, W. E.
    Views and Reviews. Lond. Nutt. 1890. 5/. N. Y. Scribner. 1890. $1.
HERFORD, (Prof.) C. H.
    Studies in the Literary Relations of England and Germany in the Sixteenth
        Century. Camb. Press. 1886. 9/. N. Y. Macmillan. 1887. 7/6.
HERTZBERG, W.
    Shakespeare und seine Vörlaufer. Sh. Jahrbuch. 15.
HIFFERNAN, PAUL.
    Dramatic Genius. Lond. 1772.
HITCHMAN, FS.
    Eighteenth Cent. Studies. Lond. Low. 1881. 12/.
HORNE, R. H.
    New Spirit of the Age. 2 v. Lond. Smith and Elder. 1844. 24/. N. Y.
        Harper. 1844.
HUDSON, H. N.
    Life, Art and Characters of Shakespeare. 2 v. Bost. Ginn. 1883. $4.
        Lond. Arnold. 21/. (Origin and Growth of the Drama in England.
        Principles of Art. Peele, Greene, Marlowe).

HUME, DAVID.
   Essays and Treatises on Several Subjects. (1: 244—54, Tragedy). 2 v. Lond. 1768.
   Philosophical Works. (3: 248—73. Of Tragedy). 4 v. Bost. 1854.

HUNT, J. H. LEIGH.
   Dramatic Essays; ed. W. Archer and R. W. Lowe. Lond. Scott. 1894. 3/6.
   (Ed.) Dramatic Works of Wycherley, Congreve, Vanbrugh and Farquhar. Lond. Routledge. 1865. 10/6.

HURD, RICHARD.
   Dissertation concerning the Provinces of the Several Species of the Drama. v. 2. Collected Works. Lond. 1811.

HUTTON, R. H.
   Literary Essays. Lond. and N. Y. Macmillan. 1888. 6/.

INGLEBY, (Dr.) C. M.
   Shakespeare Allusion Books. New Sh. Soc. 1874.
   Centurie of Prayse; the above ed. Lucy Toulmin Smith. New Sh. Soc. 1879. 21/.

IRVING, HENRY.
   The Drama: Addresses. Lond. Heinemann. 1892. 3/6. N. Y. Tait. 1892. $1.25.

JACOBS, JOSEPH.
   Essays and Reviews: from the Athenæum. Lond. Nutt. 1891. 2/6. N. Y. Scribner. 1891. $1.25.

JAHRBUCH DER DEUTSCHEN SHAKESPEARE — GESELLSCHAFT.
   (References are to Jahrbuch (Sh.))
   Weimar. 1865—

JAHRBUCH FUR ROMAN. U. ENG. SPRACHE U. LITTERATUR:
   Ed. Ebert and Lemcke. Berlin. 1859—'71. Leipzig. 1874—'76. ea. v. 12/.

JOHNSON, SAMUEL.
   Lives of the Poets. Lond. Bohn. 3 v. ea. 3/6. 2 v. N. Y. Stokes. 1888. ea. $1. 3 v. N. Y. Macmillan. ea. $1.00.

JONSON, BENJAMIN.
   Conversations with Drummond of Hawthornden. Sh. Soc. Pub. 1842.

JONES, H. A.
   Renascence of the English Drama. Lond. and N. Y. Macmillan. 1895. 7/ and $1.75.

JUSSERAND, J. J.
   English Novel in the Time of Shakespeare. Lond. Unwin. 1890. 21/. N. Y. Putnam. 1890. $6.

KELLY, W.
   Notices illustrative of the Drama and other Popular Amusements, chiefly in the Sixteenth and Seventeenth Centuries. Lond. Smith. 1864. 9/.

KLEIN, J. L.
   Geschichte des Drama's. (v. 12 & 13, Englische Drama). 13 v. in 15. Leipzig. Weigel. 1886.

KOEPPEL, E.
   Beiträge zur Geschichte des Elizabethanischen Dramas. (Engl. Studien, 18: 357—74).

LAFOND, E.
   Contemporaines de Shakespeare. Paris. 1864.

LAING, F. A. and WEISCHER, THOMAS.
   Analyses of Classic English Plays for the use of Students of English Lit. Stuttgart. Neff. 1883. mk.

LAMB, CHARLES.
   Specimens of English Dramatic Poets. Lond. Bohn. 3/6. N. Y. Macmillan. $1.00.
   Dramatic Essays; ed. Brander Matthews, w. introd. and notes. Lond. Chatto. 1893. 2/6. N. Y. Dodd. 1893. $1.

LANGBAINE, GERARD.
   Account of the English Dramatic Poets. Oxford. 1891.

LESSING, G. E.
   Werke. 20 v. in 12. Berlin.
   Selected Prose Works. Trans. Beasley and Zimmern. (Laocoon, How the Ancients represented Death, and Dram. Notes). Lond. Bohn. 1879. 3/6.

LODGE, E.
   Portraits, with Memoirs. 8 v. Lond. Bohn. ea 6/. N. Y. Macmillan. ea. $1.50.

LOWELL, JAMES R.
   My Study Windows. (Camelot Classics). Lond. Scott. 1886. 1/. Houghton. $2.00.
   Old English Dramatists. Bost. Houghton. 1892. $1.25. Lond. Macmillan. 1892. 5/.

MACAULAY, THOMAS B.
   Critical, Historical and Miscellaneous Essays. (Essay on the Comic Dramatists). 3 v. Riverside Ed. Bost. Houghton. $3.75.
   Critical and Historical Essays. 2 v. Lond. and N. Y. Longmans. 1890. $3.

MALONE, E.
   Historical Account of the English Stage. Basil. 1800.

MARMONTEL, J. F.
   Eléments de Littérature. (v. 3). 3 v. Paris. Didot. 1846.

MAZZINI, GIUSEPPE.
   Life and Writings. (v. 2). 6 v. Lond. Smith. 1864—'70.

MANZONI, A. F. T. A.
   Opere Varie. (Lettera su l'Unita di Tempo e di Luogo nella Tragedia. 60 pp.) Milano. 1845.

MCCARTHY, J. H.
   Hours with Eminent Irishmen. N. Y. Ford's Nat.'Lib. 1886. $1.00.

MCDERMOT, M.
   A Philosophical Inquiry into the Source of the Pleasures derived from Tragic Representations. Lond. 1824.

MENZIES, S.
   Royal Favorites. 2 v. Lond. Maxwell. 1865. 32/.

MERES, FRANCIS.
   Palladis Tamia, 1598. (*See* Ingleby's Centurie of Prayse). *Also* in Arber Reprints.

MERMAID SERIES.
Best Plays of the Old Dramatists; ed. Havelock Ellis.
   Beaumont and Fletcher. 2 v.; ed. St. Loe.
   Chapman; ed. W. L. Phelps.
   Congreve; ed. A. C. Ewald.
   Dekker; ed. E. Rhys.
   Ford; ed. Havelock Ellis.
   Heywood; ed. A. W. Verity.
   Jonson. 3 v.; ed. B. Nicholson.
   Marlowe; ed. J. A. Symonds.
   Massinger. 2 v.; ed. Arthur Symons.
   Middleton. 2 v.; ed. A. C. Swinburne and Havelock Ellis.
   Nero and Other Plays; Various Editors.
   Otway; ed. Roden Noel.
   Shadwell; ed. G. Saintsbury.
   Steele; ed. G. A. Aiken.
   Shirley; ed. Edm. Gosse.
   Vanbrugh; ed. W. C. Ward.
   Webster and Tourneur; ed. J. A. Symonds.
   Wycherley; ed. W. C. Ward.
      Lond. Vizetelly. 1887. Unwin. 1893— ea. v. 3/6. Bost. Little, Brown. ea. v. $1. N. Y. Scribner. ea. v. $1.

MEZIERES, ALFRED.
   Contemporains et Successeurs de Shakespeare. Paris. Charpentier. 1864. 3 fr. 50c.

MINTO, W.
   Characteristics of the English Poets from Chaucer to Shirley. Edin. Blackwoods. 1874. 9/.

MITFORD, (Mrs.) MARY RUSSELL.
   Recollections of my Literary Life. Lond. Bentley. 1888. 6/. N. Y. Harper. $1.50.

MODERN LANGUAGE NOTES.
   Ed. A. Marshall Elliott. Baltimore. 1886—

MORLEY, (Prof.) HENRY.
   English Literature in the Reign of Victoria. Lond. Low. 1882. 2/6. Leipzig. Tauchnitz. 1881. 1/6. N. Y. Putnam. 1882. $2.
   English Writers. 11 v. (20 v. intended. Author died 1894; v. 11 dealing w. Jacobean period, being completed by W. Hall Griffin). Lond. Cassell. 1887—'95. ea. v. 5/.

NEWMAN, JOHN HENRY.
: Essay on Aristotle's Poetics; ed. A. S. Cook. Bost. Ginn. 30c.

NICHOLS, J.
: Literary Anecdotes of the Eighteenth Century. 9 v. Lond. 1815.

NICHOLS, JOHN.
: The Progresses, Processions and Magnificent Festivities of King James the First. 4 v. Lond. 1828.
: The Progresses and Public Processions of Queen Elizabeth. 2d ed. 2 v. Lond. 1823.

OLIPHANT, (Mrs.) MARGARET O. W.
: Literary History of England in the End of the Eighteenth and Beginning of the Nineteenth Century. 3 v. N. Y. Macmillan. 1882. $3. 2 v. Lond. Percival. 1892. 12/.

PEPYS, SAMUEL.
: Diary (1659—'69), w. Lord Braybrooke's notes; ed. H. B. Wheatley. 8 v. Lond. Bell. 1894. ea. 10/6. 8 v. Lond. Bohn. ea. $1.50.

PERRY, THOMAS SERGEANT.
: English Literature in the Eighteenth Century. N. Y. Harper. 1883. $2.

POOLE, (Dr.) W. F. and FLETCHER, W. I.
: Index to Periodical Literature. (Poole's Index). Lond. Paul. 1893. 17/6. Bost. Houghton. 1893. $8.
: Proelss, R. Geschichte des Neueren Dramas. 3 v. Leipzig. Elischer. 1881—'83.

PUTTENHAM, GEORGE.
: Arte of English Poesie. Arber Reprints. Lond. 1869.

ROBERTSON, E. S.
: English Poetesses. Lond. and N. Y. Cassell. 1883. 5/.

ROSSETTI, W. MICHAEL.
: Lives of Famous Poets. Lond. Ward. 1885. 3/6 and 2/.

ROYER, ALPHONSE.
: Histoire Universelle du Théatre. 4 v. Paris. Franck. 1869—'71. 30 fr.

RYMER, THOMAS.
: The Tragedies of the Last Age. Lond. 1678.

SAINTSBURY, G. W.
: History of Elizabethan Literature. Lond. and N. Y. Macmillan. 1887. 7/6. $1.75. N. Y. Macmillan. Students' Ed. $1. (Ed.) Eliz. and Jacob. Pamphlets. Lond. Percival. 1892. N. Y. Macmillan. 1892. $1.00.

SARRAZIN, G.
: La Renaissance de la Poesie Anglais. Paris. Perrin. 1889. 3 fr.

SCHERER, EDM.
: Essays on English Literature trans. from French by Geo. Saintsbury. Lond. Low. 1891. 6/. N. Y. Scribner. 1891. $1.50.

SCHILLER, JOHANN CHRISTOPH FRIEDRICH.
> Aesthetic Letters, Essays and Philosophical Letters; trans. J. Weiss. (p. 309 —43, The Tragic Art). Bost. Little, Brown. 1845.

SCHLEGEL, A. W. von.
> Dramatische Kunst und Literatur. 3 v. Heidelb. 1817.
> Lectures on Dramatic Art and Literature. (*The Same*, trans. John Black). Lond. Bohn. 1886. 3/6. N. Y. Macmillan. $1.00. N. Y. Scribner. 1886. $1.50.

SCHOPENHAUER, A.
> World as Will and as Idea. Trans. Haldane and Kemp. (1 : 326—30; 3 : 212 —20, 454). 3 v. Lond. Trübner. 1883—'86. 50/.

SCOTT, MARY AUGUSTA.
> Eliz. Translations from the Italian. (Pamphlet). Baltimore. Mod. Lang. Ass. of America. 1895.

SCUDDER, VIDA D.
> Life of the Spirit in the Modern English Poets. Bost. Houghton. 1895. $1.75.

SIDNEY, (Sir) PHILIP.
> Apologie for Poetrie. Arber Reprints. Lond. 1868. Camb., [Eng.] Univ. Press. 1891. 3/. (Pitt press ser.) Bost. Ginn. 1890. 90c.

SIMPSON-BAIKIE, E.
> The Dramatic Unities. 2d ed. Lond. Longmans. 1875. 2/6.

STEDMAN, E. C.
> Victorian Poets. Lond. Chatto. 1888. 9/. Bost. Houghton. 1888. $2.25.

STEPHEN, LESLIE.
> Hours in a Library. 3 v. Lond. Smith and Elder. 1892. ea. 6/. N. Y. Putnam. 1892. $4.50.

STOW, JOHN.
> Annals. Lond. (1580). 1615. 35/.
> The Survay of London; written in 1598, by J. Stow and continued and corrected and enlarged by A. M(unday).
> Survey of London; ed. H. Morley, as London under Elizabeth. Lond. and N. Y. Routledge. 1890. $1.

SUCKLING, (Sir) JOHN.
> Poems; ed. F. A. Stokes. (Session of the Poets). N. Y. White & S. 1886. $2.00.

SWINBURNE, ALGERNON CHARLES.
> Essays and Studies. Lond. Chatto. 1888. 12/. N. Y. Scribner. 1888. $4.50.
> Miscellanies. (Congreve, Wordsworth, Byron, Landor). Lond. Chatto. 1886. 12/. N. Y. Scribner. 1886. $4.50.
> Sonnets on English Dramatic Poets. (1590—1650). Repr. Th. B. Mosher, Portland, Maine, for The Bibelot, June, 1895. (Vol. 1, 6).
> Studies in Prose and Poetry. Lond. Chatto. 1894. 9/. N. Y. Scribner. 1894. $2.50.
> Study of Shakspeare. Lond. Chatto. 1880. 8/. N. Y. Worthington. 1880. $1.75.

SYMONDS, JOHN A.
  Shakspere's Predecessors in the English Drama. Lond. Smith & Elder. 1888. 16/. N. Y. Scribner. 1884. $6.40.

TAINE, HIPPOLYTE ADOLPH.
  History of English Literature. 2 v. Lond. Chatto. 1877. 15/. 2 v. N. Y. Worthington. $3.75.

TEGG, W.
  Shakspeare and his Contemporaries. Lond. Tegg. 1878. 4/.

THACKERAY, WILLIAM MAKEPEACE.
  English Humorists of the Eighteenth Century. (Swift, Congreve, Addison, Steele, Gay, Smollett, Fielding and Goldsmith). Lond. Smith and Elder. 1888. (Pocket Libr.) 1/6. 2 v. (Half Hour Ser.) N. Y. Harper. 1879. 50c.

TIMBS, J.
  Lives of the Wits and Humorists. 2 v. Lond. Bentley. 1872. 12/.

TOMLINS, F. G.
  A Brief View of the English Drama. Lond. C. Mitchell. 1840. 4/.

ULRICI, H.
  Shakespeare's Dramatic Art; trans. L. D. Schmitz. 2 v. Lond. Bohn. 1876. ea. 3/6. N. Y. Scribner. ea. $1.40. N. Y. Macmillan. ea. $1.00.

WARD, ADOLPHUS W.
  History of English Dramatic Literature to the Death of Queen Anne. 2 v. Lond. Macmillan. 1875. 32/. (*New ed. in prep.*)

WARD, T. H.
  English Poets. Selections, w. crit. introds. by various authors. 4 v. Lond. and N. Y. Macmillan. 1888. ea. 7/6 and $5.

WARTON, T.
  History of English Poetry from Twelfth to close of Sixteenth Century. Ed. W. C. Hazlitt. 4 v. Lond. 1871. New ed. Lond. Ward & L. 1872. 6/.

WATSON, WILLIAM.
  Excursions in Criticism. Some Literary Idolatries. (On Eliz. Dramatists). Lond. and N. Y. Macmillan. 1893. 5/ and $2.

WEBBE, WILLIAM.
  Discourse of English Poetrie. Arber Reprints. Lond. 1870.

WHIPPLE, EDWIN P.
  Literature of the Age of Elizabeth. Bost. Houghton. $1.50.
  Essays and Reviews. 2 v. Bost. Houghton. 1882. ea. $1.50.

WHITE, RICHARD GRANT.
  Studies in Shakespeare. (Acc. of antecedent Eng. Drama). Lond. Low. 1885. 10/6. Bost. Houghton. $1.75.

WHITELOCKE.
  Memorials of the Eng. Affairs. 4 v. Oxford. Parker. 1853.

WHITTAKER.
  Dramatic Canons. (Galaxy, 23 : 396, 508).

WILLIAMS, JANE.
  Literary Women.

WILSON, J. GRANT.
  Poets and Poetry of Scotland. 2 v. Lond. Blackie. 1875. ea. 12/6.

WOTTON, M. E.
  Word Portraits. Lond. 1887.

III.

HISTORY OF THE ENGLISH THEATRE.

ALLEYN PAPERS.
  Illustrative of the Early English Stage; ed. Collier. Sh. Soc. Pub. 1843.

ANON.
  (Author of the Life of Quin).
  Thos. Betterton. (1635—1710). Life and Times. Lond. Reader. 1888. 7/6.

ANON.
  (Author of the Life of Betterton).
  James Quin. (1693—1766). Life, with History of Stage. Lond. Reader. (1766). 1887. 7/6.

ARCHER, WILLIAM.
  About the Theatre; Essays and Studies. Lond. Unwin. 1886. 7/6.
  Ed. Eminent Actor Series. Betterton, ed. R. W. Lowe; Cibber; The Dibdins, ed. E. R. Dibdin; Elliston, ed. A. B. Walkley; Garrick, ed. Jos. Knight; The Keans, ed. Fred. Wedmore; The Kembles; Macklin, ed. E. A. Parry; Macready, ed. Wm. Archer; The Mathews, ed. H. S. Edwards. Pub. to 1896, Macready, Betterton, Macklin. Lond. Paul. 1891. ea. 2/6. N. Y. Longmans. 1891. ea. $1.

ASTON, ANTHONY.
  Brief Supplement to Colley Cibber, Esq.; his Lives of the late famous Actors and Actresses.

BAKER, HENRY BARTON.
  English Actors from Shakespeare to Macready. 2 v. N. Y. Holt. 1879. $3.50.
  The London Stage; its History and Traditions fr. 1576—1888. 2 v. Lond. Allen. 1889. 12/. 2 v. N. Y. Scribner & Welford. 1889. $4.80.
  Our Old Actors. Popular ed. Lond. Bentley. 1881. 6/.

BOADEN, JAMES.
  Memoirs of Mrs. Siddons. (1755—1831). Lond. Gibbings. 1893. 7/6.
  Biography of John Philip Kemble. (1757—1823). Lond. 1825. 25/.

BROWN, T. A.
  History of the American Stage. N. Y. Dick. 1870. $3.00

CALNOUR, A. C.
  Fact and Fiction about Shakspeare w. some account of the Play-houses, Players, and Playwrights of his period. Lond. Williams. 1894. 6/.

CHETWOOD, W. R.
General History of the Stage, fr. its Origin in Greece down to the present time; w. memoirs of Principal Performers. Lond. Owen. 1749.

CIBBER, COLLEY.
An Apology for his Life. (Contains also Historia Histrionica, Aston's Brief Supplement and copy of Davenant's Letters Patent). Ed. Robt. W. Lowe. 2 v. Lond. Nimmo. 1889. 42/.

COHN, ALBERT.
Shakespeare in Germany in Sixteenth and Seventeenth Cent. An Account of English Actors in Germany and the Netherlands. Lond. 1865.

COLE, J. W.
Life and Theatrical Times of Kean. (1811—'68). 2 v. Lond. Bentley. 1860. 21/.

COLEMAN, JOHN.
Players and Playwrights I have Known. 2 v. Lond. Chatto. 1888. 24/.

COLLIER, J. PAYNE.
Account of Fools and Jesters. Sh. Soc. Pub. 1842.
Memoirs of Principal Actors in Sh.'s Plays. Sh. Soc. Pub. 1846.

COOK, D.
Book of the Play. Lond. Low. 1876. 24/.
Hours with the Players. 2 v. Lond. Chatto. 1881. 6/.
Nights at the Play. Lond. Chatto. 1883. 6/. 2 v. N. Y. Scribner. 1883. $6.
On the Stage. Studies of Theatrical History and the Actor's Art. 2 v. Lond. Low. 1883. 24/.

COQUELIN, C.
The Actor and his Art. Bost. Roberts. 1881. 50c.

CUNNINGHAM, P.
Extracts from the Accounts of the Revels at Court in the Reigns of Elizabeth and James; w. introd. Sh. Soc. Pub. 1842.
Story of Nell Gwyn. (1640—'91). Lond. Gibbings. 1892. 7/6.

DALY, AUGUSTIN.
Peg. Woffington. (1718—'60). Troy, N. Y. Nims and Knight. 1890. $5.

DAVIES, T.
Memoirs of the Life of D. Garrick. 2 v. Lond. 1780.

DIDEROT, D.
The Paradox of Acting; trans. W. H. Pollock, w. pref. by H. Irving. Lond. Chatto. 1883. 4/6. N. Y. Scribner. 1883. $1.25.

DORAN, (Dr.) J.
In and About Drury Lane. 2 v. Lond. Bentley. 1881. 21/.
Their Majesties' Servants; Annals of the English Stage from Thomas Betterton to Edmund Kean; ed. R. W. Lowe. 3 v. Lond. Nimmo. 1888. 54/. V. 1 and 2 of Doran's Works. N. Y. Widdleton. 9 v. $15.

DOWNES, J.
Roscius Anglicanus; History of the Stage, 1660—1706; ed. Knight. (Facsimile reprint of the original of 1708). Lond. Jarvis. 1886.

EDWARDS, H. S.
: Famous First Representations. Lond. Chapman. 1886. 6/. N. Y. Scribner. 1887. $2.40.

EGAN, PIERCE.
: The Life of an Actor. Lond. Pickering and Chatto. 1892. 14/.

FITZGERALD, PERCY HETHERINGTON.
: Henry Irving: a record of 20 years at the Lyceum. Lond. Chapman. 1893. 14/.
: The Kembles, including Mrs. Siddons and her brother, John Philip Kemble. 2 v. Lond. Tinsley. 1871. 30/.
: Life and Times of J. Wilkes. 2 v. Lond. 1888.
: Life of David Garrick. 2 v. Lond. Tinsley. 1868. 30/.
: Life of Mrs. Catherine Clive, (1711—'85). Lond. 1888. 7/6.
: Lives of the Sheridans. 2 v. Lond. Bentley. 1886. 30/. 2 v. N. Y. Scribner & Welford. 1887. $12.00.
: New History of the English Stage, from the Restoration to Lib. of Theatres. 2 v. Lond. Tinsley. 1882. 30/.
: Romance of the English Stage. 2 v. Lond. Bentley. 1874. 24/. N. Y. Lippincott. $2.

✓ FLEAY, F. C.
: Chronicle History of the London Stage, 1559—1642. Lond. Reeves and Turner. 1890. 18/. ✓

GALT, JOHN.
: The Lives of the Players. 2 v. Bost. Hill. 1831. Glasgow. Morrison. 1886. 5/.

GENEST, J.
: English Stage. Some Account of the English Stage, from the Restoration in 1660 to 1830. 10 v. Bath. Carrington. 1832.

GILLILAND, T.
: Dram. Mirror, cont. hist. of the stage, biog. and crit. acc. of all dram. writers fr. 1660, and of most distinguished actors fr. Sh. to 1807; also hist. of the country theatres in England, Ireland and Scotland. 2 v. Lond. 1808.

GODDARD, ARTHUR.
: Players of the Period. (Leading English Actors of the Day). 2 v. in 1. Lond. Dean. 1891. 1st ser. 10/6.

HALLIWELL, J. O. (Ed.)
: A Collection of ancient documents respecting the office of Master of the Revels, and other papers relating to the early English Theatre. From the orig. MSS. formerly in the Haslewood Collection. Lond. 1870. Privately printed.

HAZLITT, WILLIAM.
: A View of the English Stage; or, A Series of Dramatic Criticisms. Lond. (1818). 1854. 3/6.

HAZLITT, W. C.
: English Drama and Stage under the Tudor and Stuart Princes, 1543—1664. Roxburghe Libr. 1869.

HISTORIA HISTRIONICA.
: (Attributed to Jas. Wright). Lond. 1699. Repr. in Cibber's Life, and Dodsley's Old Plays, v. 15. (*Also* known as " A Dialogue on Old Plays and Players).''

HOGARTH, G.
: Memoirs of the Opera. 2 v. Lond. Bentley. 1851.

HUNT, J. H. LEIGH.
: Critical Essays on the Performers of the London Theatres. Lond. 1807. *Same*, sel. and ed. Wm. Archer and R. W. Lowe. Lond. Scott. 1894. 3/6.

HUTTON, L.
: Plays and Players. N. Y. 1876.

JONES, INIGO.
: Original Designs for Masques at Court; ed. Collier and Planché, w. life by P. Cunningham; portrait, plates, etc. Sh. Soc. Pub. 1848.

KELLY, MICHAEL.
: Reminiscences. N. Y. Harper. 1826.

KEMBLE, FRANCES A. (1811—'93).
: Records of my Girlhood.
: Records of Later Life.
: Further Records of my Life. Lond. Bentley. 1891. 24/. N. Y. Holt. 1891. ea. $2.

KENNARD, (Mrs.) N. H.
: Life of Elisa Rachel. (1820—'58). (Eminent Women Series). Lond. Allen. 1886. 3/6. Bost. Roberts. 1886. $1.00.
: Life of Mrs. Siddons. (1755—1831). (Eminent Women Series). -Lond. Allen. 1886. 3/6. Bost. Roberts. 1887. $1.00.

KNIGHT, JOSEPH.
: David Garrick: (1716—'79). A Biography. Lond. Paul. 1894. 10/6.
: Theatrical Notes. Lond. Lawrence and Bullen. 1893. 6/.

LAMB, CHARLES.
: Art of Stage as set out in Lamb's Essays; ed. P. Fitzgerald. Lond. Remington. 1885. 7/6. N. Y. Scribner. 1885. $3.

LEWES, G. H.
: On Actors and the Art of Acting. Lond. Smith and Elder. 1881. 7/6. N. Y. Holt. $1.50.

LENNOX, (Lord) W. P.
: Plays, Players and Play-houses at Home and Abroad. 2 v. Lond. Hurst. 1881. 16/.

LIGHTS OF THE OLD ENGLISH STAGE.
: N. Y. Appleton. 1878. 30c.

LOWE, ROBERT W.
: Thomas Betterton. (Eminent Actor Series). Lond. Paul. 1891. 2/6. N.Y. Longmans. 1891. $1.

MACREADY, W. C.
  Reminiscences and Selections from his Diaries and Letters; ed. (Sir) F. Pollock. 2 v. N. Y. Macmillan. 1875. $12.00. *Same condensed*, $1.50.

MALONE, E.
  Hist. Account of the Rise and Prog. of the Eng. Stage. Lond. 1821. (Shakespeare: Plays and Poems, ed. E. Malone, v. 3).

MARSTON, WESTLAND.
  Our Recent Actors. 2 v. Boston. Roberts. 1888. $2.00. Lond. Low. 1890. 6/.

MATTHEWS, BRANDER, and HUTTON, LAWRENCE, Editors.
  Actors and Actresses of Great Britain and the United States from the days of David Garrick to the present time. 5 v. N. Y. Cassell. 1886. ea. $1.50.
  Studies of the Stage. N. Y. Harper. 1894. $1.

MOLLOY, J. FITZGERALD.
  Famous Plays, with Discourses on the Playhouses of the Restoration. Lond. Ward. 1887. 6/.
  Life and Adventures of Edmund Kean, Tragedian. (1787—1833). 2 v. Lond. Ward. 1888. 21/. N. Y. Scribner & Welford. 1888. $5.00.
  Life and Adventures of Peg Woffington, w. pictures of the period in which she lived. Lond. Hurst. 1887. 6/. 2 v. N. Y. Dodd. 1892. $3.50.

MOORE, THOMAS.
  Life of Sheridan. (1751—1816). Lond. Longmans. 1825.

MORLEY, (Prof.) HENRY.
  Journal of a London Play-goer. Lond. Routledge. 1866. 5/.

MORRIS, MOWBRAY.
  Essays in Theatrical Criticism. Lond. Remington. 1882. 6/.

MURDOCH, J. E.
  The Stage; or, Recollections of Actors and Acting. Phil. Stoddart. 1880. $2.50.

NEVILLE, HENRY.
  The Stage: its past and present history in relation to fine art. Lond. Bentley. 1875. 5/.

ORDISH, T. FAIRMAN.
  Early London Theatres. (In the Fields). Lond. and N. Y. Macmillan. 1894. (Camden Libr.) Lond. Stock. 1894. 6/.

OULTON, W. C.
  Hist. of the Theatres of London from 1771 to 1795. 3 v. 1818. Hist. of the Theatres of London from 1795 to 1817. 3 v. 1818.

PARRY, EDWARD A.
  Charles Macklin. (1690?—1797). (Eminent Actor Series). Lond. Paul. 1891. 2/6. N. Y. Longmans. 1891. $1.

PASCOE, C. E.
  The Dramatic List. (Record of living actors). Lond. Allen. 1879. 3/6. Bost. Roberts. 1879. $5.00.

PEMBERT, T. E.
   Memoirs of Edward Aiken Southern. (1830—'89). Lond. Bentley. 1889. 16/.

READER, ARTHUR. (Pub.)
   Dramatic Publications. Lives of the Players. (Mrs. Abington, Mrs. Cibber, Mrs. Jordan, Quin).

RUSSELL, W. C.
   Representative Actors. (Chandos Libr.) Lond. Warne. 1875. 1/6.

SMITH, W. H.
   Bacon and Shakespeare. An Inquiry touching Players, Play-houses and Play-writers in the Days of Elizabeth. Lond. Smith. 1857. 5/.

STIRLING, E.
   Old Drury Lane: fifty years' recollections. 2 v. Lond. Bentley. 1881. 21/. 2 v. N. Y. Scribner & Welford. 1881. $6.00.

THE THESPIAN DICTIONARY,
   Or, Dramatic Biography of the Eighteenth Cent.; cont. sketches of the lives, productions, etc., of all the principal managers, dramatists, composers, commentators, actors and actresses of the United Kingdom.

VICTOR, BENJAMIN.
   History of the theatres of London and Dublin from 1730 to present time. (With an annual register of all plays, etc., performed at the Theatres Royal in London from 1712). Lond. T. Davies. 1761.
   From 1760 to the present time, being a continuation of the Annual Register, etc. Lond. T. Becket. 1771.

WILLIAMS, M.
   Some London Theatres. Lond. Low. 1883. 7/6.

WINTER, WILLIAM.
   Life and Art of Edwin Booth. N. Y. Macmillan. 1893. $2.25. Lond. Unwin. 1893. 10/6.

WRIGHT, J.
   The Second Generation of English Actors, 1625—1670. (This includes some valuable information respecting London Theatres during this period). Arber Reprints. Lond. and N. Y. Macmillan. (*See* Historia Histrionica).

IV.

STAGE POLEMICS.

(Chronological).

WYCLIFITE (?).
   Sermon against Miracle Plays. End of Fourteenth Cent. Reliquæ Antiquæ; ed. Wright and Halliwell. 2 v. Lond. 1841—'43.

NORTHBROOKE, JOHN.
   Treatise against Dicing, Dancing, Plays and Interludes, 1577; ed. Collier, Sh. Soc. Pub. 1843.

GOSSON, STEPHEN.
  School of Abuse containing a Pleasant Invective against Poets, Pipers, Players, Jesters and such like Caterpillars of a Commonwealth. July, 1579. Repr. Somers' Tracts, 1810. 3: 552. ed. Collier, Sh. Soc. Pub. 1841. Arber Reprints. 1868.
ANON. (In answer to Gosson).
  Strange News out of Affrik. Oct., 1579. (*Not extant*).
GOSSON, STEPHEN. (In answer to Strange News out of Affrik).
  A Short Apology of the School of Abuse. Dec., 1579. Arber Reprints. 1868.
LODGE, THOMAS. (In answer to Gosson).
  Defence of Poetry, Music and the Stage. 1580. Sh. Soc. Pub. 1853.
ANON.
  Second and Third Blast of Retreat from Plays and Theatres. 1580.
SIDNEY, SIR PHILIP.
  An Apology for Poetry. Wr. 1580? Pr. 1595. Arber Reprints. 1868. *See also. II.*
GOSSON, STEPHEN. (In answer to Lodge).
  Plays Confuted in Five Actions. 1582. Repr. Hazlitt, W. C. English Drama and Stage under the Tudor and Stuart Princes. Roxburghe Libr. 1869.
STUBBS, PHILIP.
  Anatomy of Abuses. "Of Stage-Plays and Interludes, with their wickedness." 1583. Ed. Furnivall. Sh. Soc. Pub. 1877—'82.
LODGE, THOMAS. (In answer to Gosson).
  Alarum against Usurers. (Preface). 1584. Sh. Soc. Pub. 1853.
WHETSTONE, GEORGE.
  Touchstone for the Time. (Appended to Mirror for Magistrates of Cities). 1584.
RANKINS, WILLIAM.
  Mirror of Monsters. 1587.
RAINOLDS, (Dr.)
  Overthrow of Stage-plays. 1599.
ANON.
  Histrio-mastix. *Play.* (Marston? 1599?) Pr. 1610.
HEYWOOD, THOMAS.
  An Apology for Actors. 1612. The Actors' Vindication. (2nd. ed. of above). 1658. Repr. Somers' Second Collection of Scarce ** Tracts. V. 1. 1750. Ed. Collier. Sh. Soc. Pub. 1841.
J. G.
  Refutation of the Apology for Actors. 1615.
PRYNNE, WILLIAM.
  Histrio-mastix. *Treatise.* 1633.
DRYDEN, JOHN.
  The Rival Ladies. (Dedicatory epistle, advocating the use of rhyme in drama). 1664.

HOWARD, (Sir) ROBERT. (In answer to Dryden).
   Four New Plays. (Preface, advocating blank verse). 1665.
DRYDEN, JOHN. (In answer to Howard).
   Essay of Dramatic Poesy. 1668.
HOWARD, (Sir) ROBERT. (In answer to Dryden).
   Great Favorite; or, The Duke of Lerma. (Preface). 1668.
DRYDEN, JOHN. (In answer to Howard).
   Defence of an Essay. (Prefixed to second edition of the Indian Emperor. 1668).
BAKER, (Sir) RICHARD.
   Theatrum Triumphans. (Attack on Prynne). 1670.
BLACKMORE, (Sir) Richard.
   King Arthur. (Preface). 1697.
MERRITON, G.
   Immorality, Debauchery and Profaneness. 1698.
COLLIER, JEREMY.
   A Short View of the Immorality and Profaneness of the English Stage. March, 1698.
ANON. (In answer to Collier).
   A Vindication of the Stage. (By Wycherley?) May 17, 1698.
FILMER, EDWARD. (In answer to Collier.)
   A Defence of Dramatic Poetry. May 26, 1698.
DENNIS, JOHN. (In answer to Collier).
   The Usefulness of the Stage to the Happiness of Mankind, to Government, and to Religion. June 6, 1698.
VANBRUGH, JOHN. (In answer to Collier).
   A Short Vindication of the Relapse and the Provok'd Wife, by the Author June 8, 1698.
FILMER, EDWARD. (In further answer to Collier).
   A Further Defence of Dramatic Poetry. June 23, 1698.
CONGREVE, WILLIAM. (In answer to Collier).
   Amendment of Mr. Collier's False and Imperfect Citations. July 25, 1698.
ANON. (In answer to Congreve).
   A Letter to Mr. Congreve on his Pretended Amendments). Sept. 2, 1698.
ANON. (In answer to Congreve).
   Animadversions on Congreve's Amendments. Sept. 8, 1698.
ANON. (In support of Collier).
   The Stage Condemn'd. Sept. 16, 1698.
COLLIER, JEREMY. (In answer to Congreve and Vanbrugh).
   A Defence of the Short View. Nov. 10, 1698.
ANON. (In answer to Collier).
   Some Remarks on Collier's Defence. Dec. 6, 1698.

DRAKE, JAMES. (In answer to Collier).
The Ancient and Modern Stages Reviewed. 1700.

COLLIER, JEREMY. (In answer to Drake).
A Second Defence of the Short View. 1700.

COLLIER, JEREMY. (In answer to Dennis).
A Dissuasive from the Play-house, by way of a Letter to a Person of Quality. 1703.

DENNIS, JOHN. (In answer to Collier).
The Person of Quality's Answer to Mr. Collier, containing a Defence of a Regular Stage. 1703.

ANON. (In support of Collier).
A Representation of the Impiety and Immorality of the English Stage. 1704.

ANON.
Some Thoughts concerning the Stage in a Letter to a Lady. 1704.

COLLIER, JEREMY.
A Letter to a Lady concerning the New Play-house. 1706.

FILMER, EDWARD.
A Defence of Plays. 1707.

COLLIER, JEREMY. (In answer to Filmer).
A Further Vindication of the Short View. 1708.

BEDFORD, ARTHUR.
A Serious Remonstrance in behalf of the Christian Religion against the Horrid Blasphemies and Impieties which are still used in the English Playhouses. 1719.

LAW, WILLIAM.
The Absolute Unlawfulness of the Stage Entertainments fully Demonstrated. 1726.

DENNIS, JOHN. (In answer to Law).
The Stage Defended. 1726.

www.ingramcontent.com/pod-product-compliance
Lightning Source LLC
Chambersburg PA
CBHW030320170426
43202CB00009B/1084